T3-BNO-452

LITTLE SONGS

LITTLE SONGS

Women, Silence, and the Nineteenth-Century Sonnet

AMY CHRISTINE BILLONE

THE OHIO STATE UNIVERSITY PRESS
Columbus

Library of Congress Cataloging-in-Publication Data
Billone, Amy Christine, 1972–
Little songs : women, silence, and the nineteenth-century sonnet / Amy Christine Billone.
p. cm.
Includes bibliographical references and index.
ISBN 978–0–8142–1042–0 (cloth : alk. paper) — ISBN 978–0–8142–9122–1 (cd-rom)
1. Sonnets, English—History and criticism. 2. English poetry—Women authors—History and criticism. 3. English poetry—19th century—History and criticism. 4. English poetry—18th century—History and criticism. 5. Silence in literature. 6. Smith, Charlotte Turner, 1749–1806—Criticism and interpretation. 7. Browning, Elizabeth Barrett, 1806–1861—Criticism and interpretation. 8. Rossetti, Christina Georgina, 1830–1894—Criticism and interpretation. 9. Southern, Isabella J. —Criticism and interpretation. I. Title.
PR589.S7B55 2007
821.'042—dc22
2006033726

Cover design by Melissa Ryan.
Text design and typesetting by Jennifer Shoffey Forsythe.
Type set in Adobe Palatino.
Printed by Thomson-Shore, Inc.

The paper used in this publication meets the minimum requirements of the American National Standard for Information Sciences—Permanence of Paper for Printed Library Materials. ANSI Z39.48–1992.

9 8 7 6 5 4 3 2 1

And then there it was, suddenly entire; she held it in her hands, beautiful and reasonable, clear and complete, the essence sucked out of life and held rounded here—the sonnet.

—VIRGINIA WOOLF, *To the Lighthouse*

Nay, let the silence of my womanhood
Commend my woman-love to thy belief,—
Seeing that I stand unwon, however wooed,
And rend the garment of my life, in brief,
By a most dauntless, voiceless fortitude,
Lest one touch of this heart convey its grief.

—EBB, *Sonnets from the Portuguese* #13

CONTENTS

ACKNOWLEDGMENTS

Little Songs came into being with much support. I am thankful to the English Department, the College of Arts and Sciences, and the Office of Research Administration at the University of Tennessee for enabling me through research and travel grants to spend extended periods of time at the British Library as well as to share my work on nineteenth-century women's sonnets at several informative conferences in this country and abroad. The Professional Development and Research Award that I was given by the University of Tennessee in the summer of 2003 and the Hodges Grant for Research in Lieu of Teaching that I received from the Department of English in the summers of 2002, 2003, and 2005 were useful in helping me meet my research goals.

I would like to thank the British Library for permitting me to study countless rare books and manuscripts; as a result, I was able to discover fascinating work by nineteenth-century women poets that has fallen out of the canon. I am obliged to the Department of English for granting me a sabbatical leave, which I used to finish *Little Songs.* I would like to thank my students, in particular Ann Broadhead, for their research into and insightful comments about the issues I discuss. I am indebted to Allen Dunn for the valuable feedback he provided me as I brought the last pieces of the manuscript into place. Especially, I would like to thank the head of the English department, John Zomchick, who stood by me and advised me while I worked to complete this book.

I owe an enormous amount to several scholars who served as role models even before my project began to take shape. Sandra Bermann, Claudia Brodsky, Suzanne Nash, and Susan Wolfson opened new avenues of thought for me and helped me find my voice. Esther

Schor not only read early versions for me but also assisted me in many practical ways as I brought *Little Songs* into its current form. Linda Shires has offered me thoughtful advice and encouragement. U. C. Knoepflmacher has been a tremendous source of inspiration, a helpful sounding board for my ideas, a wonderful editor, and a dear friend. Indeed, my debts to him exceed what I can express here.

I would like to thank my friends and colleagues Anne Jamison, Tamara Ketabgian, Robert T. Lehe, Joshua Mason, Natania Meeker, Yumi Selden, and Andrea Sherman, whose intelligence and compassion have guided my scholarly as well as my personal development for many years.

Scott Lewis aided me with his groundbreaking work as an editor of the Browning letters and by sharing his knowledge and ideas with me over tea in London. I greatly benefited from the extraordinarily insightful readers' reports I received after I submitted my manuscript for publication. In addition I would like to thank Sandy Crooms at The Ohio State University Press for her kindness and professionalism.

A short section of chapter 1 was printed in "Breaking 'the Silent Sabbath of the Grave': Charlotte Smith's Quiet Gaze at Grief," in *Silence, Sublimity and Suppression in the Romantic Period,* edited by Fiona L. Price and Scott Masson (New York: Mellen, 2002). A section of chapter 2 was printed in "'In Silence like to Death': Elizabeth Barrett's Sonnet Turn," *Victorian Poetry* 39, no. 4 (2001): 533–50. A brief section of chapter 1 was published in "Swallowing Sorrow: Women and the Eighteenth-Century Sonnet," *Augustan Studies* 2 (2005): 72–91.

Most of all, I want to say thank you to my family for their longstanding reassurance, understanding, and faith both in me and in my work. My father, Michael, my mother, Christine, and my sister, Nina, have spent many hours proofreading drafts of *Little Songs* and many years listening to my ideas evolve point by point. Finally, I will always be grateful to my husband, Shannon Burke, for this, as well as for everything I write.

INTRODUCTION

Silence, Gender, and the Sonnet Revival

We have only recently become aware of the instrumental role that women played in England's nineteenth-century sonnet revival.[1] Our oversight, which lasted two centuries, may have stemmed from Samuel Taylor Coleridge's shifting attitudes toward the sonnet form. In his *Sonnets from Various Authors* (1796), Coleridge selected sonnets by Helen Maria Williams, Charlotte Smith, and Anna Seward, and printed them next to his own. Of these, Smith had published her sonnets first, in her *Elegiac Sonnets* of 1784, and she seems to have restored single-handedly an enthusiasm for the disputed form.[2] But Coleridge later expressed great admiration for the sonnets of William Lisle Bowles, who had published his work just after Smith's.[3] Twentieth-century critics recapitulated Coleridge's appreciation for Bowles, hypothesizing that the latter made possible a kind of loco-descriptive poetry that Romantic writers would imitate.[4] Although Coleridge eventually dismissed his youthful enjoyment of Bowles's poetry, his earlier excitement may have persuaded modern critics to associate the sonnet revival with Bowles rather than to credit his legitimate precursor, Charlotte Smith. Indeed, Coleridge's preference for Bowles over Smith most likely resulted from his effort to distance himself from the female-dominated elegiac sonnet tradition.[5] Following Coleridge's lead, modern critics may have been complicit in their act of historical disavowal.

It is now recognized that Charlotte Smith inspired an energetic resurrection of sonnet writing: a powerful revival that would continue even into the twentieth century. In so doing, she dwarfed the accomplishments of her male precursors such as Thomas Edwards and Thomas Warton who also helped to legitimize the sonnet form.[6] In Stuart Curran's words, "[The sonnet's] rebirth coincides with the rise of a definable woman's literary movement and with the beginnings of Romanticism. The palm in both cases should go to Charlotte Turner Smith, whom Wordsworth a generation after her death accurately described as 'a lady to whom English verse is under greater obligations than are likely to be either acknowledged or remembered.'"[7] Following Smith, women poets went on to produce an outpouring of elegiac and amatory sonnets. Wordsworth read these poems and drew inspiration from them—his own first published poem in 1787 was a sonnet inspired by Helen Maria Williams—although he claimed he turned to sonnet writing because of Milton alone.[8]

While scholars now concede that women initiated the sonnet revival in England, *Little Songs* at present serves as the only book-length study devoted to a range of female sonneteers from the long nineteenth century.[9] *Little Songs* may be read as a supplement to, but more importantly, as a reconceptualization of Jennifer Wagner's *A Moment's Monument: Revisionary Poetics and the Nineteenth-Century English Sonnet* (1996). Wagner considers Wordsworth, Shelley, Keats, Dante Gabriel Rossetti, Hopkins, and Frost. She does not, however, examine any women poets of the period. A more recent study, Joseph Phelan's *The Nineteenth-Century Sonnet* (2005), updates Wagner's approach by giving space to female as well as male sonneteers. However, Phelan does not make gender his point of focus. Rather, he divides his chronological study into classes of sonnets—political, devotional and amatory. Unlike Phelan, I concentrate on nineteenth-century female sonneteers, juxtaposing well-established figures such as Elizabeth Barrett and Christina Rossetti with overlooked poets such as Anna Maria Smallpiece and Isabella Southern.[10] Through this approach, I aim to uncover a neglected element of intellectual history: how British women writers from the late eighteenth until the beginning of the twentieth century entered the lyric tradition through their use of the sonnet form.

In spite of my effort to bring non-canonical women into focus, I am not simply rendering invisible women poets visible and making muted, forgotten, or misunderstood words freshly audible. I also am exploring the connection between femininity, silence, and the sonnet that nineteenth-century women poets stress both in the themes of their poems and in their letters, prefaces, and notes. These sonneteers align femininity with what Charlotte Smith terms "blank despair," Elizabeth Barrett calls "hopeless grief," and Christina Rossetti names the "silence of love that cannot sing again." I maintain that the female poets who embraced the compressed sonnet form at a time when women could only with difficulty enter the lyric tradition were drawn to its structural affinity for reticence. Ultimately, I argue that the sonnet, better than any other form, allowed nineteenth-century women poets to investigate and promote gendered interpretations of silence.

SILENCE AND THE SONNET

Since its very origin, the sonnet has been associated with silence. As Paul Oppenheimer argues, the sonnet was the first lyric form since the fall of the Roman Empire designed not for song or for performance but for silent reading.[11] Between 1225 and 1230, the sonnet developed out of a courtly love tradition predicated on the absence or unattainability of a beloved addressee; at the same time, it broke from that tradition by developing a radically nonmusical structure.

The word "sonnet" in itself encapsulates the paradox that complicates the modern lyric. On the one hand, critics and lexicographers have assumed that the word "sonnet" (*sonnetto*) means "little song," or more specifically "little sound," and that it derives from the Italian *suono* or "sound." This notion of the sonnet's essentially musical structure leads critic John Fuller, and many others, to speak with confidence of "the sonnet's original musical setting."[12]

On the other hand, the *sonnetto*'s diminutive suffix undermines its claims to musicality. Oppenheimer explains that the first appearance of the word "sonnet" did emerge in the Italian word *sonnetto,* generally attributed to Dante's *Vita Nuova* of 1294; however, this word was never explicitly defined. The term is only critically discussed when it appears not in Italian but in the Latin word *sonitus,* of Dante's *De Vulgari Eloquentia* (before 1305). Dante places the sonnet below the *canzone* and the *ballata* because, unlike these more noble forms, the sonnet needs something from the outside (presumably music) and fails to create this quality from within. Oppenheimer notes that in classical Latin, *sonitus* can mean murmur, but usually conveys the idea of "noise as in empty sound, bombast, thunder" (181).

Furthermore, Oppenheimer posits that the Italian sonnet's peculiarly asymmetrical structure, which is built around a formal and thematic rupture or "volta," marks a radical departure from the musical lyrics of the troubadours. He notes that since no "musical settings for Petrarch's sonnets can be assigned a date earlier than 1470, well over two centuries after Giacomo [da Lentino] wrote his first sonnets," there simply may have been no prior attempt to fit words to music (178).

In contrast to traditional courtly love lyrics, early sonnets display a much more pronounced investment in *absence;* that is, the absence of any direct or implied address to a listening audience on the one hand, and the absence of multiple or dual personae on the other. Rather than engaging internal or external auditors in a performative debate, these sonnets record a process of dialectical self-confrontation through which a speaker inwardly articulates and then resolves a problem by means of the sonnet's divided structure itself. For Oppenheimer, the modern emphasis on silence introduced by the birth of the sonnet also "heralds a departure from the tradition of lyrics as performed poems and introduces a new, introspective, *quieter* mode, a mode that is to dominate the history of Western poetry for at least the next seven centuries" (187; my italics).

WOMEN AND SILENCE

In *The Madwoman in the Attic: The Woman Writer and the Nineteenth-Century Literary Imagination* (1979), Sandra M. Gilbert and Susan Gubar address the difficulty with which early women poets entered the lyric tradition. They cite Virginia Woolf's myth of Judith Shakespeare—an allegory that demonstrates why no woman poet of Shakespeare's status could have existed during the sixteenth century. Gilbert and Gubar extend Woolf's metaphor to apply in modified form throughout the nineteenth century as well. An important reason that women were denied credibility as poets during the nineteenth century, Gilbert and Gubar suggest, may have been their lack of the "aesthetic models" made possible by formal education.[13]

As Rita Felski observes in *Literature after Feminism* (2003), feminist scholars have criticized Gilbert and Gubar for relying on a homogenous and universalizing notion of "womanhood." These contemporary accounts examine how gender is inextricably linked to a number of other identity-based categories such as race, class, and sexuality.[14] Since the 1990s, critics have also, in Felski's estimation, become cautious about "the madwoman as an example of a feminist monomyth" (70). In *Eighteenth-Century Women Poets and Their Poetry: Inventing Agency, Inventing Genre* (2005), Paula R. Backsheider critiques Gilbert and Gubar's analysis, arguing that "by the end of the [eighteenth] century women poets were being recognized as one of the glories of the British nation" (382). Numerous critics observe that whatever the obstacles nineteenth-century women poets may have faced, they were in fact writing. In Anne K. Mellor's words, "between 1780 and 1830, women dominated not only the production of the novel [. . .] but also the production of poetry."[15] And Backsheider claims, "What must be obvious from this book is that barriers did not stop a larger number of talented women than we have recognized" (385).

In *Little Songs* I do not maintain that nineteenth-century women poets were silenced as in prevented from speaking; on the contrary, many of the women writers I discuss were amazingly prolific. Nor do I argue that they were silenced as in being removed permanently from literary history. As Tricia Lootens clarifies in *Lost Saints: Silence, Gender, and Victorian Literary Canonization,* "The silence around Barrett Browning—and around other poets—turned out not to be an absence."[16] Instead, poets enter and exit the canon for reasons more complex than their gender alone. What interests me is the overlapping, persistent, gendered attentiveness to silence that I have witnessed in nineteenth-century women's sonnets. I want to suggest that nineteenth-century women poets' attachment to silence results from Romantic and Victorian presumptions about normative gender and sexuality.

In *Little Songs,* I argue that Charlotte Smith, Elizabeth Barrett, and Christina Rossetti, together with their female contemporaries, linked silence to gender, albeit in shifting and at times conflicting ways.[17] Facing the historical absence of female precursors, as well as a continued artistic and intellectual silencing, and, finally, the challenge of calling attention to this social structure in their poems, nineteenth-century women's involvement with unspeakability became very elaborate.[18] These female poets needed to find ways of accentuating in words a problem that haunted and troubled them—the difficulty (if not in their minds the impossibility) of enjoying the same literary stature afforded their male counterparts—but they also needed to mask what they were articulating. It is partly for this reason that critics remain uncertain about Smith's changing status as a poet, Barrett's sentimentality and apparent conventionality, and Rossetti's professed lack of having anything to say.

Elizabeth Barrett's famous remark, "Where were the poetesses? [. . .] I look everywhere for grandmothers and see none," reminds us of the relative isolation of the nineteenth-century woman poet.[19] While Charlotte Smith was a celebrated poet during her lifetime, her reputation faded after her death (her successor, Elizabeth Barrett, most likely read none of her poetry). Anna Maria Smallpiece, a gifted Romantic sonneteer, probably was ignored even while she was still alive, as was the poet I carefully examine in chapter 4, Isabella Southern. Both Elizabeth Barrett and Christina Rossetti have suffered if not from the absence of recognition then from unfortunate acts of critical misrecognition.[20]

One of my goals in *Little Songs* is to awaken our ears and eyes to tones and configurations in nineteenth-century women's sonnets to which we have previously been deaf and blind. I do not argue that nineteenth-century female sonneteers overcome silence in favor of lyrical speech; rather, I explore how they simultaneously posit both muteness and volubility through style and theme. Ultimately, I illustrate how later nineteenth-century women writers repudiated the structural and thematic affinity for speechlessness that preoccupied their female precursors, thereby ushering in a historical period that has demonstrated an increasing respect for women poets.

BIOGRAPHICAL HAUNTINGS

Although I utilize biography in my analyses of nineteenth-century female poets, I strive to avoid the pitfalls of reductive biographical readings. As Alison Chapman explains in *The Afterlife of Christina Rossetti* (2000):

> Any feminist methodology which voices the silent, in fact, is caught up in an impossible double bind. On the one hand, in the logic of recovery, literary voices that have been silenced, repressed, or muffled from within the representational scheme need to be recovered in order to understand their contextual positions and to interrogate the construction of canonicity that

> marginalised them in the first place. [. . .] But, on the other hand, the result is to project a voice onto what has culturally become the voiceless: an act of critical ventriloquy which overturns, yet leaves in place, the methodological binary voice / silence upon which the literary canon is constructed.[21]

My intention in *Little Songs* is not so much to give voice to what has been repressed as it is to decipher the formal and thematic strategies with which nineteenth-century female sonneteers approached silence. Felski stresses a third alternative to the death of the author (promoted by Roland Barthes and Michel Foucault) and to the reading of literary works as allegories of female authorship: the careful navigation between biography and textual independence: "We can recognize that female authors have themselves been authored—that is to say, shaped by a multiplicity of social and cultural forces that exceed their grasp—without thereby denying their ability to act and to create. Similarly, we can factor the author into our readings of literary works without reducing literature to autobiography or assuming that such links determine the meaning of the work once and for all. Authorship is one strand in the weave of the text rather than a magic key to unlocking its mysteries."[22] Following this third approach outlined by Felski, I use biographical details to help decode puzzling references in nineteenth-century women's sonnets, and I pay close attention to places where women poets expose aspects of their biographical selves. As Natalie Houston and Phelan emphasize, the sonnet possessed an unusual documentary function for nineteenth-century writers and readers. In Houston's words, nineteenth-century "critical discourse about the sonnet generally assumed that it was a vehicle for truthful revelations."[23] And Phelan explains that the sonnet was repositioned "as a site of privileged autobiographical utterance within the system of poetic genres" (43). At the same time, I resist reductive biographical interpretations. Felski points out, "authors are skilled in the art of deception and concealment, in putting on masks and performing in elaborate disguise. This is the case even, or perhaps especially, when they claim to be giving accurate testimony, to be telling us the truth as it really happened" (61). In many ways, as I will show, nineteenth-century women's sonnets construct elaborate disguises which, rather than spotlighting biographical selves, as critics often assume to be the case, instead camouflage, obscure, and withhold them.[24] However, at other times, details from the authors' lives puncture these same sonnets, and it would be a mistake, I think, to cover our eyes to every biographical light that shines through.

CRITICAL RELEVANCE

This book enters into conversation with three central cross-disciplinary debates: 1) those that trace silences in literary fiction (such as Simon P. Sibelman's *Silence in the Novels of Elie Wiesel* [1995], Leona Toker's *Eloquent Reticence: Withholding Information in Fictional Narrative* [1993], Patricia Ondek Laurence's *The Reading of Silence: Virginia Woolf in the English Tradition* [1991] and Janis P. Stout's *Strategies of Reticence: Silence and Meaning in the Works of Jane Austen, Willa Cather, Katherine Anne Porter, and Joan Didion* [1990]); 2) those that discuss how silence informs theory, feminist criticism or rhetoric (such as Cheryl Glenn's *Unspoken: A Rhetoric of Silence* [2004], *Listening to Silences: New Essays in Feminist Criticism,* edited by Elaine Hedges and Shelley Fisher Fishkin [1994], *Languages of the Unsayable: the Play of Negativity in Literature and Literary Theory,* edited by Sanford Budick and Wolfgang Iser [1989], and Tillie Olsen's *Silences* [1978]); and 3) those that explore issues in gender theory (in particular I have been influenced by Judith Butler's work).[25]

While I have drawn inspiration from the recent debates about silence, I offer the single existing study of the overwhelming impact that silence makes, not only on British women's poetry but on the relationship between women's sonnets and the development of modern poetry and thought. In *Undoing Gender* (2004), Butler calls attention to the way that sexual difference functions not as a fact but as "a question, a question for our times" (177).[26] It is with the same sense of timeliness that I approach my study. Because the women poets I examine in *Little Songs* wrestle with the sonnet form during a period where the use of lyric poetry was still in many ways blocked to them, their insights into the uncertain relationship between gender and language will be of particular interest to us now. We have entered the twenty-first century with more questions than answers about a bewildering topic that we can neither put to rest nor put out of our minds. What is sexual difference? What is gender? By what are we constrained? From what are we free? The female sonneteers I investigate in *Little Songs* intelligently question the meaning of terms that continue to perplex us—female, male, femininity, masculinity, woman, and man. My choice to gather together and evaluate a group of women poets when the term "woman" remains so much in flux does not result from naïveté or presumptuousness. By questioning a term like "woman" we do not invalidate it. Rather, as Butler stresses in *Undoing Gender,* "To question a term [. . .] is to ask how it plays, what investments it bears, what aims it achieves, what alterations it undergoes. The changeable life of that term does not preclude its use" (180). My juxtaposition of British female sonneteers from the long nineteenth century likewise involves a simultaneous reliance upon and inquiry into the language we use (indeed into our very idea of language) as we struggle to conceptualize sexual difference and gender roles.

LITTLE SONGS

The first chapter of this book, "Breaking 'the Silent Sabbath of the Grave': Romantic Women's Sonnets and the 'Mute Arbitress' of Grief," explores both Charlotte Smith's confrontation with silence in her *Elegiac Sonnets* of 1784 and the responses of Smith's female contemporaries. I examine how Smith fuses silence and speech in her poems: unspeakability ("blank despair") coexists with a fragmented but sustained poetic language. To achieve this effect, Smith employs grieving masculine personifications—characters that are unable to speak or even to continue living but can only die in despair. The speaker persistently compares herself to these male figures—wanderers, mariners, pilgrims—without ever specifying the source of her own grief.[27]

At the same time, Smith pursues a number of feminized abstractions which vary between polar extremes, such as Melancholy and Hope, Solitude and Friendship. It is Smith's endless appeal to these oppositions that provides her with a constant source of poetic speech. In the final section of the chapter, I examine the responses of Smith's female contemporaries who were influenced by her poetics but who gravitated to silence in slightly different ways. Helen Maria Williams transposed Smith's elegies into a more comforting key while Anna Maria Smallpiece took issue with Williams's optimism; in spite of this similarity, Smallpiece conflicts with Charlotte Smith in the reasons that she gives for her own sorrow. While Smith's *Elegiac Sonnets* reveal varying sources of grief, Smallpiece's sonnets are all pressured by the difficulties of lesbian love—problems that Smallpiece does not explicitly verbalize; instead she communicates her struggles through ambiguity and indirection.

My second chapter, "'In Silence Like to Death': Elizabeth Barrett's Sonnet Turn," investigates Barrett's turn to the sonnet after the death of her brother in 1840. Seeing the sonnet's reticent structure as a metaphor for inexpressible grief, Barrett tries to highlight unspeakability and to find a way of undoing it. Explaining that grief must be expressed "in silence like to death" and that "poetry resembles grief," Barrett, like Smith, envisions poetry as representative of silence. While Barrett's sadness about her brother's death impeded her sonnets' ability to provide consolation in 1844, her 1850 *Sonnets from the Portuguese* appear to reverse her previous beliefs. Even though Barrett seems to translate death into life and grief into love in her 1850 sonnets, I demonstrate how Barrett's speaker actually remains haunted by death from the beginning to the end of her sequence. Barrett may speak to two people at the same time, to a dead beloved and to a living one, but she refuses to translate death into life. The only progress that takes place between 1844 and 1850 is that Barrett's sonnets at last claim to be versions of living flowers rather than dead ones. Yet while these flowers might be alive, Barrett splits them apart until they "burst, shatter, everywhere!"; what we see in the end are not living flowers but pale, bare branches. Consequently, silence functions at once as both a hinderer and a nourisher of Elizabeth Barrett's art.

My third chapter, "Sing Again: Christina Rossetti and the Music of Silence," untangles the different ways that Rossetti perplexes scholars with the tension between her restraint—her quiet voice—and with the musical nature of her poems. Silence operates on two different levels in Rossetti's poetry. First, her apparently female speaker continually reminds the reader that she cannot express herself, and second, her poetic lines cancel themselves out, producing a vagueness of situation and an unsteadiness of voice. I refer to the first category as one of "stated" silences since they are openly acknowledged, and the second category as one of "semantic" silences since they upset the exchange of ideas. And yet all of Rossetti's sonnets have a musical quality: the speaker skillfully sings that she cannot sing and also sings lyrics that seem to lack content.

In this chapter, I argue that Rossetti produces both music and silence, both women's voices and their absence. Requesting that nameless, forgotten women sing, Rossetti proves her question unanswerable. However, she does bring these women back. Unremembered women poets from history adopt many identities in Rossetti's sonnets, forcing everyone into speechlessness and also into an eternal musical request for forgotten women's impossible song. Pushing Barrett's encounter with grief one step further, Rossetti destroys her sonnet cycle "*Monna Innominata*" in its final words: "cannot sing again." But, as I will show, Rossetti follows both Smith and Barrett in her definition of silence, finally characterizing poetry as the music of inexpressivity itself.

In my fourth chapter, "'Silence, 'Tis More Cruel Than the Grave!': Isabella Southern and the Turn to the Twentieth Century," I consider how the contemporaries of and the first successors to Elizabeth Barrett and Christina Rossetti reworked the assertions made by their most celebrated female counterparts. I begin by looking at sonnets by Maria Norris, Dora Greenwell, and Michael Field, all of whom refer in their poems to Barrett and Rossetti by name. At first glance, Norris, Greenwell, and Field seem to write sonnets that thoroughly praise their poetic heroines. However, as I will illustrate, these sonnets present fundamental reevaluations of the poets they appear to extol. After a brief discussion of Norris, Greenwell, and Field, I devote a much longer section of the chapter to a study of Isabella J. Southern, whose book *Sonnets and Other Poems* (1891) finds fault with Barrett's and Rossetti's work.[28] While Barrett never read Charlotte Smith and while Christina Rossetti rejects Barrett by name in *Monna Innominata,* Southern addresses Barrett and Rossetti without ever telling us their names (although she obviously has read them). Refusing to designate who Barrett and Rossetti are, Southern tirelessly repeats and alters their sonnets in her own works. I propose that later nineteenth-century women sonneteers' movement away from the kind of silence that absorbed their female predecessors anticipates modern and contemporary thought.

Unlike recent interpretations that have stressed the importance of male sonneteers from Wordsworth to Frost, this book makes a case for the vital role women sonneteers have played in literary history. With voices that still remain almost too faint for us to hear, nineteenth-century women poets wrote on two different levels—mutely and musically—complexly gendering the double function of sonnets, and, by extension, of all lyric poems, as at once soundless and harmonic "little songs."

CHAPTER ONE

Breaking "the Silent Sabbath of the Grave"

Romantic Women's Sonnets and the "Mute Arbitress" of Grief

William Wordsworth's frequently cited praise of Charlotte Smith as "a lady to whom English verse is under greater obligations than are likely to be either acknowledged or remembered" prophesied both Smith's historical impact and her disappearance from the early Romantic canon.[1] Even though current attention to Romantic women writers has generated interest in Smith's *Elegiac Sonnets*—first published in 1784, the start of the nineteenth-century sonnet revival—critics remain perplexed by the collection's failure to elegize any constant source of grief. The sonnets shift between translations from Petrarch, poems supposedly written by Johann Wolfgang von Goethe's Werter, amatory lyrics by many characters from Smith's own novels, apparent elegies for her dead daughter, and those that mourn unstated causes.[2] At the same time, these poems repeatedly evoke a "blank despair" that language cannot ameliorate.

Charlotte Smith's concentration on unutterable despair may indirectly account for her long-term disappearance from the early Romantic canon. Until recently, Smith's historical successor William Lisle Bowles had taken her place as the most well-known late-eighteenth-century sonneteer. Our earlier confusion about Smith's instrumental role in the sonnet's rebirth seems to have derived from Coleridge's preference for Bowles over Smith, a partiality quite possibly influenced by the extremity of Smith's apparent grief. It is as if by foregrounding a fundamental silence whose cause poetry cannot articulate and whose antidote no language can provide, Smith quieted her sonnets to the point where they ceased to be heard at all.

Our current appreciation for Romantic women writers has brought Smith back into focus, but her sonnets' refusal either to justify or to alleviate sorrow poses some crucial problems. Throughout the *Elegiac Sonnets,* Smith describes grief as final, wordless, and unalterable, persistently tying her speaker to inaudible mourners; conversely, she continues to speak through ten widening volumes that draw from an enormous intertextual base and even appear in several of her own novels. The speaker's poetic voice manages to swing from muteness to loquaciousness as it concurrently extinguishes itself and expresses the varying sentiments of a wide range of people. Over the course of this chapter, I will investigate the conflict between "blank despair" and expansive speech in the *Elegiac Sonnets* in order to unpack Smith's gendered manipulation of these terms. In so doing, I will juxtapose the *Elegiac Sonnets* with Thomas Gray's famous "Sonnet [on the Death of Mr. Richard West]" (1775) as well as William Lisle Bowles's *Fourteen Sonnets, Elegiac and Descriptive* (1789). Unlike Gray and Bowles, Smith emphasizes loss at the expense of regeneration. Ultimately, I will argue that the *Elegiac Sonnets* juxtapose two poetic modes—vacancy and regeneration—without ever allowing one to take precedence over the other. By recognizing poetry's dual status as music and as silence (a gendered relation that the sonnets break down), Charlotte Smith modernizes the sonnet form, successfully transposing lyric poetry itself from a major to a minor key.

In the last part of this chapter, I examine the approaches of Smith's female contemporaries—sonneteers who at once admired Smith's work and resisted it. In particular, I discuss sonnets by Helen Maria Williams and Anna Maria Smallpiece. Williams's sonnets adopt a more reassuring tone than Smith's elegies. Meanwhile, Anna Maria Smallpiece takes issue with Williams (openly in "To Miss Williams, on Reading her Sonnet to the Strawberry"). While Smallpiece resents Williams's consolatory approach, she, too, differs from Smith in the similarly obscured but unrelated cause that motivates her grief. As I will illuminate in the next two chapters, through the complex gender alignments that they design and in the bond between silence, grief, and the poetic function that they generate, Charlotte Smith, Helen Maria Williams, and Anna Maria Smallpiece foreshadow sonnets by their successors Elizabeth Barrett and Christina Rossetti.

ELEGY AND BIOGRAPHY

Critics are still inclined to root Smith's underlying source of grief in biographical details—the narrative of her doomed marriage to a reckless gambler who brought her with him to debtors' prison and failed to provide for their numerous children. Smith herself called attention to these distresses in prefaces to the *Elegiac Sonnets*, prefaces which, by evoking readers' sympathy, helped to market her poems.[3] Although she turned away from poetry to novels for financial reasons (she ultimately wrote ten novels over a ten-year period), her sonnets inspired the nineteenth-century revival of the sonnet form. The *Elegiac Sonnets* appeared in nine expanding editions during Smith's lifetime, and a tenth after her death.[4] Curiously, Smith's poems evade the very biographical readings that she commercially promoted.

As Esther Schor has shown, Charlotte Smith's need to revise and extend her elegies throughout her life forced her to keep justifying the remarkable persistence of her sorrow. She had to write new prefaces that "would attest even more adamantly to the constancy and continuity" of her grief.[5] Schor makes it clear that much like Bowles's own subsequent prefaces (though with very different results) Smith's "prefatory claims escalate" (61).[6] In her prefaces to the first and second editions, Smith does not identify her cause of mourning (she calls it simply "some very melancholy moments") (3); in the third and fourth editions, she speaks of poems that are actually not new at all (3); it is only in the sixth edition of 1792 that she explains to a friend how her family has not "obtained the provision their grandfather designed for them" (5). The preface to the second volume of her poems, published in 1797, accounts for the length of time the edition took by citing her "pecuniary inconveniences," the death of her daughter and her own failing health (6–12).

Smith's quietness about the source of her mourning through five publications of her poems, and within her individual sonnets, awakens curiosity in the reader. Daniel White suggests that "by their very ineffability," "the insults and inconveniences" that Smith faced "must be described over and over again."[7] If, in the eighteenth century, "critics hardly ever reviewed her poems without commenting directly on her personal life," the same also holds true today.[8] The introduction to the 1992 edition of Smith's poems begins with a long description of her hardships: not only was she "living with her wastrel husband in a London debtors' prison," but she would bear twelve children and grew up motherless since "she was three."[9] Before we learn anything about the *Elegiac Sonnets,* we are informed that "all told, she had a good deal to be elegiac about" (1). At the same time, in Jerome McGann's words, "The peculiar force of Smith's *Elegiac Sonnets* [. . .] comes from the fact that they are *not* elegies for some particular person or persons. *Lacrymae rerum,* they meditate a general condition."[10]

The biographical trend in Smith criticism may have led contemporary scholars to commit the same errors as many of her sympathetic eighteenth-century readers.[11] Janet Todd explains how, during the Georgian era, the assumption that biography and literature were interconnected was a part of all kinds of sentimental writing.[12] However, this interrelationship between life and textuality does not valorize biographical readings of sentimental poems. As Todd explains, the link between writing and experience does not mean that the former exactly imitates the latter, as most criticism of Smith's work maintains. Instead, sentimental convention suggests that it is in life that literature is imitated rather than the reverse. Given the anti-autobiographical nature of the *Elegiac Sonnets* (which in its final version contains thirty-six sonnets written by ventriloquized voices), our biographical interpretations could over-simplify her poems. Focusing on Smith's life might even result once again in the erasure of her poetry from the very Romantic canon that we are currently committed to reassessing.

Our need to explain Smith's grief biographically may correspond to her recent reentry into the Romantic canon. Two of the poets I will examine, Elizabeth Barrett and Christina Rossetti, were often discussed in biographical terms when feminist criticism first revitalized an interest in them. Sandra Gilbert's and Susan Gubar's *The Madwoman in the Attic* (1979) may have inspired this renewal of interest. Between 1986 and 1988, well-known Barrett scholars such as Angela Leighton, Helen Cooper, Margaret Forster, and Dorothy Mermin all published key studies on Barrett's poetry. In Rossetti's case, only one book had been published on her poetry since 1930 when Antony Harrison wrote *Christina Rossetti in Context,* which did not appear until 1988. Because over twenty-five years has passed since Barrett and Rossetti returned to the canon, earlier biographical readings have now been pushed aside. Charlotte Smith, on the other hand, was not fully rediscovered until 1993 (the publication date of Stuart Curran's collection of her poems).

Over the past ten years in Smith criticism the shift away from biography has begun to occur. For example, in 1996, Adela Pinch touched upon Smith's elaborate, nonbiographical configurations, explaining that Smith's sonnets "highlight the *literariness* of the melancholy they express. From the first sonnets onward, they seem to argue that their melancholy may indeed be caused by the strange effects of reading and writing."[13] However, while Pinch demonstrates that "Smith's sonnets are like echo chambers, in which reverberate direct quotations, ideas, and tropes from English poetry," her premise is that the *Elegiac Sonnets* at once repeat past literary devices *and* assert the author's individual sentiments (60): "Smith's poems claim simultaneously that the feelings in them are derived from the transmission of literary tropes and that their authority comes from their personal idiosyncrasy" (68). For example, the fact that Werter's beloved is named Charlotte creates a strange combination of emotions. As Smith is also a Charlotte, she appears to be both the communicator and the receiver of Werter's feelings. This model illustrates how in her sonnets Smith at once plays the role of object and subject. Because of Smith's complicated sympathy with her own emotions, it becomes difficult for readers to understand the circumstances surrounding her feelings—"whether they are real or fictive, where they come from, to whom they belong" (66).

While Pinch accurately calls attention to the way that Smith plays the roles of both object and subject, her theory does not totally account for alignments between Smith's speaker and the male characters. For instance, it is not immediately clear from Pinch's argument how poems ostensibly narrated by male speakers, poems that refer to no female characters, engage in the same strategy as Smith's Werter sonnets. Nor is it obvious how Smith's Petrarchan translations, which surely do speak to a female character, tie their authorial persona to Laura except in terms of gender—surely an overly simple analogy to draw. Instead, personal idiosyncrasies only stand out in the *Elegiac Sonnets* because every possible device is set into motion to cover them up.

In *Charlotte Smith: Romanticism, Poetry and the Culture of Gender* (2003), Jacqueline M. Labbe stresses the importance both of biography and theatricality in the *Elegiac Sonnets.* In Labbe's view, Smith calls attention to her autobiographical self in the *Elegiac Sonnets* through an extensive apparatus—for example, the prefaces Smith attached to the sonnets, the engravings accompanying several of the sonnets, the frontispiece (which presented a picture of the author to her readers), and other marginal matter, including the extensive notes Smith wrote to explain hidden elements to readers.[14] Labbe admits that due to this apparatus, she, like Smith's contemporaries, often wants to equate the varying speaker of Smith's sonnets with the author: "Because of the strength and persistence of this embodied 'I,' even modern readers, myself included, have been prone to see Smith's poetic speaker(s) as more or less unmediated versions of Charlotte Smith herself."[15] At the same time, Labbe recognizes the theatricality of Smith's sonnets, acknowledging that "[e]ven as she pursues a project of writing the sorrows of Charlotte, Smith overturns the very subjectivity this relies on: her manipulation of selfhood reflected in her abstraction of the 'I' results in poetry that is simultaneously highly personal and emptied of personality altogether" (*Charlotte Smith* 91).

According to Labbe, on the one hand, Smith "writes poetry that emphasizes straying, exile, alienation and mystique" (*Charlotte Smith* 11). In so doing, she places her ostensibly female speaker in traditionally male roles. On the other hand, "Smith peppers many of her novels with sonnets spoken or written by both male and female characters, which she then includes in her *Elegiac Sonnets* either without attribution or without revealing the poem's original speaker. The most obvious result is that a poem first written from a man's point of view is usurped by a feminine speaker" (104–5). Finally, Smith writes several sonnets clearly from a male point of view, such as her translations from Petrarch or her sonnets supposedly written by Werter. Labbe believes that by personalizing the *Elegiac Sonnets* and distancing them from herself, Smith makes it necessary for the reader to approach her poems in two different ways.

In 2005, Joseph Phelan underscored Smith's use of the "confessional dimension" of the sonnet form but recognized that such privileged autobiographical utterance became disguised or encrypted within the heavily rule-governed sonnet shape.[16] Phelan maintains that this double quality of "expressiveness and decorum" made "the sonnet form so attractive [. . .] in particular to the women poets of the early nineteenth century" (46–47). In 2005, Paula R. Backsheider takes "the formal characteristic of the double voice" that other critics have observed in Smith's sonnets and pushes it one step further.[17] According to Backsheider, rather than writing primarily autobiographical poems, Smith was above all writing a sonnet sequence constructed through "artifice and performance" (326). In Backsheider's opinion, Smith "works very hard to make it impossible to deny that the sonnets are art and artifice" (328).

I would like to reformulate the tension between sincerity and concealment within the framework of silence and speech. Relating grief to silence in the *Elegiac Sonnets,* Smith's speakers appeal to a wide list of often-conflicting feminized abstractions in order to seek comfort for their despair. While these abstractions are feminized as is the "self" that Smith presents to us in her prefaces and engravings, she continually relates her speaker to speechless male victims (the "poor mariner," the "unhappy exile," the "lone wanderer"). Varying the identity of her speaker, Smith calls attention to the interchangeability of gender roles, dissolving the boundary between the femininity that inspires speech and the masculinity that lacks access to it. As I will show, poetry, for Smith, results from two contrary movements: a progression toward unspeakability and toward extensive verbalization—the *Elegiac Sonnets* vibrate incessantly between these polar extremes.

"THE LUCID LINE": TWO READINGS

In order to illustrate how the double pull between silence and voice intertwines with gender references in Smith's *Elegiac Sonnets,* I will do a close reading of two paradigmatic sonnets: Sonnet 85 (which lacks a title) and Sonnet 86 ("Written near a port on a dark evening"). As Sonnets 85 and 86 appear in one of Smith's novels, *The Young Philosopher* (1798), they enable me to show how the interplay between fictional and poetic worlds complicates and enhances Smith's project throughout the *Elegiac Sonnets.* Furthermore, as Sonnet 85 is written by a female character (Mrs. Glenmorris) and Sonnet 86 is written by a male character in reply (George Delmont), the pendant permits a study of 1) how the imagery and tone of Smith's sonnets vary depending on the gender of the fictional characters behind them; 2) how masculinity and femininity enter into conversation with one another throughout Smith's collection; and 3) how Smith manipulates gendered personifications in her sonnets.[18]

We learn from *The Young Philosopher* that a female and a male character write Sonnet 85 and Sonnet 86, respectively. In fact, George Delmont (the "young philosopher" himself) composes Sonnet 86 in direct response to Sonnet 85, after receiving the first from his correspondent, Laura Glenmorris. In *The Young Philosopher,* characters therefore send the sonnets to each other by post as a kind of statement and reply. Smith ties the characters' sonnets to their financial hardships. The novel's premise is that a mother and her daughter (Laura and Medora Glenmorris) have left their home in America to resolve a dispute about Medora's deserved inheritance, while Mr. Glenmorris remains abroad. Living in seclusion, they are frequently visited by George Delmont, a friend of their caretaker. George and Medora fall in love, but financial problems interfere with their marriage. Mrs. Glenmorris learns that not only will Medora probably not earn the money to which she is entitled but the two of them possess barely enough to sustain themselves due to ambiguous difficulties Mr. Glenmorris is having in America. Delmont, then, becomes entangled in the gruesome financial issues of his gambling, bad-natured older brother, and consequently loses all of his own meager sums as well. While he is away, endeavoring to resolve these problems, Mrs. Glenmorris writes him a letter in which she includes one of her own recent sonnets (what will become Sonnet 85 in the *Elegiac Sonnets*). Absorbed with his comparable problems, George Delmont composes a sonnet for Mrs. Glenmorris (Sonnet 86), which he intends as an answer to her own. The two sonnets read as follows:

LXXXV

The fairest flowers are gone! for tempests fell,
And with wild wing swept some unblown away,
While on the upland lawn or rocky dell
More faded in the day-star's ardent ray;
And scarce the copse, or hedge-row shade beneath,
Or by the runnel's grassy course, appear
Some lingering blossoms of the earlier year,
Mingling bright florets, in the yellow wreath
That Autumn with his poppies and his corn
Binds on his tawny temples[.]—So the schemes
Rais'd by fond Hope in youth's unclouded morn,
While sanguine youth enjoys delusive dreams,
Experience withers; till scarce one remains
Flattering the languid heart, where only Reason reigns!
(Curran, *The Poems of Charlotte Smith* 73)

LXXXVI
WRITTEN NEAR A PORT ON A DARK EVENING

Huge vapours brood above the clifted shore,
Night on the Ocean settles, dark and mute,
Save where is heard the repercussive roar
Of drowsy billows, on the rugged foot
Of rocks remote; or still more distant tone
Of seamen in the anchor'd bark that tell
The watch reliev'd; or one deep voice alone
Singing the hour, and bidding "Strike the bell."
All is black shadow, but the lucid line
Mark'd by the light surf on the level sand,
Or where afar the ship-lights faintly shine
Like wandering fairy fires, that oft on land
Mislead the Pilgrim[.]—Such the dubious ray
That wavering Reason lends, in life's long darkling way.
(Curran 74)

In *The Young Philosopher,* Sonnet 85 addresses both the premature approach of Autumn and Mrs. Glenmorris's financial concerns. "The fairest flowers are gone!" represents lost income, also corresponding to lost youth with the hope it entails.[19] This statement becomes clearer when the title of the novel is considered together with its reference to George Delmont and, through him, to Mr. Glenmorris—"philosophers" who are related because of their lack of interest in trivial events and social conventions. The very quality of "reason" unfortunately causes Mr. Glenmorris to lose the money he needs to support his family. Delmont has no interest in pursuing a well-paying career (philosophy itself is his main interest), and this, combined with his brother's actions, makes him incapable of helping the Glenmorrises or of realizing the marriage that everyone feels should come about.

I propose to read Mrs. Glenmorris's sonnet in light of the neoclassical gendering of personifications. The first articulated gender designation occurs in line 9—the opening of the sestet. Here, the masculine gender of Autumn surfaces not once but three times—"That Autumn with *his* poppies and *his* corn / Binds on *his* tawny temples" (my italics). It is important to juxtapose this maneuver with the masculinization of Autumn in Thomson's *The Seasons,* which Smith quotes in Sonnet 27. The "fairest flowers," clearly feminized entities (especially given their link to the beautiful Medora), are apparently violated by masculine "tempests," "the day-star," and "Autumn" himself. We see, then, a replacement of femininity with masculinity—a point that is reinforced by the extension of flowers to "fond Hope" (gendered feminine in eighteenth-century writing), which "withers" with the sudden intrusion of Fall.

Even though Smith shows how Hope is replaced by Experience in Sonnet 85, she refers to "Experience" just like "Hope" in the feminine.[20] This gendering sets up within Sonnet 85 the vibration between poles that femininity (as opposed to masculinity) brings about in Smith's poems. It is as though an aggressive masculine force—Autumn—demands the movement from one feminized extreme to the other (from Hope to Experience). This fluctuation between feminized terms (culminating in the forfeiture of one in favor of the other) may result from a destructive masculine energy.

As much sense as this gendered interpretation of Sonnet 85 makes, the ending couplet complicates our reading. The phrase "where only Reason reigns!" seems to gender "Reason" masculine, if we consider the poem's implicit reference to male "philosophers." However, in Sonnet 38, Reason abdicates "*her* throne" (38; my italics). Thus, the final phrase may in fact return not to masculinity but to femininity. Moreover, the sonnet's concluding line rules out everything that precedes it: Autumn, Hope, and even Experience. At the end, "*only* Reason reigns!"—an exclamation that recalls the poem's opening cry: "The fairest flowers are gone!" (my italics).

Ultimately, femininity might gain rather than lose supremacy in Sonnet 85, with Reason instead of "the fairest flowers" most fully associated with it.[21] But how can this reading apply to a poem that also asserts masculinity's binding control? Strangely, Smith *does* gender Autumn feminine in her famous Sonnet 34, "To Melancholy," which opens, "When latest Autumn spreads *her* evening veil" (34; my italics). Smith's reliance on Thomson's masculine gendering of Autumn implies that she should masculinize the term. A quick, triple gendering of Autumn in Sonnet 85 ("*his* poppies," "*his* corn," "*his* tawny temples")—the only instance of explicit gendering in Sonnet 85—calls our attention to its masculinity, while the announcement "When latest Autumn spreads *her* evening veil" (the first time the term is gendered in the *Elegiac Sonnets*) alerts the reader to its femininity from the outset (my italics).

As a result, Sonnet 85 leaves us with two conflicting interpretations. On the one hand, it seems that an intrusive masculine energy (Autumn) propels the movement from a feminine Hope to an equally feminine Experience, finally subverting this dynamic altogether so that only masculine Reason reigns. On the other hand, Smith genders Reason feminine in Sonnet 38 and Autumn feminine in Sonnet 34. It seems that one model of femininity (as "the fairest flowers" and "Hope") is overcome by another: an opposing model of femininity like Experience and Reason. By gendering Autumn masculine and by omitting Reason's gender in Sonnet 85, Smith supports my initial reading. At the same time, within the *Elegiac Sonnets* as a whole, Autumn's masculine gender is called into question, Reason is explicitly feminized, and our second reading comes to hold as much force as the first. To understand how both of these readings apply to the sonnet, it is important to remember that in Sonnet 85 neither the flowers, the day-star, Hope, Experience, the heart, or Reason are openly gendered in any way. At last, we confront Autumn's ambiguous, shifting gender in the collection as a whole. Gender relations do not disappear from Smith's sonnets as a result of this disturbance; rather, gender becomes all the more apparent as the methods we use for understanding how it operates break down.

After receiving Sonnet 85, the "young philosopher," George Delmont, replies to Mrs. Glenmorris first in the form of a letter and then as a sonnet of his own. His letter repeats many of her sonnet's complaints: "'You can imagine,' said he, 'nothing more unlike my former self than I am at this moment.—I now enjoy nothing as I did five years since,—when I passed two months in wandering over Wales—and yet I am in perfect health'" (*The Young Philosopher* 181). He consciously writes his sonnet as a response to hers: "Satiated as I, and as I suppose two-thirds of the reading world have been with sonnets [a comment on the sonnet revival that Smith herself helped to initiate], yours from Upwood has reconciled me to them, and even tempted me, as I traversed the beach, to sonnetize myself—" after which his poem "Written near a port on a dark evening" follows (181).

Backsheider explains that Sonnet 86 "was written to be spoken by Delmont in *The Young Philosopher* as he waits for favourable winds to sail" (334). But in her reading she makes no mention of Sonnet 85. A closer analysis of Smith's novel encourages us to read Sonnets 85 and

86 side by side (as Smith's own readers would have done). Delmont's sonnet contrasts with Mrs. Glenmorris's most obviously in its references to sublimity as opposed to beauty. His adjectives—"huge," "dark," "mute," "rugged," "repercussive," "remote," "distant," "deep," "black," "dubious," "long," and "darkling"—echo Edmund Burke's discussion of the sublime in *A Philosophical Enquiry into the Origin of Our Ideas of the Sublime and Beautiful* (1757), a discussion with which Smith was surely familiar. In Burke's analysis, the sublime is "vast," "dark," "rugged," "solid and massive" (like the "rocks remote"), and even associated with privation: "All *general* privations are great, because they are all terrible; *Vacuity, Darkness, Solitude* and *Silence.*"[22] On the other hand, Mrs. Glenmorris's choice of adjectives corresponds to beauty rather than sublimity: "fairest," "bright," "yellow," "unclouded," "sanguine," and "languid." This distinction between the beautiful and the sublime divides Sonnet 85 and Sonnet 86, mirroring the different genders of the two poems' speakers. Burke imposes a gendered difference between the two terms, relating beauty to femininity; he says, "The beauty of women is considerably owing to their weakness, or delicacy, and is even enhanced by their timidity, a quality of mind analogous to it" (106).

While they differ with respect to beauty and sublimity, Sonnets 85 and 86 share many common images. Mrs. Glenmorris personifies falling "tempests" at the opening of her poem just as Delmont brings to life "huge vapours" that "brood" over the shore. Her "rocky dell" reappears as his "rocks remote," while her "delusive dreams" of "sanguine youth" reoccur in Delmont's poem as the ship-lights' glow that misleads the pilgrim. Formally as well as thematically, Delmont repeats the previous poem's structure. Sonnet 85's initial couplet, "fell / dell," echoes midway through 86 as "tell / bell." Moreover, Sonnet 85's second rhyme, "away / ray," inverts in Delmont's concluding couplet as "ray / way."

Delmont extends Sonnet 85's concluding exclamation, "where only *Reason* reigns!" to the warning, "Such the dubious ray / That wavering *Reason* lends, in life's long darkling way" (my italics).[23] Whereas Sonnet 85 ends with the rule of reason alone, Sonnet 86 appears to take this point a step further. Moving lost beauty into the realm of sublime darkness, Delmont shows how even reason becomes suspect in the end. Now no flowers appear in the poem at all but instead cliffs, the ocean, rocks and black shadow. The "lucid line" of reason wavers in Sonnet 86 where before it simply ruled, preeminent; in the fashion of "wandering fairy-fires," reason misdirects the lost traveler. In Backsheider's words, "Trained to trust his reason, Delmont has learned through suffering and observation that reason, like the 'lucid line' between surf and sand—which is, indeed, an illusion as the line shifts with each wave—does not make things clear" (335).

In Sonnet 86, silence and darkness eventually transmute into sound and light, a process that seems to stress masculinity over femininity. In the first two lines we hear a triple echo: "huge," "brood," and "mute." Thus, night settles down, in silence, among massive vapours. However, the second two lines reverse this emphasis on silence. As "shore" finds its rhyme in "roar," so "mute" transforms into "foot." The phrase "repercussive roar" might similarly describe poetry, particularly sonnets, which work through a reverberation of sounds. The movement from "mute" to "foot" reinforces this idea of the lyric, in which lines move rhythmically from one foot to the next. Further in the distance, one can hear the "tone / Of seamen, in the anchored bark, that tell," not unlike poetic speakers, and one can even discern "one deep voice alone / Singing the hour, and bidding 'strike the bell.'"

Just as silence gives rise to lyrical sound in Delmont's sonnet, the darkness with which the poem opens expands into light. The "night o'er the ocean" that "settles, dark and mute" (after which "all is black shadow") resolves into a "lucid line / Mark'd by the light surf on the level sand." As "lucid line" ends the poetic line, it refers back to its own structure, just as the marking of the surf on the "level sand" highlights the sonnet's own highly balanced, cadenced form. In a reversal of Mrs. Glenmorris's sonnet, Sonnet 86 replaces defeated beauty with the sublime and seems to recreate poetry not as lost "fairest flowers" but as "one deep voice alone" that sings the hour and bids, "Strike the bell." Delmont's emphasis on masculinity, both in echoes of Burke's sublime—"huge," "clifted," "roar," "rugged"—and in the characters who are able to speak, sing and call—"seamen," "one deep voice alone"—opposes Mrs. Glenmorris's contrary stress on withered fairness and also her final exclamation that "only [feminine] Reason reigns!"

At the same time, Delmont's sonnet struggles to undo itself like Mrs. Glenmorris's and other poems throughout Smith's collection. Neither the seamen telling the watch relieved nor the "one deep voice alone" counteract the darkness that the settling night brings.

It is only at the start of the sestet that both darkness and muteness disappear: "All is black shadow, but the lucid line / Mark'd by the light surf on the level sand." Lucidity here suggests both light and reason just as the "light surf" carries ideas of color and also of weight. The light surf that "marks" a "lucid line" on a "level" surface carries with it at once sound and brightness. As in Sonnet 85, Sonnet 86 strips itself of gendered distinctions—the line of retreating ocean waves, which inscribes a steady, luminous and echoing trail, holds no apparent gender at all. But this image only makes sense when we look at the spaces *between* each line of the poem. In writing, letters are all "black shadow"; the "lucid line" (after which the line itself breaks) suggests the path of blankness that splits rather than constitutes poetic lines.

Importantly, at the start of Delmont's last quatrain, Sonnet 86 becomes sonorous: "A*ll* is b*l*ack shadow, but the *l*ucid *l*ine / Mark'd by the *l*ight surf on the *l*eve*l* sand" and "All is black sha*d*ow, but the luci*d* line / Mark'*d* by the light surf on the level san*d*" (my italics). This use of alliteration recalls the repeating sounds of water that offer us brilliant paths no longer of language but of absence and departure. Smith's collection takes us to the moment when waves hit the sand with repercussive, Petrarchan roars; however, it also takes us to a time of vanishing, where only the white markings of the ocean's disappearance remain.

SMITH'S USE OF PERSONIFICATIONS

In my reading of Sonnet 85 and Sonnet 86, I call attention to the importance of gendered personifications in the *Elegiac Sonnets.* Over the course of her *Elegiac Sonnets,* Smith shows nearly every feminized abstraction to be fundamentally reversible. While Friendship is compared to the "fair moon" and invoked as "O Nymph!" in "To Friendship," in "To Solitude," coveted aloneness is likewise addressed "Ah, Nymph!" (31, 27). Fancy, the "Queen of Shadows," is opposed to a feminized Reason, which in one sonnet "abdicates her throne" (and this feminization of Reason was crucial to my reading of Sonnet 85). Tranquility, the "beauteous sister of the halcyon peace" (40), is sharply contrasted with "wild Phrenzy," which is awakened from "her hideous cell" (43). Nature, associated with nurturing and childhood innocence in "To the South Downs" (15–16), is elsewhere related to a feminized worldliness: "The spot where pale Experience hangs her head" (and we also observed how Experience took the place of feminized Hope in Sonnet 85) (44).

Smith draws conflicting feminized personifications from her role models: William Collins, James Thomson, John Milton, William Hayley, and William Cowper, among others. But her work makes a startling turn: the *Elegiac Sonnets* relentlessly create feminized *abstractions* (there are more than twenty-five in her sonnets, such as "Melancholy," "Hope," and "Night") while, on the other hand, masculine figures are particularized. This latter category is almost entirely composed of silenced individuals such as the pilgrim, the woodman, the captive, the lunatic, the seaman, and the wanderer. In other words, while both feminized and masculinized personifications traditionally were used alternately, both in abstract and particular form, the *Elegiac Sonnets* create a radical gender imbalance. In accordance with the poetic conventions she follows, Smith makes use both of typical feminized universals and masculinized particulars, but she refuses to bring in masculinized abstractions. Over and over she refers to the traditionally masculine "despair" in her sonnets without gendering it (failing to use such words as "he," "his," "him," etc); nor does she gender other masculine forces like "time," "genius," "pride," "judgment," or "oppression" (a word that echoes throughout the collection). This gender disequilibrium sets Smith's work apart from the neoclassical background in which it takes root.

Smith's twist in gender distinctions is all the more remarkable when we compare her work to that of her predecessors. Collins's "The Passions: An Ode to Music" (1747) exemplifies the models against which Smith was positioning her poems: he refers to "music," "hope," "pity," "melancholy," and "cheerfulness" in the feminine, yet calls to "fear," "anger," "despair," "revenge," "sport," and "joy" in the masculine.[24] Likewise, "Autumn" in Thomson's *The Seasons* (1727), which Smith quotes in Sonnet 27, alludes to "wisdom," "quiet," and "morning" in the feminine, but masculinizes "hunger," "Autumn," and "the power of philosophic melancholy."[25] Milton's "L'Allegro," which Smith quotes in Sonnet 57, refers to "Mirth" and "Liberty" in the feminine and "brooding darkness" and "Laughter" in the masculine.[26] And Hayley, to whom Smith dedicates the *Elegiac Sonnets,* refers in his "Essay on Painting" to "Painting," "Fancy,"

"Friendship," "Fame," "Beauty," "Ign'rance," "Art," "Perfection," and "Glory" in the feminine, and "the travell'd Artist," "Fashion," "Genius," "Judgment," "Pride," and "Time" in the masculine.[27]

Like Smith's feminized generalizations, her masculinized embodiments divide into two categories, both of which connect to forms of silence. While feminized abstractions remain muted, they nonetheless inspire speech in a way that Smith's male incarnations cannot. Instead, Smith describes male figures either as having nothing of substance to say, or else, due to desperate circumstances, as being unable to speak at all. She often uses the term "blest" to designate her first category of male personifications—those who are devoid of feeling and thought. For example, the "blest" shepherd in Sonnet 9 "Lies idly gazing—while his *vacant* mind / Pours out some tale antique of rural love" (18; my emphasis). The shepherd is clearly oblivious to the feminized abstraction of Melancholy. Smith writes, "Ah! *he* has never felt the pangs that move / Th' indignant spirit" (18). Although the shepherd sings a "tale antique of rural love," Smith suggests that he has never known true love or its connection to heartbreak. "Nor *his* rude bosom those fine feelings melt, / Children of Sentiment and Knowledge born, / Thro' whom each shaft with cruel force is felt, / Empoison'd by deceit—or barb'd with scorn" (18). Immune to these "fine feelings," the shepherd's bosom is "rude" and his mind is "vacant," for he is excluded from both reason and fancy, both grief and love.[28]

Similar to the shepherd in Sonnet 9, the "hind" in Sonnet 31 is "blest" because of "thoughtless mirth" and a "careless head" (34). The woodman in Sonnet 54, with his toil "oppress'd," also is granted a "careless head," "momentary rest," and "a sweet forgetfulness" (49). Likewise, in Sonnet 57, the hind is more "blest" than those who trust to dependence (51). Even the lunatic in Sonnet 70 murmurs to the water with "hoarse, half-utter'd lamentation" (61). This inarticulateness exemplifies the condition of all Smith's unreflecting shepherds: lacking reason, the lunatic can hardly speak, and has no audience but the sea. Ironically, Smith's speaker covets the fate of the shepherd and the madman; in 31, she says, "Ah! what to me can those dear days restore" (34); in 54, "Ah! would 'twere mine" and "Would I could taste, like this unthinking hind" (49). The lunatic himself inspires jealousy: "I see him more with envy than with fear" (61). Dependent and "oppress'd," the speaker craves the "blest" quietness that she will never, until death, be able to obtain.

While Smith cannot condone boyish insanity, her speakers relate intimately to a parallel vision—that of the exiled and silenced wanderer. The last six lines of Sonnet 12 read:

> Already shipwreck'd by the storms of Fate,
> Like the poor mariner, methinks, I stand,
> Cast on a rock; who sees the distant land
> From whence no succour comes—or comes too late.
> Faint and more faint are heard his feeble cries,
> 'Till in the rising tide the exhausted sufferer dies. (20)

This comparison between the dejected speaker and a displaced male traveler is repeated in Sonnet 43: "The unhappy exile, whom his fates confine / To the bleak coast of some unfriendly isle, / [. . .] perhaps may know / Such heartless pain, such blank despair as mine" (41).

In Sonnet 36, a similar identification between the speaker and weakened masculinity gives Smith the opportunity to consider silence in relation to creativity. Here, roses and the "flowers" of "Poesy" may distract both the poem's "lone Wanderer" and the speaker from their troubles, respectively; however, both individuals fail to find relief. Rest for these figures is no better than the "distant sail" for a mourning exile: "But darker now grows life's unhappy day, / Dark with new clouds of evil yet to come, / Her pencil sickening Fancy throws away, / And weary Hope reclines upon the tomb; / And points my wishes to that tranquil shore, / Where the pale spectre Care pursues no more" (37). As Fancy, and presumably Smith's own poetic impulse, throws her pencil away in disgust, the speaker's wish for comfort points to the silence of the grave.

By positing both Hope and Sorrow as courted feminine love objects, Smith carries the Petrarchan tradition into a new context; she uses amatory motifs so that the speaker's grief (its source unspecified) can be expressed and to some extent overcome. Pursuing feminized abstractions as though they themselves were the love objects, the speaker can move from grief for the loss of what she has loved to the love of this very grief, exclaiming "Oh Melancholy!—such thy magic power, / That to the soul these dreams are often sweet, / And soothe the pensive visionary mind!" (35). Verbalizing her desire for Hope and Sorrow, she fuels her poetry and finds redemption through it. But the male wanderers to whom she compares herself find no such solace. They cannot speak at all, let alone make poetry or music; their grief is incommunicable, a "feeble cry" or "blank despair." It has no single cause, no possible cure. In the end, Smith's exiled male personae merely wish to die.

SMITH'S DEPARTURE FROM GRAY

Smith's construction of grief as both hopelessly inarticulable and lyrically reversible diverges from earlier models. Her work is certainly indebted to Thomas Gray's "Sonnet [on the Death of Mr. Richard West]" (published posthumously in 1775), which Curran designates as "the motive force underlying the entire Romantic revival of the sonnet."[29] Although Gray's sonnet is most well known today for Wordsworth's critique of its highly figured style, Schor argues that "Wordsworth's announced forfeiture of Gray's legacy is disingenuous" (57). Not only did Gray's sonnet influence Wordsworth's own poetic style but, in Schor's view, we need "a more complex account than Wordsworth's of the fabulous reflexivity which was Gray's legacy to the elegiac sonneteers of the 1770s, 1780s, and 1790s—a reflexivity which Wordsworth mistook for solipsism" (57). By writing an Italian sonnet with Miltonic diction, Gray sets into motion a double inheritance from Shakespeare's reflexive sonnets, on the one hand, and from Milton's elegies for lost paradise on the other. Gray's octet-sestet Italian structure in fact retains the Elizabethan quatrain, doubled to compose the octet (abababab), and an enlarged quatrain (cdcdcd) in the form of the sestet. Schor notices allusions between the sites Adam lists in the landscape ("this Tree," "these Pines," "this Fountain")—locations that he would revisit with his sons if he were not in exile—and parts of the body—ears, eyes, heart, breast—that had once taken pleasure in Gray's lost friend.

Since Gray grounds elegiac poetry in both the Shakespearean and Miltonic traditions, it makes sense for Smith and Bowles to derive from his sonnet the prerogative to present an ambiguous grief by referring to Shakespeare, Milton, and even Gray himself. In addition to many other citations she makes to Gray, Smith footnotes "And fruitless call on him—'who cannot hear'" by directing her readers to "Gray's exquisite Sonnet; in reading which it is impossible not to regret that he wrote only one" (81). Clearly Gray made a major impact on Smith's work. However, a close reading of Gray's sonnet elucidates Smith's revision of her precursor's technique:[30]

In vain to me the smiling mornings shine,
And reddening Phoebus lifts his golden Fire:
The birds in vain their amorous Descant join;
Or cheerful fields resume their green attire:
These ears, alas! for other notes repine,
A different object do these eyes require.
My lonely anguish melts no heart but mine;
And in my breast the imperfect joys expire.
Yet morning smiles the busy race to cheer,
And new-born pleasure brings to happier men:
The fields to all their wonted tribute bear:
To warm their little loves the birds complain:
I fruitless mourn to him that cannot hear,
And weep the more because I weep in vain.

From the first line, Gray's poem prepares the reader for its repetitive structure. The opening words "In vain" first reappear in line 3 of the introductory quatrain and also conclude the poem itself. Serving as the sonnet's conclusion, the word "vain" is echoed twice in the sestet with "men" and "complain." But "men" resembles "mine"—the most recent occasion of the sonnet's opening rhyme. Thus, the ending of the first line, "shine," which next connects to "join" and "repine," in a sense also echoes "vain." As "shine" audibly resembles "Fire" ("attire," require," "expire"), Gray composes his whole sonnet around variations on one single rhyme. Moreover, two additional words in the poem's opening line occur later on: "smiling mornings" transposes to "morning smiles" in line 9, the start of the sestet. We see a final mirror of this structure in the closing line in which "smiling" becomes "weep," repeated twice, and "mornings" breaks into the word "more." Falling on the fourth syllable, "more" refers back to the preceding line where "mourn" occurs at syllable 4 as well. Thus, the word "mornings," which introduces the sonnet, doubles as "mourning"—"morning [mourning] smiles" which causes the speaker to "weep the more," although both activities occur "in vain."

Gray's play with reverberations extends to more nuanced layers than the simple repetition of words. His second quatrain begins, "These ears, alas!" which, as Schor suggests, echoes the list of sites Adam hopelessly desires to revisit. But visually we notice a tie between "These ears" and "tears," which helps to explain Gray's use of "alas!" just afterwards (considering that someone other than

Gray named the sonnet after his death, the poem itself does not tell us that a person's presence is desired until line 13). This pattern recurs in the sonnet's second to last line: "I fruitless mourn to him that cannot hear." Containing four hard "t"s (and one soft "t"), the line juxtaposes its final "t" with "hear," creating a nearly perfect echo with "tear"—a notion that will immediately resurface in the poem's conclusion: "And *weep* the more because I *weep* in vain" (my italics). This particular word game is furthered by line 13's excessive use of hard "t" sounds; we observe that, in contrast, the sonnet's successive line contains none. The only other line in the sonnet with as many as four hard "t"s (and two soft "t"s) is line 10: "The fields to all their wonted tribute bear." Again we remark that the last letters before "bear" are "te," creating one more subtle imitation of "tear."

Gray's indirect repetition of the word "tear" serves not only to confirm that he will continue to "weep the more." The first play on "tears" in line 5 immediately follows the line, "Or cheerful fields resume their green attire." In this way, "[t]ears" falls at the exact syllable as "cheer" from the previous line. When "cheer" recurs as an introductory rhyme in the sestet, we see this association once again, with the word "tear" created by the bordering of "cannot" and "hear" in line 13. This double alliance between "cheer" and "tear" serves a parallel function to the coupling of "morning smiles" and "weep the more."

Expressing grief to a person who is already dead automatically implies that the listener "cannot hear." For Gray to engage in this kind of mourning means, then, that he will "weep the more" precisely because his tears necessarily fall "in vain." In truth, he is not mourning *to* the absent or deceased object of grief—his phrases, "other notes," "a different object," and "mourn to him" in no way indicate that he speaks to Richard West himself. Rather, "cannot hear" recollects "These ears"; tears in the poem (because of a desired but unavailable listener) motivate Gray to reproduce grief "in vain" for both the speaker and the reader. Hence, the word "mourn" echoes "new-born" since the poem will give birth to itself (like the fields that "to all their wonted tribute bear") again and again. This helps to make sense of the smooth transition between "mourn," "more," and "morning"—"tears" turn imperceptibly into poetic "cheer" and vice versa. In this way, "cheer" falls into the same structure as "tear"; following the word "to," "cheer" also echoes "tear." All three rhymes in the sestet, then, convey the idea of tears. The blurring of "cheer" and "tear," together with the repetition of "in vain," links the first and last lines of the poem. The weeping speaker weeps the "more" through his endlessly recurrent poem, and as a result his "morning" / "mourning" continues to smile in good cheer.

Constructed around essentially one single rhyme, Gray's sonnet communicates a principle of limitless poetic energy. In spite of its apparent references to emptiness ("cannot hear," "fruitless"), Gray's sonnet highlights a regenerative lyrical process. Although Smith draws inspiration from Gray, her poems foreground an inexpressibility that she can never convert into language or counteract. Like Gray, Smith fuses "tears" ("Melancholy," "Night," "Solitude") with "cheer" ("Hope," "Fortitude," "Friendship"). However, gender plays a part in this combination for Smith that it does not play for Gray. By feminizing both "Melancholy" and "Hope" (Gray's "tears" and "cheer"), Smith shares other neoclassical poets' approaches to personification. Yet Smith departs from her counterparts by foregrounding expressionlessness. This pull toward voicelessness not only distinguishes Smith from her precursors like Gray; it also marks a definitive contrast between her work and that of her own contemporary, William Lisle Bowles.

BOWLES'S DEPARTURE FROM SMITH

As I have shown, it was Bowles and not Smith who became most enthusiastically aligned with the revival of the sonnet form, an incorrect association perhaps first initiated in Coleridge's *Biographia Literaria* (1817). The Coleridge-Bowles affiliation was repeated in the twentieth century by prominent critics such as W. K. Wimsatt and M. H. Abrams.[31] Nevertheless, Bowles first published his *Fourteen Sonnets, Elegiac and Descriptive* anonymously in 1789 whereas Smith's *Elegiac Sonnets* appeared in 1784. Therefore, as Sylvia Mergenthal points out, Bowles was "historically speaking one of Smith's successors, and indeed imitators."[32] Perhaps after being accused of plagiarizing Smith, Bowles retitled his second edition, of 1789, *Sonnets Written Chiefly in Picturesque Spots, During a Tour,* as though distressed by the connections readers had drawn between his sonnets and Smith's earlier collection. He further disassociated himself by using his own name in this second edition instead of retaining his anonymity.

Coleridge's preference for Bowles's work over Smith's helps to explain Smith's disappearance from the Romantic canon and her replacement by Bowles, who ought to have occupied instead a place as her legitimate successor. The depressive Coleridge may have preferred the relative resilience of Bowles's work to Smith's more absolute despair. Brent Raycroft convincingly argues that Bowles's sonnets are more intellectual than Smith's "only in the sense that they grant consolatory power to reflective distance."[33] While Smith's sonnets often "attempt to convey the almost insupportable nature of the speaker's suffering, almost dramatized by the failure of consolation," we find "no such rhetoric of anguish or moral indignation" in Bowles's work (Raycroft 376). Raycroft suggests that Coleridge's compromise was to prefer the sonnets of a poet who was influenced by Smith, but whose melancholy comes closer to nostalgia than despair. Whereas Abrams accounts for Coleridge's appreciation of Bowles through the loco-descriptive poetics of Bowles's early sonnets, Raycroft argues that it "was Bowles's tone, the relative lightness of his melancholy, that appealed to Coleridge" (380).

Bowles's sonnet "To the River Itchin," on which Coleridge most likely did base his own "Sonnet to Otter" (although, as Raycroft explains, no written record exists of this borrowing), resembles Gray's in key aspects:[34]

SONNET VIII
TO THE RIVER ITCHIN, NEAR WINTON

Itchin, when I behold thy banks again,
Thy crumbling margin, and thy silver breast,
On which the self-same tints still seem to rest,
Why feels my heart the shiv'ring sense of pain?
Is it, that many a summer's day has past
Since, in life's morn, I carol'd on thy side?
Is it, that oft, since then, my heart has sighed,
As Youth, and Hope's delusive gleams, flew fast?
Is it that those, who circled on thy shore,
Companions of my youth, now meet no more?
Whate'er the cause, upon thy banks I bend
Sorrowing, yet feel such solace at my heart,
As at the meeting of some long-lost friend,
From whom, in happier hours, we wept to part.

Introducing his sonnet with the act of beholding "again," Bowles prepares us (as does Gray) to read the poem repeatedly. The final quatrain might summarize our relationship to the sonnet, over which we bend "sorrowing" as it reaches its conclusion, yet feel "such solace" at heart because we are reencountering it once more. The weeping in the sonnet's conclusion (and Bowles uses the same word—"wept"—as Gray does in his final line) doubles as an experience of friendly reunion with "happier hours." Just as they do for Gray, tears transform into "cheer" or "solace." It is also the act of reading that provides this kind of transformation: the river's "crumbling margin" mirrors the cracking border of a book's page. When the speaker sang at the river's "side" in "life's morn," he also soon "sighed" as youth and hope quickly disappeared; the homophone here, "side" and "sighed," evokes an image of the "side" of a sheet of paper, the end of a poem's line—at which place these words fall. The speaker's "shiv'ring sense of pain" results either from the length of time that has passed since he sang at the river's "side" or from the way he has since "sighed" as Youth and Hope fled. In the end, singing and lamenting alternate between each other to create a "shiv'ring sense" both of pain and enjoyment that good poetry makes possible. As the speaker "bend[s] / sorrowing" at the start of his final four lines, he repeats his sonnet's "turn" or "bend" into its last quatrain, a structural move that imitates the sadness of the poem's theme (made up of turns or bends from one time in life to the next) as well as the extreme comfort of the poem's form itself (simulating the happy reunion with a long-lost friend).

Like Gray, Bowles differs from Smith by emphasizing regeneration in contrast to irreparable loss. Stressing sorrow far less than the "solace" that comes to take its place, Bowles identifies his pain with a "shiv'ring" between songs and sighs that recalls poetic energy itself. Like Gray, Bowles grieves the departure of companions; however, for Bowles, weeping to part in "happier hours" becomes a more optimistic emotion at the sonnet's end when his lost friend (the river itself) is met again. Smith's language and overall accentuation is entirely different: while her sonnets constantly revive themselves by fluctuating between extremes, they simultaneously assert a "blank despair" that counterbalances this revival. In contrast to Gray and Bowles, who underscore the continuity and consolation that poetry offers in the face of sorrow, Smith activates a powerful countermovement to inarticulable and unredeemable loss.

Bowles's sonnets do resemble Smith's in unmistakable ways. Like hers, they apostrophize (in addition to rivers and landscapes) such generalized concepts as Evening, Poverty, and Time. Like hers, Bowles's poems associate the movement of the mind with literal footsteps through nature: his first sonnet begins, "As slow I climb the cliff's ascending side" (1); his seventh ends, "When I am wand'ring on my way alone" (8); in "Sonnet IX," we learn that he attends Poverty's "rugged paths with pleasure" (10). In more general terms, Bowles often refers to imagined others who wander just as he does: in "Sonnet IV: To the River Wenbeck," he envisions "him who passes weary on his way" (5); in his fifth sonnet, "To the River Tweed," he pictures "a stranger, that with wand'ring feet / O'er hill and dale has journey'd many a mile" (6); in "Sonnet VI," he thinks of those that "wander 'mid [Evening's] lonely haunts / Unseen" (7); in "Sonnet X: On Dover Cliffs," he imagines that "On these white cliffs. . . . Sure many a lonely wanderer has stood" (11); in "Sonnet XII: Written at a Convent," the speaker wonders "If chance some pensive stranger, hither led" (13). Likewise, Smith begins her sequence, "The partial Muse has from my earliest hours / Smiled on the rugged path I'm doom'd to tread" (13). In her fourth sonnet, "To the moon," she exclaims, "Queen of the silver bow!—by thy pale beam, / Alone and pensive, I delight to stray" (15). She titles Sonnet 42, "Composed during a walk on the Downs, in November 1787" (40). In Sonnet 62, she says, "O'er the cold waste, amid the freezing night, / Scarce heeding whither, desolate I stray" (55).

Like Smith, Bowles apostrophizes feminized abstractions, while at the same time either removing their gender or simply not referring to masculinized generalities. Instead, Bowles's male personifications are individual characters, very similar to those we find in Smith's sonnets. While Bowles feminizes "Sorrow" (2), "Charity" (3), "Pity" (3), "Spring" (6), "Genius" (10), and "Peace" (15), he refers instead to naturalized male personifications such as the "fainting wretch" (3), the "cheerless pilgrim" (5), the "stranger" (6), the "poor man" (10), and the "lonely wanderer" (11).

I want to suggest that Bowles and Smith identify their masculinized personifications with real-life individuals instead of with more general representations because they aim to identify their speakers with these semi-allegorical human personalities. It is Bowles's "fainting wretch" (3), "cheerless pilgrim" (5), "stranger" (6), "poor man" (10), and "lonely wanderer" (11) who best illustrate his own speaker's grief. Similarly, Smith's "Poor wearied pilgrim" (15), "poor mariner" (20), "unhappy exile" (41), "breathless Captive" (50), and "darkling Pilgrim" (64) most intimately share her speaker's forlorn sentiments.

Although they use very similar personification techniques, Bowles and Smith nevertheless produce contradictory results. By associating his speaker with wandering male personifications, Bowles appeals to feminized abstractions (in sum, to Nature herself) for comfort and finally does obtain the relief that he seeks. Smith, on the other hand, stages two projects at once: she appeals to conflicting feminized abstractions; at the same time, she persistently aligns her speaker with speechless male sufferers who can do nothing but die in despair (unlike what happens in Bowles's sonnets, nature provides no solace for Smith's "poor mariner," "unhappy exile," and "lone wanderer"). By writing from the point of view of male and female characters, Smith draws her voice both from the femininity that inspires speech and from the masculinity that precludes it. Therefore, while her sonnets derive much of their complexity from the double function that gender serves in them, they also do their best to overcome such divisions through their openness to the interchangeability of gender roles (as the speaker plays both men's and women's parts), of languages (Petrarch's Italian to Smith's English, for example) and of genres (from poems to novels and vice versa).

THE TURN TO ROMANTICISM

Smith's curious play between gendered personifications dramatizes the transition from neoclassical to Romantic writing. To understand this transition, it is important to observe how Smith's masculinized personifications forecast Wordsworth's later revisions of neoclassical abstractions.[35] Wordsworth eliminates the whole range of abstract personifications that Smith chooses to feminize. However, Wordsworth shifts to natural agents (the Leech-Gatherer, the Discharged Soldier, the Blind Beggar, and the Philosopher Child)—representatives that retain many elements of their allegorical heritage. Where

Wordsworth suppresses formal allegory (figures no longer proclaim their allegorical identities as do Death, Melancholy, Hope, etc.), he effectively takes these generalized personifications and naturalizes them.

In the case of Milton's memorable incarnation, "Death,"—a figure that plays a similar role to all abstract personifications—this embodiment oscillates between its status as a physical thing and as a universal principle. Steven Knapp describes Milton's "Death" as swinging "between the fixed materiality of a literal agent and the figurative transparency of a nominal abstraction."[36] Knapp explains that "Death" is the ideal personification in that it cannot be described: it "corresponds to the impossible doubleness of personifications in general" (36).[37] But sublimity involves doubleness, too; the sublime experience includes identification as well as differentiation. Over-identification with a sublime force (the breakdown of all contrast between reason and empirical consciousness), Knapp reminds us, leads both Kant and Coleridge to the issue of fanaticism. The protection against fanaticism, for Kant, depends on the negativity of the sublime: "On the other hand, this pure, elevating, and merely negative exhibition of morality involves no danger of *fanaticism,* which is the *delusion* [*Wahn*] *of wanting to* SEE *something beyond all bounds of sensibility,* i.e., of dreaming according to principles (raving with reason). The exhibition avoids fanaticism precisely because it is merely negative. For *the idea of freedom is inscrutable* and thereby precludes all positive exhibition whatever."[38] In other words, one must simultaneously realize the ultimate inadequacy of the self—the distance between the self and the sublime object—and experience a positive movement of self-affirmation through unification with the vast energy. What makes a personification sublime is the way it both prohibits the individual's identification with it—the abstraction clearly cannot and does not exist in human form—and also the way it announces its own impossibility. As Knapp shows, the personification is the perfect fanatic, "both devoid of empirical consciousness and perfectly, formally conscious of itself" (83). What is reassuring about this perfection, what offers the other side of its double character, is "its sheer and obvious fictionality" (83).

The Wordsworthian figure that might most closely approach formal reflexiveness is the Blind Beggar, whose identity is contained in the inscription he wears around his neck. By concealing this personification's allegorical nature, Wordsworth emphasizes "a discrepancy between the agent's natural status and its sudden acquisition of a quasi-allegorical resonance" (Knapp 106). Stating his identity and purpose through a sign he wears while remaining incapable of writing or reading the inscription, the Blind Beggar takes on a haunting semifictional status. His character becomes mysteriously self-enclosed. For Wordsworth, it is this discordance between naturalistic and allegorical tendencies that translates into imaginative power.

By converting masculinized personifications into real-life beings (the wanderer, the mariner, the pilgrim) as opposed to formal concepts, Smith anticipates Wordsworth's own shift to natural agents. Smith's naturalized masculinized personifications remain slightly more general than Wordsworth's Blind Beggar and Leech Gatherer; the "wanderer" and "pilgrim" come closer to formal personifications than do Wordsworth's. However, while Smith's forlorn male embodiments proclaim only the knowledge of their existence as such, with no hope for changed circumstances, they remain completely naturalized next to their feminized counterparts such as Melancholy and Hope.

Unlike Wordsworth, Smith does not draw inspiration from her immediately successful and failed identification with these natural yet half-fictional beings. Rather, she makes it clear that her easy sympathy with one kind of silenced masculinized personification contrasts with a different model: her swing between opposing feminized abstractions. Smith's manipulation of these two gendered models of personification stages and even prophesies the very historical progression in which her own lyrics take place.

SWALLOWING SORROW: CHARLOTTE SMITH'S FEMALE CONTEMPORARIES

Women poets such as Anna Seward, Helen Maria Williams, Mary Robinson, Anna Maria Smallpiece, Mary Bryan, Martha Hanson, and Jane Alice Sargant followed Charlotte Smith by producing an outpouring of elegiac and amatory sonnets.[39] Curran thus insists that this rediscovery of the sonnet form "coincides with the rise of a definable woman's literary movement [in poetry] and with the beginnings of Romanticism," declaring that the late-eighteenth-century sonnet revival matches that of the sixteenth century in its force (*Poetic Form and British Romanticism* 30–31).

In this section, I want to examine the responses of Smith's female contemporaries, who were preoccupied with Smith's poetics but who resisted her double stance—one toward limitless verbalization (made possible by an appeal to conflicting feminized personifications) and the other toward "blank despair" (embodied in naturalized male personifications such as the mariner, the pilgrim, the exile, and the wanderer, whose predicaments the speaker claims to share). While Anna Seward resented Smith's successes, other eighteenth-century women writers such as Helen Maria Williams closely emulated her work. But as I will show, Williams moved Smith's elegies into a more consolatory sphere. Anna Maria Smallpiece, on the other hand, gracefully repudiated Williams's approach (very explicitly in her sonnet, "To Miss Williams, on Reading her Sonnet to the Strawberry"). Although Smallpiece seems to renounce Williams's appeals for consolation, thus returning to Smith's bleaker view of inconsolable grief, she clashes with Smith in the vastly different but equally gender-specific reasons that she gives for her anguish. Smith, Williams, and Smallpiece consequently gender their grief in three opposing ways, all of which involve suppression. In part because these women felt they could not openly verbalize their unhappiness about normative gender roles, they essentially spoke without moving their lips in poems that address elusively shifting or inexplicable sorrow. As a result, eighteenth-century women writers turned in huge numbers to a lyric form that they wholeheartedly revitalized: the sonnet, which, more than other kinds of poetry, manages to sing through compression and restraint.

Helen Maria Williams composes sonnets that read as consoling reiterations of Charlotte Smith's grief.[40] Not only does Williams make heavy use of apostrophe, but her titles all call attention to this device: together with her translation of Bernardin St. Pierre's *Paul et Virginie* (1795), she includes eight original sonnets—"To Love," "To Disappointment," "To Simplicity," "To the Strawberry," "To the Curlew," "To the Torrid Zone," "To the Calbassia-Tree," and "To the White Bird of the Tropic." Some of her other well-known sonnets include "To Hope," "To Twilight," and "To the Moon."[41]

Like Smith and Bowles, Williams removes the gender of masculinized abstractions, feminizing their counterparts. In her *Paul and Virginia* sonnets, she addresses Disappointment as a "relentless nymph!" (214); "To Simplicity" begins "Nymph of the desert!" (215); in "To the Calbassia-Tree," Friendship casts "*her* soothing shade / [. . .] Ah! not in vain *she* lends her balmy aid: / The agonies *she* cannot cure, are less!" (219; my italics). But while Disappointment, Simplicity, and Friendship remain feminized, the male gender drops away from such conventional abstractions as "love" (213–14, 219) and "despair" (213), instead attaching itself to specific individuals.

Although Williams uses natural rather than abstract masculinized personifications, she does not refer to unhappy wanderers, pilgrims, exiles, and mariners. Instead, she genders *birds* male, such as "the curlew" (217) and "the amadavid-bird" (218). In these figures the speaker identifies herself: the curlew "blends his melancholy wail" with "the murmurs on the sea-boat shore," and the speaker cries out, "Like thee, congenial bird! My steps explore / The bleak lone sea-beach, or the rocky dale, / And shun the orange bower, the myrtle vale, / Whose gay luxuriance suits my soul no more" (217). Despite her complaint that the amadavid-bird spreads "his gay plumes" for the pathway of light alone (while she is relegated to a twilight space) (218), as "nature's child" she desires still to haunt the bold recesses "where yon tall cliffs are rudely pil'd / Where towers the palm amidst the mountain trees, / Where pendent from the steep, with graces wild, / The blue liana floats upon the breeze" (215). Overall, instead of sympathizing with unhappy pilgrims and drowning mariners, Williams associates herself with masculinized free creatures in flight—"the white bird of the tropic," for example, who marks "the bounds which torrid beams confine / [. . .] Oblique, enamour'd of sublimer day" (220).

Helen Maria Williams might sweeten the bitterness of Charlotte Smith's voice, but other of Smith's female successors such as Anna Maria Smallpiece do not share this gentleness of tone. In "To Miss Williams, On Reading her Sonnet to the Strawberry," Smallpiece's self-deprecation and praise of Helen Maria Williams's work read as deliberately extreme:[42]

O! sweetest minstrel of green England's Isle,
Who from your native fields, now far away,
While you revert to your primeval May;
To blushing fruits, that did your youth beguile,
And wild woods teeming in gay Summer's smile,
Ah! as you frame the soft expressive lay,
And carol sweetly childhood's playful day;
Youth's happy season seems renew'd awhile,
For I like you these white wing'd hours retrace,
Their transient bliss, their faded prime deplore;
Yet could my pen paint with your vivid grace,
The sweet illusion might gay youth restore;
Luxuriant fancy all its hopes replace,
And to eternal Summer fondly soar.

Here, Smallpiece describes Williams's poetry as the sweet caroling of "childhood's playful day," which through "sweet illusion" and "luxuriant fancy" is able to restore gay youth. She recognizes that Williams is currently exiled in France (as "from [her] native fields," she is "now far away"), but she also believes that Williams as a poet is still able to "revert to [her] primeval May" because her poetry alleviates sorrow. Smallpiece, on the other hand, who identifies with Williams's sufferings ("For I like you these white wing'd hours retrace, / Their transient bliss, their faded prime deplore"), allegedly lacks the artistic ability to relieve her own pain. She forewarns us of this shortcoming in her preface: "I have only with great humility to submit [these compositions] to the Public, soliciting their indulgence for the melancholy that pervades them, which, unfortunately for the writer, has not been affected" (iii).

Smallpiece is right about the extraordinary lushness and sensuality of Williams's sonnet, "To the Strawberry":[43]

The Strawberry blooms upon its lowly bed,
Plant of my native soil!—the lime may fling
More potent fragrance on the zephyr's wing;
The milky cocoa richer juices shed;
The white guava lovelier blossoms spread:
But not like thee to fond remembrance bring
The vanish'd hours of life's enchanting spring,
Short calendar of joys for ever fled!

> Thou bidst the scenes of childhood rise to view,
> The wild-wood path which fancy loves to trace;
> Where, veil'd in leaves, thy fruit of rosy hue
> Lurk'd on its pliant stem with modest grace:
> But, ah! when thought would later years renew,
> Alas, successive sorrows crowd the space!

In Williams's sonnet "To the Strawberry," as Backsheider has observed, we observe a number of resemblances to Smith's sonnets: "The beautiful, nationalistic salute to the strawberry, the global stretch to limes, cocoa, and guava, followed by the comparison of childhood to the sorrowful present, compresses compositional strategies and content from some of Smith's best sonnets" (347). However, Backsheider does not call attention to the primary difference that I see between Williams's work and Smith's—the shift Williams's sonnets enact from bleakness to contentment and even to joy. Twelve out of the sonnet's fourteen lines contain positive images: "blooms," "potent," "fragrance," "milky," "cocoa," "richer," "white," "guava," "lovelier," "fond," "enchanting," "joys," "childhood," "wild-wood," "fancy," "fruit," "rosy," "pliant," "modest," "grace," and "renew." With the exception of line 8 and line 14, the poem reads euphorically. Because the sonnet is in an Italian rather than Shakespearean form, the impact of the last two lines, which do not rhyme, is reduced as the speaker concludes, "But ah! when thought would later years [about which we know nothing] renew, / Alas, successive sorrows crowd the space!"

Smallpiece's inability (or unwillingness) to imitate Williams's reassuring style brings her quality of voice closer to Charlotte Smith's gloomy tone. Like Smith, Smallpiece also feminizes abstractions such as the Muse, Pity, Health, Fate, Ev'ning, Memory, Hope, Reason, and Illusion.[44] Like Smith, too, and in contrast to Williams, she transforms her male personifications into human individuals such as the Sinner, the Trav'ller, the Sailor, the Peasant, and the musing Poet.[45] But where Smith provides many different sources of grief for her speakers, Smallpiece gives readers the unsettling impression that *one* source of grief persists throughout her collection. In fact, it appears as though Smallpiece's (presumably female) speaker has been (a) in love with another woman and (b) rejected by this woman who, while she may have cared for the speaker, ultimately did not feel romantic love in exchange. If we ignore this subtly staged drama, Smallpiece's collection as a whole ceases to make logical sense, and it is perhaps for this reason that during the Romantic period she was rejected and ignored by her readers, reemerging before our eyes now as an entirely unknown poet.[46]

Smallpiece writes in her preface, "To those who have suffered from long sickness; to those who have stood

> Around the death-bed of their dearest friends,
> And mark'd the parting anguish;

To those who have suffered by the keen sting of ingratitude, these effusions may not be unacceptable, and may perhaps be read with kindred sympathy; as under the pressure of such feelings they have generally been written" (iii–iv). In Smallpiece's sonnets themselves, however, these three sources of grief—sickness, death of a friend, and ingratitude—get tangled up together. The sequence confuses "faithless" and "faithful" friends and then complicates this problem by grieving a friend's death.[47] But it is not clear whether the departed friend was in actuality faithless or faithful to the speaker.

Smallpiece uses the trope of wandering to define not only her passages of thought but also her relationship with a "sister dear, sweet partner of [her] walk" from whom she must separate (6). Such separations occur throughout her poems, with reasons varying from the friend's move to another place, to the friend's unfaithfulness in her love (for the speaker), to the friend's death. However, bizarre conflations occur between these different categories. For example, "Fate decrees" that the speaker and the "sweet partner of [her] walk" should live apart in Sonnet VI; at the end of the poem, the speaker hopes that "She may relent, and to this throbbing heart / The friend sincere, and flow'ry path restore; / Together then we'll live, and fondly prove, / That absence long has not diminish'd love" (6). By "She," in "She may relent," the speaker presumably means "Fate," but the words might also be read as pertaining to her "friend sincere" who has become faithless (that is, romantically attached to someone else); her only hope is that this friend will relent and devote herself once again to the speaker's "throbbing heart."

This confusion between feminized abstractions and specific real-life women recurs throughout Smallpiece's sonnets. The latter part of "Sonnet III: Written in Ill Health" reads "If o'er thy cheek the loose-zon'd goddess, Health, / With coral finger, spread her rosy hue, / Far art thou bless'd . . . / Nor more would I at little ills repine, / Were her full eye, and sparkling lustre mine" (3). Although neoclassical poets typically anthropomorphized abstractions, Smallpiece's description of Health's "coral finger," "full eye," and "sparkling lustre" humanizes the abstraction in an unmistakably sensual way. In particular, the last line, "Were her full eye, and sparkling lustre mine," suggests that the speaker yearns to possess a desired female other. It is as though the speaker's "ill health" *derives* from her sorrow that her friend does not regard her with a "full eye."

Clearly, Smallpiece could not make the powerfully homoerotic subtext of her sonnets explicit at the time when they were published. Thus, she obscures this latent theme by confusing abstractions with literal women characters, and by suggesting that her grief stems from many socially acceptable sources (her own sickness, the death of friends, "ingratitude" toward the faithless, which, although Smallpiece never uses this term, *might* designate male rather than female lovers). As a result of these ambiguities, her poems do not, however, lessen the pressure that homoerotic love places on them; instead this strain only increases due to the weight of its unsayability.

Charlotte Smith and William Lisle Bowles align their speakers with cheerless pilgrims and unhappy exiles. In contrast, Smallpiece speaks in "Sonnet IV: To Charity" of a "poor hopeless sinner" who "fears to die" (4). She never explains *what* this sinner has done but she trusts "that Heav'n, unlike the worldly friend / Forgives weak man, and knows he must offend" (4). If this "poor hopeless sinner" (interestingly gendered masculine) illustrates an aspect of the speaker's own situation—that is, her homosexual desires—she prays for forgiveness in heaven, as she cannot find divine charity in her "worldly friend."[48] Impossible love, then, may reside at the source of the speaker's grief: impossible just as was Petrarch's love in his amatory sonnets—because Laura did not reciprocate his speaker's affections *and* because of her death—yet more extreme. For Smallpiece, physical love between two women was socially unthinkable; her speaker's homoerotic desires may not only have been unrealizable due to faithlessness, death, and physical separations, but to an outside observer her desires also would have seemed morally unjustifiable.

In conclusion, like Petrarch, Charlotte Smith suggests that the lyric is communicated and sustained by constant verbalization to silent oppositions; however, Smith also insists that poetry guards at its center a fundamental speechlessness. This double function of the lyric becomes complexly gendered in Smith's work: traditionally linked to fluency, masculinity falls mute just when poetry's emptiness is exposed, while femininity becomes agile and resilient at this same moment. But this reversal (as Smith's incessant regendering of poetic speakers reveals) is counteracted by a silence that cannot be gendered at all, a blankness that relates all poets (male or female) to exiled wanderers who can never enter into language although they utter inaudible cries.

Two of Smith's female successors, Helen Maria Williams and Anna Maria Smallpiece, find alternate ways of confronting the irrevocable loss of voice that Smith makes evident. Williams more soothingly expresses a similar kind of grief and Smallpiece replaces Smith's constantly shifting sorrow with one single source of socially unacceptable and hence unsayable suffering—the torments of unrealizable lesbian love.

Like Smallpiece, Thomas Gray confuses grief for lost homoerotic love (due to death) with the impossibility of its realization in life; his beloved friend may not be able to hear him speak his love in "Sonnet [on the Death of Mr. Richard West]," first, because this friend is dead, and second, because romantic love between men was at that time unspeakable.[49] But, as we have seen, by beginning and ending his sonnet with the same phrase, "in vain," Gray gives the futility of his voice endless strength. In turn, his unforgotten sonnet can now be identified as the initial catalyst propelling the entire eighteenth-century revival of the sonnet form. Anna Maria Smallpiece, on the other hand, enjoyed no such destiny. She was presumably unappreciated during her lifetime and like the often-disparaged sonnet or "little song" itself, her very name—"Smallpiece"—mimics the inconsequentiality of her verse, which even today remains unknown. But in order to rediscover early women writers' work, we must learn to listen to minor poets in new ways. In addition to inspiring the nineteenth-century sonnet revival, Romantic women's sonnets initiate an awakening preoccupation with silence: they pinpoint the enigmatic bond between poetry and the unsayable that troubles modern thought. As I will analyze in my next chapter, Elizabeth Barrett wrote that "poetry resembles grief." Early Romantic women poets certainly prophesize this claim, mourning for a language that will never unite with itself because it bumps constantly against namelessness as does Charlotte Smith's "pensive visionary mind" (35).

CHAPTER TWO

"In Silence like to Death"

Elizabeth Barrett's Sonnet Turn

In 1840, Elizabeth Barrett was already a highly acclaimed poet. By the age of thirty-four, she had published three major works: *An Essay on Mind, with Other Poems* (1826); a translation of Aeschylus's *Prometheus Bound* (1833); and *The Seraphim and Other Poems* (1838). However, 1840 also marked the date of Barrett's favorite brother Edward's death by drowning. So devastated by his death she could not speak of her grief, Barrett was convinced that "this long silence, embracing the most afflictive time of [her] whole life" could be neither verbalized nor transcended (*The Brownings' Correspondence* [hereafter *BC*] 5:43). Consequently, she began to question the redemptive model of lyric poetry to which she had previously subscribed. In this chapter, I suggest that Edward's death awakened Barrett's interest in the sonnet form. Although she began publishing poetry as early as 1820, she did not print her first three sonnets until 1838. Her 1844 collection, on the other hand, included twenty-eight sonnets, and in 1850 she published fifty sonnets.[1]

With her turn to the sonnet, Barrett found a formal metaphor to represent silence and grief.[2] She responded to the sonnet tradition primarily in the context of two approaches: the amatory model according to which poets drew a source of lyrical potency from the absence or unattainability of a beloved addressee, and, alternatively, the Wordsworthian version (itself a recasting of Milton), whereby the unresponsiveness of nature or of a contemplated other is converted into the mind's encounter with the sublime.[3] Becoming for her, as it did for almost every major poet of the nineteenth century, a synecdoche for lyric poetry in general, the sonnet thus put Barrett into dialogue with her most prolific Romantic precursor in the field—a man who, perhaps not uncoincidentally, had lost his own brother to drowning.[4] The result was a collision between poetic modes. Rather than adopting Wordsworth's revisionary sonnet poetics as a means of resolving her preoccupation with unutterable grief, Barrett put forth a competing model that reevaluated the Wordsworthian sublime. Unlike Wordsworth, Barrett enlisted a non-recuperative version of negativity as a framework for her sonnets, and as a key to her understanding of lyric poetry in general.[5] By critiquing Wordsworth, Barrett wrote herself into the male lyric tradition; in so doing, she confronted the "silence of [her] womanhood"—a silence ultimately interchangeable, I will argue, with her feminized grief and with the generative limits of poetry itself.[6]

BARRETT'S SONNET TURN (1844)

Elizabeth Barrett's view of lyric poetry was radically called into question when her brother died.[7] Her letters from this period chart, as Angela Leighton has remarked, "how heavy a burden of feeling the idea of silence carries."[8] Eleven years after the incident, Barrett wrote to her friend Mrs. Martin, "There is only one event in my life which never loses its bitterness; which comes back on me like a retreating wave, going and coming again, which was and *is my grief—I never had but one brother who loved and comprehended me.*"[9] Explaining that "one stroke ended [her] youth" (*BC* 5:281), Barrett entreated her correspondents to "say no more," to avoid speaking of her grief: "*Do not speak of that,* dear Mr. Horne. And for the rest, you see that there is nothing to say. It is a 'blank, my lord.'" (*BC* 7:354).

Barrett's remarkable inability to verbalize her grief (she wrote to Mary Russell Mitford, "I cannot write of these things—you see I cannot—I cannot write or speak—I never have spoken—not one word—not to Papa—never named that name anymore") creates a silence that appears to be, in Leighton's words, "imaginatively unredeemable" (*BC* 5:169; Leighton, *Elizabeth Barrett Browning* 81). Barrett's referral to her grief as "a blank" importantly echoes Charlotte Smith's unspecified source of mourning or "blank despair." Leighton speculates, "It is perhaps a characteristic of the female imagination to desire that silence which is an abdication of all poetic power, rather than a culmination of it" (*Elizabeth Barrett Browning* 83). While Barrett viewed her grieving silence as unredeemable, this experience led her not to renounce poetic power but, rather, to define the nature of lyric poetry more confidently and complexly than she had ever done before.

In November 1841, she wrote to Mitford of her grief, "I beseech you to say no more. [. . .] My head turns to write. I never knew DESPAIR before those days—never. And the grief I had felt before so lately,—nay, all my former griefs & I have had many, were bruised out of my heart by one" (*BC* 5:169–70). One year later, she explained to the artist, Benjamin Haydon, "I love poetry *unto death*" (*BC* 6:140). And she reported to her brother, George, "I am writing such poems . . . allegorical-philosophical-poetical-ethical . . . synthetically arranged! I am in a fit of writing—could write all day & night" (*BC* 7:242).

There is a striking contrast between Barrett's simultaneous insistence on helpless silence ("I cannot write of these things . . . I cannot write or speak") and poetic productivity ("I am in a fit of writing—could write all day and night"). Her affirmation to Haydon, "I love poetry *unto death*," constructs poetry as a bridge between love and potential grief. Shortly after this declaration, she explicitly made the connection between poetry and grief; she wrote to Mitford, "Yes—poetry is divine. It resembles grief in rending asunder our conventionalities, . . . but does so singing instead of sighing. It transfigures the great humanity into the sense of its *To-come*" (*BC* 6:219). From serving to counteract and compensate for grief, poetry for Barrett thus became, in part, a formal metaphor for grief itself.

This last observation best accounts for Barrett's turn to the sonnet form. She wrote to Mitford at this same time, "The sonnet structure is a very fine one, however imperious, and I never *would* believe that our language is unqualified for the very strictest Italian form. I have been exercising myself in it not unfrequently of late" (*BC* 6:111). Just as grief "*rend[s] asunder* our conventionalities," the Petrarchan sonnet, "the very strictest of Italian form," breaks apart conventional form through the structural and thematic gap between octave and sestet (Oppenheimer 3). Furthermore, if poetry communicates grief "singing instead of sighing," then the sonnet or "little song," with its focus on sonority and its claim to music, might best be able to achieve this conversion from silence to song.[10]

"I WRITE UNDER THE EYES OF WORDSWORTH"

Although Barrett first met Wordsworth in 1836, her closeness to "the great poet" coincided with her substantial turn toward sonnet writing in 1842 (*BC* 6:118).[11] In September of that year, Elizabeth Barrett's cousin, John Kenyon (responsible for Barrett's acquaintances with both Wordsworth and Browning), sent her "several little branches & buds out of Wordsworth's garden" (*BC* 6:31). The near-mythical symbolism of this event was not lost on Barrett, who had orchestrated the exchange by originally requesting that Mr. Kenyon "supplicate *for himself*"; however, Kenyon refused to "bear the ignominy of such fantastic sentimentality" and mentioned her name (*BC* 6:31). After receiving the poet's gift, Barrett wrote to her brother George that "prophecies are ominous: but I do trust that the Muses will interpose with all manner of invisible dews & secure the sprouting" (*BC* 6:31). Intimately familiar with the common Victorian tropological identification of poetry with flowers, Barrett was aware that her double request (first, for "branches and buds" from Wordsworth's garden, and second, for the Muses to "interpose" and "secure the sprouting") might be interpreted as a bold desire to take part in the Laureate's poetic power.[12]

Just one month after this event, Barrett received another reminder of Wordsworth: an unfinished portrait of the poet by Haydon. She explained, "I write under the eyes of Wordsworth! [. . .] Mr. Haydon the artist, with the utmost kindness has sent me the portrait he was painting of the great poet—an unfinished portrait! and I am to keep it until he wants to finish it. Such a head! such majesty!—and the poet stands musing upon Helvellyn! And all that,—poet Helvellyn & all,—is in my room!!" (*BC* 6:118–19). Barrett was so impressed by the painting that she composed a sonnet in response to it, which she sent to Mitford, and to Haydon, who forwarded it to the poet himself:

ON A PORTRAIT OF WORDSWORTH BY B. R. HAYDON

Wordsworth upon Helvellyn! Let the cloud
Ebb audibly along the mountain-wind
Then break against the rock, and show behind
The lowland valleys floating up to crowd
The sense with beauty. He with forehead bowed
And humble-lidded eyes, as one inclined

> Before the sovran thought of his own mind,
> And very meek with inspirations proud,
> Takes here his rightful place as poet-priest
> By the high altar, singing prayer and prayer
> To the higher Heavens. A noble vision free
> Our Haydon's hand has flung out from the mist:
> No portrait this, with Academic air!
> This is the poet and his poetry.
> (Barrett, *The Complete Works,* vol. 2, 228)

Wordsworth not only acknowledged the sonnet; he critiqued it as well, taking issue with her choice of the word "ebb" in line 2 and with her original lines 11 and 12:[13]

> The conception of your Sonnet is in full accordance with the Painters intended work, and the expression vigorous; yet the word "ebb" though I do not myself object to it, nor wish it altered, will I fear prove obscure to nine readers out of ten.
>
> "A vision free
> And noble Haydon hath thine art released,"
>
> Owing to the want of inflections in our language this construction here is obscure. Would it not be a little [better] thus?—I was going to write a small change in the order of the words, but I find it would not remove the objection. The sense as I take it, could be somewhat clearer thus, if you could tolerate the redundant syllable:
>
> "By a vision free
> And noble, Haydon, is thine Art released."

Having inscribed her own initials (Elizabeth Barrett [Moulton] Barrett) beneath Wordsworth's name in the first word of the sonnet's second line, Barrett preferred not to acknowledge Wordsworth's criticism that the word "ebb" would "prove obscure to nine readers out of ten."[14] Instead, she let the word stand, signaling a brave self-inscriptive gesture similar to that which had motivated her recent request for seeds out of Wordsworth's garden.[15] Nor did Barrett accept Wordsworth's proposed changes to lines 11 and 12. She did alter these lines (Mitford had found fault with them as well) but the revision was her own: "A noble vision free / Our Haydon's hand has flung out from the mist." Barrett's unwillingness to defer to Wordsworth's criticisms directs our attention (as do biographical details) to the critique her sonnet puts forth of the very poet it purports to eulogize.

At first glance, Barrett's "On a Portrait of Wordsworth by B. R. Haydon," written in Petrarchan form, appears to be constructed according to a double structure of praise. The octave compliments Wordsworth directly, placing the poet in a natural setting ("Wordsworth upon Helvellyn!") and describing, first the natural scene, then the poet himself whose apparent unity with nature prepares for a sublime revelation. The sestet seems to accomplish this shift by subsuming both nature and poet under Haydon's portrait ("Takes here his rightful place as poet-priest"), thereby converting the poet's introverted, contemplative silence into divinely inspired song ("singing prayer and prayer / To the higher Heavens"). The object of praise now moves from the poet to the painting ("A noble vision free / Our Haydon's hand has flung out from the mist"), appearing to reveal how art (both Wordsworth's and Haydon's) can transcend its generic limitations ("No portrait this with Academic air! / This is the poet and his poetry").[16]

The transition from poet to painting, however, suggests a more involved reading: a further displacement from painting to poetry. Barrett's admiration of Wordsworth is subtly critical in tone. Wordsworth's bowed forehead and "humble-lidded eyes" parody his egotistical self-scrutiny ("as one inclined / Before the sovran thought of his own mind"), and his meekness belies his "inspirations proud." Wordsworth is shown to be both impotent and self-important. The turn away from this caricature toward the "noble vision" of Haydon's portrait, a move that creates the illusion of song, is also problematized, usurped by a further turn away from both image and song toward the site of Barrett's own writing.

This final shift becomes apparent in the last tercet, which reads, "Our Haydon's hand has flung out from the mist: / No portrait this, with Academic air! / This is the poet and his poetry." The syntactical ambiguity of the original lines "A vision free / And noble, Haydon, hath thine art released" is telling, as is Wordsworth's revision, "By a vision free / And noble, Haydon, is thine art released." Barrett's initial rendering is ambivalent: the lines indicate either that a free and noble vision has released Haydon's art, or that Haydon's painting has released a noble vision. Wordsworth interestingly chose the first and least likely of these interpretations, preferring to think that art is finally transcendent to its object as well as to its motivating inspiration.

In fact, the ambiguity of Barrett's first version indicates that the painting and its subject matter may be equally insignificant. By releasing an already free vision, rather than rendering it transcendent, transforming it into song or prayer, Haydon's artwork may instead be discarding it. In so doing, the artwork shows itself to be superfluous, "released" by the useless pretensions of its self-consciously denied "Academic air." This dual release whereby both vision and painting are dismissed or "flung out" permits Barrett's acquisition of artistic power. From nature to poet to portrait, her sonnet moves in order from artistic object to artist to artwork, finally turning inward to its own form. The concluding tercet, "Our Haydon's hand has flung out from the mist: / No portrait this, with Academic air! / This is the poet and his poetry," re-defines the sonnet's object from "portrait" to "poet" to "his poetry," thereby reversing the order in which these concepts are developed over the course of the poem. Supplanting first one, then the other of these terms with the potentially self-referential article, "this," Barrett's sonnet assumes the position of Wordsworth's poetry itself.

SILENT-BARE: TWO APPROACHES TO THE SUBLIME

Although Barrett duplicates and responds to many of Wordsworth's own poetic techniques in her sonnet on Haydon's portrait, the 1844 sonnets also foreground a crucial difference: her reassessment of the sublime.[17] For Wordsworth, the passage from absence to presence and back again occurs through both a debilitating breakdown of the faculty of representation and a recuperative turn toward potency and self-affirmation. As J. Hillis Miller has observed, the recognition of an "oscillation between consciousness and nature, life and death, presence and absence, motion and stillness" is "the characteristic endpoint of any careful reading of Wordsworth's best poems."[18] However, Miller does not remark that to his list of binaries we might add silence and speech; nor does he note how "oscillation" (another word for Romantic irony) is often propelled by the sublime, which activates different forms of silence.

Miller recognizes that an "encounter with the blankness of an irresolution is an essential component of any thoughtful reading of Wordsworth's shorter poems. This irresolution is constituted by the 'suspens vibratoire,' in Mallarmé's phrase, of enigmatic juxtapositions among the words of the poem" (68). If Wordsworth's encounter with "blankness" is his meeting with the sublime itself, then the "vibratory suspense" of meaning in his poems is kept in motion by the simultaneously annihilating and rehabilitating effect of these collisions. Barrett enlists the sonnet as a means of revising Wordsworth's poetics on precisely these points.

Considering Wordsworth's view of incarnative language as "not what the garb is to the body but what the body is to the soul," Karen Mills-Courts speculates that Wordsworth's language incarnates by establishing a relationship between thought and the world as thought.[19] Wordsworthian incarnation is not an attempt to embody an external force, Mills-Courts explains, but rather it presents thought as *self*-consciousness. Incarnating thought in words by contemplating itself as a "thing," the mind enters into intimate proximity to death, for, in so doing, it objectifies itself, as though it were a fragment of the external world. Wordsworth's poetry thus incarnates, Mills-Courts notes, in very much the same way that a ruin does; anticipating Derrida's discussion of signs in *Writing and Difference,* Wordsworth's language appears "somewhat like the architecture of an uninhabited city, reduced to its skeleton by some catastrophe of nature or art. A city no longer inhabited, not simply left behind but haunted by meaning and culture. This state of being haunted, which keeps the city from returning to nature, is perhaps the general mode of presence or absence of the thing itself in pure language."[20]

Wordsworth's effort to establish a relationship in his sonnets between thought and the world as thought connects with his approach both to silence and to sublime revelation. It is on specifically these points that Barrett takes issue with him. By focusing on two juxtaposed sonnets, Wordsworth's "Composed Upon Westminster Bridge, Sept. 3, 1802" and Elizabeth Barrett's "Grief" (1844), I will demonstrate 1) how Wordsworth translates his understanding of self-consciousness into poetic form and 2) how Barrett debates this argument:

COMPOSED UPON WESTMINSTER BRIDGE
SEPT. 3, 1802

Earth has not anything to show more fair:
Dull would he be of soul who could pass by
A sight so touching in its majesty:
This City now doth, like a garment, wear
The beauty of the morning; silent, bare,
Ships, towers, domes, theatres, and temples lie
Open unto the fields, and to the sky;
All bright and glittering in the smokeless air.
Never did sun more beautifully steep
In his first splendour, valley, rock, or hill;
Ne'er saw I, never felt, a calm so deep!
The river glideth at his own sweet will:
Dear God! the very houses seem asleep;
And all that mighty heart is lying still!
(Wordsworth, *The Poetical Works of Wordsworth* 214)

Wordsworth's "Composed Upon Westminster Bridge," Barrett's favorite sonnet of his, is typical of his sonnet poetics in general.[21] It begins with a series of negations: "Earth has *not* anything to show more fair," "Dull *would he be* of soul who could pass by" (a figure nonexistent in the poem), "The beauty of the morning, *silent, bare,*" "All bright and glittering in the *smokeless* air" (my italics). The roundabout opening posits that the sight the poem exposes is "touching," which hints that the sonnet is working "incarnatively," with its subject matter (the City or, most accurately, the mind itself) embodied: i.e., rendered tangible. At the same time, the view of the City wearing the beauty of the morning "like a garment" recalls Wordsworth's warning: unlike representational language, "incarnative" language is "not what the garb is to the body but what the body is to the soul." This alerts the reader to the operative negativity in the octave. The scene is not in fact "touching" at all but rather is situated at a remove from the poem's mode of signification. In other words, the sonnet may not present thought itself but may only represent it, just as the City only wears (not as its body but as a mere "garment") the beauty of the morning.

The phrase "silent, bare" is followed by a chain of images, which culminates in the verb "lie." Falling at a line break, this word carries the weight of a double meaning, as if the long catalogue of images that the octave describes is "belied" by the negativity of the poem's representational mode. Wearing the morning sunlight's beauty "like a garment" (and the poem performs the same gesture, Wordsworth implies), "this City" is unable to be *touched;* its beauty is a form of emptiness.

With the turn from octave to sestet, negativity takes on a new quality. As Miller has shown, the "negatives and quasi-negatives" in Wordsworth's sonnet on Westminster Bridge "have a strange power to create as a shimmering mirage lying over their explicit assertions the presence of what they deny" (Miller 72). The fall into deception in the first part of the poem gives rise to a positive movement in the second with the introduction of the word "Never." Subtly repositioning the negativity of absence in the past tense ("Never did sun"), the sonnet appears to overcome its limitations; the gap between octave and sestet (in which the sublime turn takes place) enables the lyric "I" to emerge in a positive movement of self-affirmation ("Ne'er saw I, never felt, a calm so deep!"). Mute representation is transformed into an incarnative exclamation, "Dear God!" which brings (or which endeavors to bring) divine presence into the poem as a result of the speaker's newly asserted self-awareness. However, the final line "And all that mighty heart is lying still!" echoes the hint at deception from the octave ("temples lie"), suggesting that the incarnative moment permitted by an encounter with recuperative negativity is necessarily reabsorbed into vacant representation.[22] Ultimately, the sublime aspect of "this City" (or this Language), Wordsworth suggests, is the way that it reflects presence and absence, life and death. The sight *is* touching (i.e., it can both be incarnated and arouse pathos), only not as the view of an inhabited city but rather as that of a haunted mental architecture, "reduced to its skeleton by some catastrophe of nature or art" (Derrida 5).

Barrett's 1844 sonnet "Grief" clearly reworks Wordsworth's "Composed Upon Westminster Bridge":

GRIEF

I tell you, hopeless grief is passionless;
That only men incredulous of despair,
Half-taught in anguish, through the midnight air
Beat upward to God's throne in loud access
Of shrieking and reproach. Full desertness,
In souls as countries, lieth silent-bare
Under the blanching, vertical eye-glare
Of the absolute Heavens. Deep-hearted man, express
Grief for thy Dead in silence like to death—
Most like a monumental statue set
In everlasting watch and moveless woe
Till itself crumble to the dust beneath.
Touch it; the marble eyelids are not wet:
If it could weep, it could arise and go.
(Barrett, *The Complete Works,* vol. 2, 230)

Both sonnets are written in Petrarchan form, which in itself is not unusual, but, significantly, the poems also share a similar choice of rhymes. One of the rhyme schemes in both octaves ends in "are / air"; two of these rhymes are identical—Wordsworth's "smokeless air" appears in Barrett's sonnet as "midnight air"; Wordsworth's fifth line ends with the word "bare" and so does the sixth line of Barrett's sonnet. But what is even more striking, these two lines share identical second to last words: *silent.* This strange coupling of words, "silent, bare" for Wordsworth, and "silent-bare" for Barrett, is very provocative.

In Wordsworth's sonnet, "silent, bare" is followed by a long chain of images that in a way contradict the supposed nakedness of the scene.[23] The City may be silent, but silence does not include bareness, Wordsworth submits, and the division between these two terms by means of a comma, "silent, bare," allows for their differentiation. But in Barrett's sonnet (and she was frequently criticized for her use of composite words), the modifiers combine to form a single word: "silent-bare." Hence, her view of silence includes exposure in a way that Wordsworth's does not, and her use of negativity will not inspire a self-affirmative turn through the sublime.[24]

Like Wordsworth, Barrett fills her octave with negatives: "hopeless," "passionless," "desertness," "silent-bare." But unlike Wordsworth, she does not convert them into positives. Rather, the impossibility of achieving this conversion in the face of hopeless grief becomes her sonnet's theme. The word "full" in the fifth line thus ironically increases absence rather than opposing it ("Full desertness"). Her assertion that "only men incredulous of despair . . . Beat upward to God's throne" recalls Wordsworth's sonnet, where the utterance "Dear God!" signals, however ambivalently, the very upward turn that Barrett denies.

The "*deep*-hearted man" whom Barrett instructs may well designate the Wordsworthian speaker who naively exclaimed, "N'er saw I, never felt, a calm so *deep!*" (my italics). Her repeated allusion to men as those in need of teaching ("That only *men* incredulous of despair," "deep-hearted *man*") echoes Wordsworth's recurring masculine pronouns ("Dull would *he* be," "In *his* first splendour," "at *his* own sweet will"), suggesting that these masculine embodiments are all in need of correction by a potentially female speaker who claims better to understand the non-recuperative silence of grief ("I tell you") (my italics).

Barrett's extension of "full desertness" from "countries" to "*souls*" recalls Wordsworth's "Dull would he be of *soul* who could pass by / A sight so touching in its majesty" (my italics). Wordsworth's "silent, bare" landscape might seem touching to one who is not "dull of soul." But Barrett's "silent-bare" grief refers to the "desertness" of souls as well as to that of countries, for her grieving silence looks like death itself, and her speechless mourner, who stands in for both poet and poetic language, is also death-like, unable to cry or to move. Still, Barrett's use of simile should not be oversimplified. She writes that "poetry *resembles* grief" and her sonnet on grief bears out this identification: "in silence *like* to death," "most *like* a monumental statue" (my italics). But while grief imitates silence and silence mimics death, poetry should not be equated with silence and death through its identification with grief. Nor is poetry truly silent. Rather, Barrett proposes that poetry stands in metaphorical relation to these terms without being equivalent to them; its task is to act like silence while it speaks or sings.

Where Wordsworth's exclamation "Dear God!" reaches beyond the scope of his poem in a haunting (because finally unsuccessful) invocation of the divine, Barrett turns inward to her poem's form: "Touch it." Entreating the reader to "touch" the statue that functions as a metaphor for her own poem, she restates Wordsworth's "sight so touching." One cannot in the end touch Barrett's crumbling metaphor for grief any more than one can come into contact with the sight of Wordsworth's dead City. But both poets make evident poetry's incarnative potential: Wordsworth's sonnets incarnate the mind in contemplation of its own absence, and Barrett's incarnate pure absence itself.

Both Wordsworth and Barrett explore poetry's ghostliness in their sonnets; both poets negotiate the interplay between representation and incarnation. In both cases, sonnets indirectly address the poets as well as their poetic language: Wordsworth's silent City/Language and the poet who traverses it are both to some extent dead; Barrett's monumental poet/language is made of stone, unable to breathe or to speak. However, a key difference separates their respective approaches. Where Wordsworth creates a sublime transition from one kind of silence to another (from non-recuperative to recuperative silence, representation to incarnation, and back again) Barrett eliminates his form of the sublime altogether. Instead, silence in her grieving sonnets functions as complete nothingness. Retreating further and further inward to the core of their own speechlessness, these sonnets nonetheless produce inscriptions for a language that will never overcome its own intrinsic death, not even momentarily by means of a sublime revelation. Her sonnets thus resemble Charlotte Smith's reiterations of "blank despair" more than they do Wordsworth's troubled sublime.[25]

FROM RENEWAL TO HOPELESSNESS: TWO READINGS

Through my close reading of the two intertextually related sonnets, Wordsworth's "Composed Upon Westminster Bridge" (1802) and Barrett's "Grief" (1844), I have illustrated how the poets' differing positions on silence and the sublime manifest themselves in poetic form. Barrett's revision of Wordsworth becomes more complicated when two terms explicitly enter into her response to him—nature and femininity. In Stone's words, "the very sublime imagery that the young Barrett turned to in representing the mind's power was inflected by paradigms that excluded her female experience" (*Elizabeth Barrett Browning* 66–67). It is precisely Barrett's dual admiration and rejection of Wordsworth's poetics that I want to explore here. To clarify how Barrett renegotiates the relation between nature, femininity, and the sublime (indeed, between these terms and the function of poetry itself), I will now juxtapose two revealing sonnets, Wordsworth's "September, 1815" and Barrett's "Irreparableness" (1844).

SEPTEMBER, 1815

While not a leaf seems faded; while the fields,
With ripening harvest prodigally fair,
In brightest sunshine bask; this nipping air,
Sent from some distant clime where Winter wields
His icy scimitar, a foretaste yields
Of bitter change, and bids the flowers beware;
And whispers to the silent birds, 'Prepare
Against the threatening foe your trustiest shields.'
For me, who under kindlier laws belong
To Nature's tuneful quire, this rustling dry
Through leaves yet green, and yon crystalline sky,
Announce a season potent to renew,
'Mid frost and snow, the instinctive joys of song,
And nobler cares than listless summer knew.
(Wordsworth, *The Poetical Works* 209)

Wordsworth's sonnet typically begins with plenitude, which is conveyed, just as in his sonnet on Westminster Bridge, through negation: "While not a leaf seems faded; while the fields, / with ripening harvest prodigally fair"; it then reveals that this fullness in fact covers up for death. Like many of his other sonnets, this poem enacts, on one level, the discovery of a revelatory quality in loss itself. In the sestet, the emergence of the poetic speaker coincides with the realization of potency and renewal. Nature is here transposed into the arena of thought, and the persona can look upon the seasonal death of nature as the mind's own inevitable and continual death. Both of these deaths might be perpetually overcome, Wordsworth suggests, through self-consciousness, as the mind projects itself onto nature while at the same time distancing from it. This glimpse of death thus proves more conducive to poetry ("the instinctive joys of song") than presence and changelessness.

As in the sonnet on Westminster Bridge, Wordsworth's seeming revelation leads back to emptiness at the end; with its homophonic resonance, the word "knew," which closes the sonnet, reminds us of how "listless summer" must itself be made "new," transplanting the poet out of his "tuneful quire" into a state of vacancy in which no voice rouses "the silent birds." The poem's conclusion thus sets into motion the process of death out of which the speaker will emerge, bewildered, into song.

Like "Grief," Barrett's 1844 sonnet "Irreparableness" mourns the death of a Wordsworthian vision of poetic language:

IRREPARABLENESS

I have been in the meadows all the day
And gathered there the nosegay that you see,
Singing within myself as bird or bee
When such do field-work on a morn of May.
But, now I look upon my flowers, decay
Has met them in my hands more fatally
Because more warmly clasped,—and sobs are free
To come instead of songs. What do you say,
Sweet counsellors, dear friends? that I should go
Back straightway to the fields and gather more?
Another, sooth, may do it, but not I!
My heart is very tired, my strength is low,
My hands are full of blossoms plucked before,
Held dead within them till myself shall die.
(Barrett, *The Complete Works,* vol. 2, 229)

Barrett's first quatrain, with its flowers and song, recalls Wordsworth's lines, "With ripening harvest prodigally fair, / In brightest sunshine bask." Just as Wordsworth introduces "this nipping frost," so Barrett's speaker explains how "decay has met [her flowers]." The poems thus resemble each other in terms of their initial structures. But glaring differences appear in their sestets. Wordsworth's cheerful (albeit threatened) inhabitant of "Nature's tuneful quire" contrasts sharply with Barrett's inconsolable persona who will not transform death into regeneration. Wordsworth's sense of death is in part that it "announces a season potent to renew." But Barrett's loss is absolutely irrevocable.

While seeming to provide an unambiguous example of Barrett's investment in non-recuperative silence, "Irreparableness" also invites misinterpretation. The poem's first addressee, "you," who "see[s]" a nosegay may or may not see what the speaker does when *the speaker* and not the reader looks at her dead flowers: "*I* look upon my flowers, decay" (my italics). Furthermore, the initial addressee is replaced by or extended into "sweet counsellors, dear friends" who give the speaker advice as to her predicament. But the adjective "sweet" here relates back to the scent of the *living* flowers in the meadow. There is thus great complexity as to the identity of the poem's addressee, what this addressee sees, and the status of the various flowers the poem invokes. Are they alive or dead?

We might argue that the flowers in question are *both* alive and dead. The speaker's failure to unite with nature leads to death, which poetry may, if nothing else, make visible: "the [dead] nosegay that you see." But this decayed, embodied nature is also granted a voice, a *life.* For poetry might not be equivalent to silence and death but, as established before, it might operate metaphorically for these terms.

There is, however, a further dimension to the "*sweet* counsellors, dear *friends*" whom the speaker asks for advice: an echo from Barrett's 1838 sonnet, "To Mary Russell Mitford in her garden"—"Benignant *friend,* I will not proudly say / As better poets use, 'These *flowers* I lay,' / Because I would not wrong thy roses *sweet*" (my italics). If in her sonnet to Mitford, Barrett ironizes conventional femininity, in "Irreparableness" this dismissiveness is shown to culminate in impotence and death. The renunciation of femininity/nature (coy in her sonnet to Mitford—"I will not proudly say") results in failure and grief ("I have been in the meadows all the day . . . But, now I look upon my flowers, decay").

As in Barrett's letter to Mitford, written at the same time as the composition of "Irreparableness," the resemblance between poetry and grief is apparent here, but this time with a twist. Barrett's claim that "poetry resembles grief but does so singing instead of sighing," that "it transfigures the great Humanity into a sense of its *To-come,*" is completely reversed in "Irreparableness" in which "sobs are free / *To come* instead of songs" (my italics). Poetry, it seems, does not only imitate grief; it *presents* grief by enacting its own petrification into "everlasting watch and moveless woe."

In "Irreparableness," it is as if Barrett turns to Mitford herself (her "benignant friend") for help with a problem that her dismissal of Mitford in 1838 has in a sense brought about. Generalizing this unique addressee into multiple "sweet counsellors, dear friends," she echoes her previous sonnet's conflation of woman with flowers (i.e., with nature and art): "I would not wrong thy roses sweet." Since this living, feminized nature doubles as a dead bouquet, Barrett implies that the presentation of nature (or of anything in the external world) is an impossible task for poetry. At the same time, she makes an incarnative claim: failure is itself rendered visible—"the [lifeless] nosegay that you see." But because these flowers continue to exhibit the potential for speech ("what do you say?"), they disturb her sonnet as a specter of Mitford's "nature-true," feminized words and also as a reminder of the "branches and buds out of Wordsworth's garden" that she has given over to the Muses so that they can "secure the sprouting." Barrett's opposition to Mitford's femininity and to Wordsworth's sublime does not remove but rather reinscribes the pressure these forces exert on her work.

THE SILENCE OF MY WOMANHOOD: BARRETT'S *SONNETS FROM THE PORTUGUESE*

Even though Barrett's despair after her brother's death blocked her poems' access to recuperation in 1844, her 1850 *Sonnets from the Portuguese* appear to invert her earlier assumptions. Recent critics trace a progression in the *Sonnets* from silence, sadness, death, and weakness to speech, joy, life, and strength. Helen Cooper outlines the progression the sonnets trace. "The *Sonnets* fall into three groups: in 1 and 2 the speaker portrays woman as the object of man's love, 3–40 record the speaker's wavering between objectifying herself and claiming her own creative and sexual subjectivity, and 41–44 demonstrate the poet's arrival at her own subjectivity, which displaces her allegiance to the conventions of the male tradition and reveals her confidence in the voice which that subjectivity elicits" (108). Tracing a similar progression to the one noted by Cooper, Jerome Mazzaro argues that in the *Sonnets from the Portuguese* Barrett adapts the "terror and physicality" of "Wordsworth's own evocations of the sublime"—his use, for instance, of transgressed boundaries and spatial metaphors—to "her own encounter late in life with love" (166). Barrett's goal in the sequence, Mazzaro claims, is to lead the reader along with the speaker from bewilderment to clarity, from fear to the self-affirmation made possible by devotion to another human being. On the whole, Mazzaro grounds his argument about *Sonnets from the Portuguese* in the way that the speaker passes from feelings of grief, mystification, and inadequacy to the realization of love, clarity, and self-worth. Traveling from one extreme to the next, Barrett seemingly repeats Wordsworth's similar movements from thoughtless happiness (i.e., her own childhood memories) to terror and death (the premise of her sequence) to the reconciliation of subject and object and the elevation of the spirit (in Barrett's case, the discovery of love).

While the *Sonnets from the Portuguese* do have a happy ending, I am hesitant to accept critics' ready interpretation of the development from the emptiness of grief to the exultation of love that the poems appear to illustrate.[26] Rather than renouncing death in favor of love, the speaker remains haunted by death from the beginning to the end of her sequence. If in her first sonnet, the speaker, weeping, mistakes love for death, she rejects her suitor in the second sonnet because God has "laid the curse / So darkly on [her] eyelids" that "if [she] had died, / The deathweights, placed there, would have signified / Less absolute exclusion" (5). The third sonnet concludes, "And Death must dig the level where these agree" (9). In the fifth sonnet, she claims that not even her Beloved's reputation as a poet will shield him from the "great heap of grief" that lies hid in her (17). (And we need to keep the ambiguity of the Electra reference in mind as the sequence unfolds.) In the tenth sonnet, the speaker proclaims that "love is fire" (33). But this implies that it is "the torch" of her own love that she extinguishes at her suitor's feet in Sonnet 13 (45).

In Sonnet 15, she asserts that she looks on him "Beholding, besides love, the end of love, / Hearing oblivion beyond memory!" (53). In other words, seeing her Beloved immediately reminds her of the object of her grief. Sonnet 17 commands the Beloved to choose whether she should be a hope, a sad memory, a shade, or a grave. In Sonnet 18, as Alison Chapman remarks in her article on *Sonnets from the Portuguese* and mesmerism, the speaker offers her Beloved a lock of her hair, proclaiming that he will find there the "kiss [her] mother left . . . when she died" (63).[27] Sonnet 19 explains how the speaker will place her Beloved's lock of hair on her chest "to lack / No natural heat" until her heart "grows cold in death" (67). In Sonnet 22, she wishes that she and her Beloved might be isolated in a "place to stand and love in for a day, / With darkness and the death-hour rounding it" (79). Sonnet 23 begins, "Is it indeed so? If I lay here dead, / Would'st thou miss any life in losing mine?" (83). While it may be true that, as Mazzaro argues, the "heavy heart" metaphor shifts associations, what remains important, I think, is that the heart's heaviness is in no way *reduced* by love. This is why the octave and the sestet of Sonnet 25 begin "A heavy heart"/"My heavy heart"; the turn that one would expect here is denied (91). In Sonnet 33, the speaker invites her Beloved to call her by her pet name so that his "mouth" may be "heir to those who are now exanimate" (115).

In Sonnet 35, the speaker asks, surprisingly without ever answering, "If I leave all for thee, wilt thou exchange / And be all to me? [. . .] / [. . .] Nay, wilt thou fill that place by me which is / Filled by dead eyes too tender to know change?" (123). As she implies in Sonnet 35, Barrett's speaker states in Sonnet 39 that she is in "death's neighborhood" (135). Sonnet 41 asks the Beloved to teach the speaker how to project her meaning into the future so that people should "salute / Love that endures, from Life that disappears!" (143). Even if we do not interpret Sonnet 43, which begins, "How do I love thee? Let me count the ways," as a recapitulation of the daughter's deceptive speech in *King Lear,* it is important to note that the last words of the poem refer once again to death, "if God choose, / I shall but love thee better after death" (151).

While the speaker makes incessant references to death throughout the sequence, she specifically relates her grief to the link between silence and gender in Sonnet XIII:

XIII

And wilt thou have me fashion into speech
The love I bear thee, finding words enough,
And hold the torch out, while the winds are rough,
Between our faces, to cast light on each?—
I drop it at thy feet. I cannot teach
My hand to hold my spirit so far off
From myself . . me . . that I should bring thee proof
In words, of love hid in me out of reach.
Nay, let the silence of my womanhood

Commend my woman-love to thy belief,—
Seeing that I stand unwon, however wooed,
And rend the garment of my life, in brief,
By a most dauntless, voiceless fortitude,
Lest one touch of this heart convey its grief.
(Barrett, *A Variorum Edition* 45)

"Sonnet XIII" echoes Barrett's 1844 revisions of Wordsworth. The octave begins with a refusal to speak that ends up suggesting inability. "I drop it at thy feet" shifts to "I cannot teach." Sharon Smulders explains how this inability to speak is reflected in the sonnet's imperfect rhymes: "This struggle emerges in the second quatrain in which 'off' and 'proof' rhyme in an 'ill-sounding' manner with the first quatrain's 'enough' and 'rough.' Likewise, the sestet's 'womanhood' rhymes imperfectly with 'wooed' and 'fortitude.' Thus, the near rhymes at the center of the sonnet mirror its concern with words' deficiency, especially for a female speaker."[28] In "Love's Measurement in Elizabeth Barrett Browning's *Sonnets from the Portuguese*," Margaret Reynolds calls attention to the paradoxical position in which this silence places Barrett: "But a womanly silence is not going to get the *woman-poet* very far. If a woman keeps silent she risks, first of all, objectification, commodification, she does not speak out herself, but can only be spoken. And if a poet is silent, how then is she a poet? And a poet is what Barrett Browning is, therefore she has to speak."[29] Yet the situation presented here is more complicated than this. The difficulty posed by articulation, for Barrett, arises from a limitation intrinsic to representational language's role as a distancing act: "My hand to hold my spirit so far off / From myself . . me. . ."[30] In the sestet, Barrett links incarnation to femininity—"the silence of my womanhood"—which permits visibility: "*Seeing that* I stand unwon" (my italics).

What is atypical about this sonnet, however, is that grief is explicitly *excluded* from the poem: "Lest one touch of this heart convey its grief." The discernible silence of the speaker's "womanhood" is only related to grief in that it reflects the divisiveness, the gaps, of representational language in general: "hold my spirit so far off"; "that I stand un[one]." In this sense, incarnation is not necessarily tied to femininity as such; it is an intrinsic part of the failure and refusal to speak that all poetry plays out: the torch of discursive speech is dropped, extinguished, and in the darkness we see language's bright holes. Masculinity appears to reside in the obscurity that persists after representational language has been rejected and femininity in the perceptible silence that emerges out of this darkness. But as this silence reveals both the constraints and the clarity of the language that has fallen away, the feminine/masculine polarity breaks down into tropological circulation.

The insight that "Sonnet XIII" offers to our reading of Barrett's sonnet poetics is how biological gender—the particularity of the body—contains true grief, true unspeakability as opposed to the silence that appears in poetry as visible absence and loss.[31] Poetry may present grief—an act that involves Wordsworthian self-consciousness ("you see"; "now I look"): in the leaping and turning sonnet structure, we catch a backward/forward glimpse of our own graves. But unlike Wordsworth, Barrett directs her vision not from the world at the end of the world, from life at death and back again; she gazes from beyond the grave at the gravestone, from the end of the world at a world that has died.

The statue that has already crumbled but that Barrett commands us to "touch" and the decayed flowers that we "see" may only contain poetry's central grief in their tie to an invisible gender that we will never find words for or catch sight of although poetry stretches it out to us—"held dead"—with full hands. We will never see the poet's "woman-heart beat," feel her touch. Barrett knows this is a grief that poetry protects us from—the grief of the body, of the *gendered* hand ("see here it is / I hold it towards you," Keats said)—and at the same time frighteningly invites us to think about.[32]

If Barrett's speaker is so overcome with grief that she has no access to the love hidden in her "out of reach," what is the status of her grief at the end of *Sonnets from the Portuguese?* In 1844 Barrett grieved the irreparable loss of nature because it prohibited her from sharing Wordsworth's experience of the sublime. What, then, takes place in 1850? In the final sonnet of her sequence, Barrett instructs her beloved to see the correct colors of her poems/flowers: "Instruct thine eyes to keep the colours true, / And tell thy soul, their roots are left in mine" (155). But these lines echo Sonnet 8, where she explains, "For frequent tears have run / The colours from my life"

(27). In terms of what the speaker herself has seen throughout the sequence, she clarifies in Sonnet 15, "But I look on thee .. on thee .. / Beholding, besides love, the end of love, / [. . .] As one who sits and gazes from above, / Over the rivers to the bitter sea" (53). Here, it is imperative that we open our ears to the two different meanings of the word "thee"; at first the speaker refers to her beloved, but when she repeats the same word, she shifts her address to the person who died in "the bitter sea."

We need to pay careful attention to the way the same sort of repetition works throughout the sequence. The mystic Shape that appears to her in the first sonnet, and that she mistakes for death, might be the bond of love between her and the dead; if he were a ghost figure, arriving to remind her of his prior claim on her, this would explain the extremity of her rejection of the living suitor in Sonnet 2, which otherwise seems to lack a justifiable cause.

The biographically informed reading that I am proposing here—the assumption that Barrett and her speaker are one and the same in the *Sonnets* and that her dead brother and her living suitor enter into fierce competition with each other for her love—is the kind of interpretation that I want to be cautious about. Exploring Barrett's informed response to Luis de Camões's life and writings in the *Sonnets* (an intertextual connection that helps to explain her choice of title, *Sonnets from the Portuguese*), Barbara Neri asserts, "In EBB's case, biographical awareness has weakened the autonomy of her *Sonnets from the Portuguese;* as a result, the history of amatory poetry has lost the importance of her contribution."[33] It is only, I think, fair and possible to use biographical information to help us understand poems to the extent that biographical details are supported by the poems themselves.

How do Barrett's *Sonnets from the Portuguese* interact with hidden biographical information? Do the sonnets ask us to read them side by side with biographical secrets that they expect us to know? For reasons I will elaborate on here, I believe that they do. No critic has contested the intersection between Barrett's *Sonnets* and her life story. Neri concedes that "[t]he autobiographical nature of EBB's *Sonnets* is undisputed and need not be argued" (66). And Houston discusses the various ways that the *Sonnets* construct an "authenticity effect" in order to encourage such biographical readings. Victorian readers believed the sonnet form in general offered access to writers' actual experiences: "Victorian critical discourse about the sonnet generally assumed that it was a vehicle for truthful revelations" (Houston, "Affecting Authenticity" 103). As Joseph Phelan explains, Smith's *Elegiac Sonnets* "helped to position the sonnet as a fundamentally autobiographical form" (43). Wordsworth continued this tradition by describing his own sonnets as "Transcripts of the private heart"; in Phelan's words, "this phrase sums up the attempt in the work of Wordsworth and many of his contemporaries to reposition the sonnet as a site of privileged autobiographical utterance within the system of poetic genres" (43).

The sonnet's documentary function was heightened in the case of the amatory sequence. The reason for this, both Houston and Phelan suggest, developed from the reception of Shakespeare's sonnets during the nineteenth century. The full text of Shakespeare's 1609 sonnets was only published as part of his complete works in Edmond Malone's 1780 edition. Malone's edition, which included a biography of Shakespeare, created a picture of Shakespeare's character and encouraged readers to speculate about connections between his biography and his sonnets: "This popular reading of Shakespeare's sonnets as a kind of autobiography created a widespread understanding of the sonnet form itself as truthful and documentary" (Houston, "Affecting Authenticity" 104). As a result of this new understanding of Shakespeare, Wordsworth's 1827 meta-sonnet "Scorn not the Sonnet" claimed that "with this key / Shakespeare unlocked his heart"; one reason that this sonnet was so often quoted in nineteenth-century sonnet criticism and appeared so often in sonnet anthologies was that it resonated so well with Victorian assumptions about the sonnet's autobiographical sincerity. We need to appreciate Barrett's decision to write an amatory sequence with an understanding of the historical context that shaped her approach to the form. In Houston's words, "Because Victorian writers and readers assumed the sonnet form to be autobiographically truthful, Barrett Browning's choice of the sonnet sequence to explore her new love relationship would seem to reinforce the emotional authenticity of the *Sonnets'* content" (Houston, "Affecting Authenticity" 105).

Beyond her choice of form alone, Barrett employs other techniques to create impressions of authenticity in her sequence. She refers in the *Sonnets* to facts we along with Victorians know to be true—Browning's career as a poet, letters they write to each other, her past griefs, her age, her illness. Houston observes that, "The close intensity of their conversation and correspondence is highlighted by

Barrett Browning's frequent use of ellipses and rhetorical questions. Despite the many literary allusions in her series, the overall effect of her language is colloquial, another hallmark of authentic expression. Language and details from everyday life also contribute to the authenticity effect of the *Sonnets*" (Houston, "Affecting Authenticity" 110). Barrett presents these sonnets as part of a private conversation.

Ultimately, I think we need to both open and close our ears to details from Barrett's biography. Her sonnets must stand alone, but at the same time the sonnets invite us to read them alongside a biographical and epistolary life. Barrett simultaneously wants to speak and wants to preserve silence on the subject of her grief. We need to allow her to do both. She knew she was writing to an audience who understood her personal story. Even before her correspondence was available for all to read, many details from her life were known by the public. This knowledge permitted her to remain silent about what she would rather not explicitly name. Beyond this knowledge, she used silence to allow her to perform tricks of address that even it would appear her readers in general would not be aware of.

Throughout the sequence, doubling plays a disquieting role. Other critics have noticed the strange effects of doubling in *Sonnets from the Portuguese.* Dorothy Mermin provides an intelligent reading of how doubling complicates the speaker's position. However, she does not account for the dual status of the addressee, which, in my view, provides a necessary key to our understanding of the sequence as a whole. Mermin discusses how, through the doubling of identities, Barrett transforms the Renaissance sonnet sequence. Barrett's speaker plays both the part of the beloved female addressee from earlier amatory sequences and the part of the amorous male poet. In Mermin's words, "She is the reluctant object of a poet's courtship, but she is also the sonneteer [. . .] This is not a reversal of roles, but a doubling of them. There are *two* poets in the poem, and *two* poets' beloveds, and its project is the utopian one of replacing hierarchy by equality."[34] The two beloveds that Mermin refers to here result from the speaker's split role. Following Mermin's interpretation, the speaker acts both as lover and beloved, both as active and passive, both as in possession of language and in resistance to it; consequently, the beloved's role, too, divides. The beloved is at once the object of the speaker's love (the glorified male poet) and part of the speaker (her silent resistant side). While I agree with Mermin that Barrett's divided identity as lover and beloved troubles the sequence, I think we need to add another level of meaning to our understanding. The beloved is also the speaker's lost love, the dead one, the one who won her heart first. Her love of the seductive living man remains an upsetting betrayal of this first love, for whom she feels grief that refuses to be overcome.

Mermin shows how the kind of doubling that she uncovers in the *Sonnets*—the speaker's occupation of two different roles, that of silent, resistant beloved and eloquent, overcome lover—becomes more unsettling due to conflicts between these two identities. Since Barrett's speaker plays the part of "the traditionally humble lover" *and* the part of "the object of desire whose beauty is a necessary premise of the sequence," we end up facing "a devaluation of the erotic object that casts the whole amorous and poetical enterprise in doubt."[35] This dual status—between masculinity and femininity, worship and humility, speech and silence—could provide a fertile ground for irony. However, Mermin stresses that while the "persistent doubling of roles accounts for most of the disconcerting strangeness of *Sonnets from the Portuguese,*" Barrett does not even appear to notice the possibilities for irony that these anomalies and contradictions provide (Mermin, "The Female Poet" 364). Because she never acknowledges the ironic potential of her double stance, "she runs the risk of leaving us disoriented and uneasy" (Mermin, "The Female Poet" 365).

I agree with Mermin that wit dominates Barrett's letters in a way that it does not drive her poems; however, the sort of doubling that I see operating in the *Sonnets from the Portuguese* does, I believe, depend on a subtle kind of irony. This is not the kind of irony that inspires laughter. And it is rendered more acute by its precarious relation to allegory. Indeed, irony and allegory have an odd way of dissolving into one another in Barrett's *Sonnets.*

In "The Rhetoric of Temporality," Paul de Man investigates the meaning of the terms "allegory" and "irony" and explains their differences as well as their intersections. According to de Man, in the case of both allegory and irony, "the sign points to something that differs from its literal meaning and has for its function the thematization of this difference."[36] For de Man, allegory relies on "the tendency of language toward narrative, the spreading out along the axis of an imaginary time in order to give duration to what is, in fact, simultaneous within the subject" (225). De Man demonstrates the fundamentally profigurative pattern of allegory with one of Wordsworth's Lucy Gray poems (223–24):

> A slumber did my spirit seal;
> I had no human fears:
> She seemed a thing that could not feel
> The touch of earthly years.
>
> No motion has she now, no force;
> She neither hears nor sees;
> Rolled round in earth's diurnal course,
> With rocks, and stones, and trees.

"A slumber did my spirit seal" describes two stages of consciousness, one belonging to the past when the speaker lay in a kind of sleep, falsely and fearlessly believing that "She seemed a thing that could not feel / The touch of earthly years." The shock of the poem occurs in the blank space between the two short stanzas—the time when "she" dies. Even though there is no real disjunction in the speaker (the poem is written from the point of view of a self that realizes a past error and now understands mortality in a new way), this demystification takes place in the poem as part of a temporal sequence. The first stanza shows us error, the death occurs between the two stanzas, and the last stanza reveals new insight. This difference in perspective "has been spread out over a temporality which is exclusively that of the poem and in which the conditions of error and of wisdom have become successive" (225).[37] While allegory depends upon temporal progression, irony "is the reversed mirror-image of this form" (225). Rather than spreading out across time, "irony appears as an instantaneous process that takes place rapidly, suddenly, in one single moment" (225). If allegory is diachronic, irony is synchronic in nature.

The doubling that Mermin highlights in the *Sonnets* does not involve irony, it would seem, because Barrett's speaker develops over the course of the sequence. Barrett's speaker may begin the courtship in a resistant role; however, her insecurities about her health, age, and attractiveness progress and transform themselves by the end of the sequence. Following Mermin's reading, Barrett does not so much say one thing and mean another; rather, she says one thing and then corrects herself later on. In other words, even though Barrett's speaker may try to occupy various positions at once (for example, that of beloved resistant female object of a male poet's attention and that of humble poet lover), she does not remain a shy unwilling beloved; obstacles seem to fall away and the sequence culminates in reciprocal love and marriage.

I want to add to this discussion of *Sonnets from the Portuguese* the double role played by the addressee. When Barrett uses the word "thee," she at times refers to one person and at times to another. Irony results from the simultaneity with which she often speaks to two beloved addressees, the living and the dead. Allegory results from our sense that one addressee exists in the past tense while the other exists in the present. Confusion surfaces due to questions about which mode Barrett is operating in—that of irony or that of allegory. Does the ghost of the dead beloved stand beside the living male poet, reminding her of his prior claim on her? Or does the dead beloved exist only as a memory that the living poet will help her to overcome? Finally, might the living poet serve as a reincarnation of the dead beloved so that the speaker can marry him without betraying her former love?

Complexly maneuvering between irony and allegory, Barrett repeatedly punctures her sonnets with doubts and uncertainties. Rather than resisting ambiguity, we need to make space for this indistinctness to shine clearly before us. Doubtfulness about the status and identity of the person with whom the speaker interacts appears as the theme of Sonnet 1. As the speaker thinks of Theocritus singing of "the sweet years, the dear and wished for years," she sees "in gradual vision through [her] tears, / The sweet, sad years, the melancholy years, / Those of [her] own life." Suddenly she becomes aware of "a mystic Shape" that moves behind her and draws her "backward by the hair" (1). When the Shape's voice asks, "Guess now who holds thee," her immediate answer is "Death." While this could indicate her own death, it seems the mystic Shape also operates as a ghost from the past. Pulling her backward—in a sense from the present toward the past—the Shape competes with her present suitor.

When the "silver answer" proclaims, "Not Death, but Love," this statement has ironic potential. The Shape functions as two figures at the same time—the dead and the living beloved. Leighton comments on this passage: "In the first sonnet of the sequence, the 'Shape' that suddenly draws the speaker 'backward by the hair' is mistakenly greeted as 'Death' not 'Love.' The memory of Bro runs through these poems like an alternative inspiration that at times rivals this new" (*Elizabeth Barrett Browning* 105). But this transition also raises the possibility of a shift to the second scenario—one of allegory. The speaker may be haunted by the memory of the dead, but the living beloved arrives to help her put her sadness behind her. This is how Chapman reads Sonnet 1: "The 'mystic shape' with its powerful agency forces her to begin to exchange death for love, figured autobiographically as respectively her dead brother Bro (for whose death at sea she held herself responsible) and Browning."[38] She is in fact wrong when she thinks the mystic Shape is a ghost from the past; she must reevaluate what is happening and recognize a new figure on the scene. She must turn from the past to the present.

Sonnet 1 also contains another possibility for the identity of the mystic Shape. He seems to be one person but is in fact another. Time collapses. The shadow from the past mutates into a new possibility for the future. The Shape simultaneously plays the role of two people (an instance of irony) and yet hints at the dissolution of one person and his replacement by another (an instance of allegory). Finally, the vision suggests the possibility of reincarnation, which aligns an awareness of the past with an appreciation of the present and suggests their interchangeability. Our awareness both of simultaneity and transition takes us to the border between irony and allegory. This interchange leads us beyond irony and allegory—to a place where disparate terms fuse into one.

Our confusion is shared by the speaker. She misjudges the identity of the mystic Shape. Even once the masterful voice corrects her (a voice not identified as masculine or feminine), certain problems remain unsolved. The ghost from the past might not be arriving to take her into the afterlife but instead to declare his love for her—to remind her of her prior commitment to him. This is the interpretation the speaker appears to take because in Sonnet 2 she explains that while human beings and nature would be powerless to "part us," God has intervened.

Like Sonnet 1, Sonnet 6 can be read in various ways. We are given reason to believe that the speaker addresses not the living but the dead beloved in this poem. It must be read in light of the previous sonnet, which begins "I lift my heavy heart up solemnly, / As once Electra her sepulchral urn" (17). In Sonnet 5, she asks her living beloved to "Behold and see / What a great heap of grief lay hid in me, / And how the red wild sparkles dimly burn / Through the ashen greyness." Here, Barrett asks us to read her allusion to Sophocles as a reference to her own brother's death. Looking in her living beloved's eyes, she overturns the ashes at his feet and tells him that if he waits beside her, the wind will blow the dust up, and the fires of her grief will "scorch and shred" his hair. His head will not be protected by his poetic fame. This sonnet suggests that the speaker's commitment to her dead beloved cannot be trampled underfoot by her living suitor. Competition will result—the dead will not be forgotten but will return to seek revenge. In Sonnet 6, she appears to speak to her living beloved when she opens the poem, "Go from me" (21). (Sonnet 5 concludes "Stand further off then! go.")

Yet, Sonnet 6 also reads as possibly addressed to the dead beloved. The turn from octave to sestet reads "The widest land / Doom takes to part us, leaves thy heart in mine / With pulses that beat double" (21). And when God hears "that name of thine," He "sees within my eyes, the tears of two" (21). But it is not clear how Doom has parted the speaker and the amorous kindly poet. This line seems rather to refer to Barrett's dead beloved—he who remains nameless even in her grieving sonnets. In Sonnet 9, the speaker says she will not give the poet "any love . . . which were unjust" (31). She corrects this position in Sonnet 10, when she claims that "love is fire" (33). But this line recollects Sonnet 5: "those laurels on thine head, / O my belovèd, will not shield thee so, / That none of all the fires shall scorch and shred / The hair beneath" (17). In Sonnet 10, she says, "*I love thee* . . mark! . . *I love thee!* . ." in the same way that she later repeats "I look on thee . . on thee" in Sonnet 15: "But I look on thee . . on thee . . / Beholding, besides love, the end of love, / Hearing oblivion beyond memory! / As one who sits and gazes from above, / Over the rivers to the bitter sea" (33, 53).[39] It appears in Sonnet 15 that she speaks to the living beloved with her first use of the word "thee" but then switches to the dead beloved with her second use of the word. The second "thee" thus takes her "to the bitter sea"—the scene of her brother's death. (At first the repetition, thee / thee, reads as an instance of irony; as the poem progresses, we see allegory in motion—the first "thee" stands in for the living beloved; the second "thee" passed away in the bitter sea.)

Barrett begins Sonnet 20, "Beloved, my Beloved" (71). In Sonnet 27, she proclaims, "My own, my own. / [. . .] And I who looked for only God, found *thee!* / I find thee" (93). In Sonnet 33, she asks her beloved to call her by her pet name, mourning the "clear / Fond voices, which, being drawn and reconciled / Into the music of Heaven's undefiled, / Call me no longer" (115). The turn from octave to sestet occurs with the phrase "Silence on the bier," which leads at the start of the sestet to "While I call God . . call God!" This inspires her to ask her beloved to "Be heir to those who are now exanimate." Sonnet 35 begins with a question that the speaker is not able to answer, "If I leave all for thee, wilt thou exchange / And be all to me?" (123). Critics often mock this sonnet for its apparent triteness—particularly the poem's concluding lines, "Yet love me—wilt thou? Open thine heart wide, / And fold within, the wet wings of thy dove." For example, Cooper describes these lines as involving "unfortunate and cloying images" (35). However, no one calls attention to the fact that these lines take the place of the answer to the question that introduces the shift from octave to sestet: "If I leave all for thee, wilt thou exchange / And be all to me?" Instead of answering the question, the sestet begins, "That's hardest. If to conquer love, has tried, / To conquer grief, tries more . . . as all things prove; / For grief indeed is love and grief beside." The final tercet attempts to comfort the speaker's Beloved since he cannot fill the place inside her that is occupied by "dead eyes"—he cannot replace her grief with his love. Barrett solves this problem by changing the sonnet's emphasis from the fact that her Beloved can never be "all" to her to her desire for him to love her anyway: "Alas, I have grieved so I am hard to love. / Yet love me—wilt thou?" Critics should pay closer attention to Sonnet 35's essentially somber tone as well as to its urgent implications for the sequence as a whole—the speaker remains haunted by death throughout the entire courtship cycle.

To conclude my discussion of the progression that takes place during Barrett's sonnet-writing career, I will juxtapose Sonnet 44 in *Sonnets from the Portuguese* with Barrett's 1844 "Irreparableness." Thematically, these two sonnets relate to flowers, and structurally they reveal a key development in Barrett's poetics:

XLIV

Belovèd, thou hast brought me many flowers
Plucked in the garden, all the summer through
And winter, and it seemed as if they grew
In this close room, nor missed the sun and showers.
So, in the like name of that love of ours,
Take back these thoughts which here unfolded too,
And which on warm and cold days I withdrew
From my heart's ground. Indeed, those beds and bowers
Be overgrown with bitter weeds and rue,
And wait thy weeding; yet there's eglantine,
Here's ivy!—take them, as I used to do
Thy flowers, and keep them where they shall not pine.
Instruct thine eyes to keep the colours true,
And tell thy soul, their roots are left in mine.
(Barrett, *A Variorum Edition* 155)

The editor of the *Variorum Edition,* Miroslava Dow, summarizes in a footnote that this final sonnet celebrates Browning's gift of flowers, which he brought to Barrett as long as he could—"usually from his mother's garden, and surprisingly long into the winter and very early in the spring. Throughout the correspondence Elizabeth thanked Browning repeatedly for the flowers" (155). And Dow stresses how Barrett's letters "frequently mention Browning's flowers to her, her gratitude, her astonishment at the fact that they seemed to thrive in her close room where she could not keep flowers and plants alive for long before his" (156). Leighton, too, has observed how flowers function in the Brownings' courtship correspondence. In "Stirring 'a Dust of Figures': Elizabeth Barrett Browning and Love," she discusses the double meanings of flowers in the Brownings' letters.[40] She reminds us of an often-forgotten section of Robert Browning's famous opening letter to Barrett, the letter in which he links his love of his poetry to his love for her: "so into me has it gone, and part of me has it become, this great living poetry of yours, not a flower of which but took root and grew—oh how different that is from lying to be dried and pressed flat, and prized highly and put in a book" (I:3). According to Leighton, "This opening gambit supplies both correspondents with a wealth of playful variations on the theme of flowers. In them, the usual priorities of what is lived and what is written are upset"

(222). Barrett tells Browning that poetry "is the flower of me," adding that "the rest of me is nothing but a root, fit for the ground and the dark" (I:65). Responding to Barrett's flower reference here, Browning writes, "this is all the flower of my life which you call forth and which lies at your feet" (I:353). Ultimately, Barrett concludes her sequence with a comparison between her thoughts (that is, her sonnet sequence itself) and the flowers that Browning has given her.

In her article "'Medicated Music': Elizabeth Barrett Browning's *Sonnets from the Portuguese*," Sharon Smulders argues that Barrett uses flower imagery in her *Sonnets* in order to rehabilitate a diseased tradition. Being a highly self-reflexive writer, Barrett alludes with this imagery to several intertexts: her courtship correspondence with Robert Browning, the Renaissance amatory lyric tradition, and her own 1844 *Poems*. According to Smulders, "Love—prescribed as a cure rather than diagnosed as a sickness—reprieves her from death, releases her into new life, and provides her with a way to effect the same transformation in a genre plagued by infirmity" (210). Smulders notes that "the green world is conspicuously absent from the beginning of the sequence"; by contrast, the subsequent sections of *Sonnets from the Portuguese* are rich with flower imagery: "In addition to palm-trees and wild vines, the sonneteer mentions flowers (sonnets 20, 21, 34, 40), lilies (sonnet 24), asphodel (sonnet 27), cowslips (sonnet 33), 'green leaves with morning dews impearled' (sonnet 42), rue, eglantine, and ivy (sonnet 44)" (207). And Smulders relates the early part of the sequence to "the scenery of 'Full desertness' ('Grief') described in the 1844 sonnets" (207). In Smulders' view, the "difference between the sonnets of 1844 and those of 1850 clarifies just how Barrett Browning uses natural imagery to indicate the woman's renewed commitment to life. In her valedictory sonnets, she refigures the Romantic trope of man's alienation from nature for a female speaker and so replaces the open vistas of fields and meadows with images of decay and enclosure" (207). For example, Smulders reads "Irreparableness" as tacitly identifying the female poet with her flowers, which have been broken from their roots. These dead blossoms become, in Smulders' words, "a funereal bouquet" (208). Smulders maintains that this is not at all the case in the *Sonnets from the Portuguese*. While "Irreparableness" suggests "the 1844 speaker's irreparable disconnection from youth, song, freedom, and ultimately life, the flowers of *Sonnets from the Portuguese* focus on vital connections and surprising reconnections" (208).

I think Smulders does a good job of highlighting certain important transitions that take place between Barrett's sonnets of 1844 and 1850. However, I would like to push my interpretation one step beyond Smulders's conclusion about *Sonnets from the Portuguese*—that Barrett "uses natural imagery to indicate the woman's renewed commitment to life" (207). Barrett's final claim in Sonnet 44 that the flowers of love have been translated into her poetry is disrupted by how the colors of these sonnets have been washed away by her tears. God knows, Barrett tells us in Sonnet 8, that "frequent tears have run / The colours from my life" (27). Have not these sonnets also been made bare, just as, in Sonnet 29, she commands her "palm-tree" to set its "trunk all bare" so that its bands of greenery (i.e., her thoughts) will drop "heavily down" and "burst, shattered, everywhere" (105)?[41] Smulders argues that "the speaker's colours, reduced to 'so dead / And pale a stuff' by 'frequent tears' (sonnet 8), take on the verdant hues of nature that, in turn, inform poetry—what Browning had, for his part, called 'heart and life and *myself*'" (210). Here she makes a perhaps too easy assumption that good poetry requires "the verdant hues of nature." And Mary B. Moore argues about the last two lines of Sonnet 44: "This trope brilliantly echoes and transforms the female poet's self-portrayal as faded 'stuff' in sonnet 8, suggesting that the male poet's love and his erotic gaze itself return her color. Color in a sense is the responsive blush of the female poet to her sexual role as erotic object. The colors' truth suggests both that the male gaze is true to the female poet and that it elicits truth from her, in the form of true colors. It helps her to show her true colors."[42] In my analysis, the speaker's "true colors" have been washed away. Lack of literal color does not equal lack of power, however.

It has always been known that the *Sonnets from the Portuguese* were not translations from the Portuguese, and I think it is clear that the speaker's dead beloved fails to be cleanly translated into the figure of the living beloved. In her 1844 sonnet, "Grief," Barrett rewrites Wordsworth's Westminster Bridge sonnet, telling him that because grief "lieth silent-bare," it must be expressed "in silence like to death" (*The Complete Works*, vol. 2, 230). There, she relates the mourner to a statue set in "everlasting watch and moveless woe," and she orders us to "Touch it; the marble eyelids are not wet: / If it could weep, it could arise and go." Just as Wordsworth brings us into contact with the "unimaginable touch of time" while he posits the impossibility of doing so, in 1844 Barrett advises us to touch her moveless statue of grief even as she acknowledges that it may already have crumbled "to the dust beneath." Similarly, in 1850, "this heart" from Sonnet 13 does touch us, it does "convey its grief" at the same time that the speaker protects us from her anguish by "rend[ing] the garment of [her] life" through the "silence of [her] womanhood" (46).

Wordsworth belongs to "nature's tuneful quire" even though he must always pass through silence in order to get there, whereas Barrett constructs a voiceless realm from which she will never depart. It is in this silence that we must learn to see and hear her invisible heart. She may speak to two people at the same time, to a dead beloved and to a living one, but she refuses ever neatly to translate death into life. The only progress that takes place between 1844 and 1850 is that Barrett's poems at last claim to be versions of living flowers rather than dead ones. Yet while these flowers might be alive, Barrett splits them apart until they "burst, shattered, everywhere!"; what we see in the end are not living flowers but pale, bare branches. Barrett might shift her theme to love in *Sonnets from the Portuguese,* but she qualifies this love with references to grief. Her beloved is left behind in the literal garden with Mary Russell Mitford. And while Wordsworth passes through confusion to clarity and back again, Elizabeth Barrett ceaselessly repeats her tears, those "sighing years / Re-sighing on [her] lips renunciative," her endless double appeals to God and God, thee and thee (31).

CHAPTER THREE

Sing Again

Christina Rossetti and the Music of Silence

Elizabeth Barrett's well-known 1845 complaint—"where were the poetesses? [. . .] I look everywhere for Grandmothers & see none"—reads ironically when we consider that Barrett's figurative poetic grandmother, Charlotte Smith, died in 1806, the very same year that Barrett was born (*BC* 10:14). Like Smith who develops an intricate system of personifications in order to mute the gender norms that she so dramatically overthrows, nineteenth-century women poets also seem to silence the female lyric tradition that they themselves initiated. Smith translates Petrarch and impersonates Werter in her sonnets rather than earlier women writers or literary figures; because of her "reverent love of the grandfathers," Barrett insists it is "not in the filial spirit" that she is deficient (*BC* 10:14). Christina Rossetti took this refusal to acknowledge her female predecessors one step further; she unambiguously writes against her own most preeminent female precursor, Elizabeth Barrett—this gesture provides the framework for Rossetti's celebrated sonnet sequence, "*Monna Innominata.*"[1] Rossetti not only refuses to mimic Barrett's "happy" writing style, but she also assumes a more reticent poetic voice.[2] Such restraint raises compelling questions, for critics remain perplexed by the double function of poems that seem to stay unusually quiet and yet to sing.

In his 1971 article, "The Lyric Voice of Christina Rossetti," Curran complains that Rossetti writes "quiet lyrics" and "has so little to say," even though he grants her "a true lyric voice" and allows that she possesses the "not inconsiderable gift of felicitous music."[3] Much feminist criticism repudiates this underestimation of Rossetti's work. But from a feminist perspective Rossetti's writing still remains elusive. Like Curran, who cannot reconcile her poems' musicality with their apparent lack of content, current readers have difficulty understanding whether Rossetti writes poems that participate in a critique of gender or whether she acknowledges her poetry's failure to achieve feminist goals.[4] Does Rossetti view gender as, in Judith Butler's words, "complexly produced" and "not as clear or as univocal as we are sometimes led to believe"? (*Undoing Gender* 212).[5] Or does Rossetti admit her inability to transform gender relations in her poetry? Both our past and our present concerns converge around the issue of silence: for Curran, Rossetti seems to have "so little to say"; for many contemporary critics, her poems seem actively to embrace reticence as all that nineteenth-century women had available to them. Rossetti's inability to describe, sing, or recall presents "beguiling puzzles" to the modern reader.[6]

I propose that silence operates on two different levels in Rossetti's poetry. First, her ostensibly female speaker reminds the reader that she cannot express herself, and second, her poetic lines contradict themselves, creating an ambiguity of context and an instability of voice. I will refer to the first category as one of "stated" silences since they are explicitly declared, and the second category as one of "semantic" silences since they disrupt communication.[7] Rossetti's speaker sings that she cannot sing and also sings lyrics that seem to lack substance. Several contradictions emerge from this interplay between silence and sound. By singing that she cannot sing, does Rossetti achieve the very goal that she professedly denies herself? Do the "semantic" silences in Rossetti's poetry lead to no meaning whatsoever—a defect that Rossetti apparently links to femininity—or do they demand an alternative mode of reading? In other words, does Rossetti confirm or refute historical stereotypes about women's incapacity to produce good poetry?

As this study emphasizes, the sonnet itself reflects the pressure that most critical accounts of Rossetti's work have underlined: an interchange between silence and sound.[8] Rossetti's poetry bridges the same gap between formal compression and musical potential that the sonnet structure traverses. It is perhaps for this reason that Rossetti embraced the sonnet frame—also adopted by her brother Dante Gabriel, notably in his 101-sonnet sequence, *The House of Life*

(1870–1881). Christina Rossetti first developed her skill as a sonneteer in the summer of 1848 when she and her brothers played with *boutes-rimés,* a game of writing sonnets to a given set of end rhymes.[9] Rossetti did write in many different forms: her 1,057 poems include the longer narratives, *Goblin Market, Repining, The Prince's Progress, The Iniquity of the Fathers upon the Children, Three Nuns, The Lowest Room,* and *From House to Home.* However, it is important to recognize that sonnets make up almost one-fifth of Rossetti's total work.[10] Publishing many individual and coupled sonnets, she printed six sequences during her lifetime, and another came out after her death. In August 1881 her collection, *A Pageant and Other Poems,* included four sequences: *"Monna Innominata: A Sonnet of Sonnets"* (fourteen sonnets), *"Later Life: A Double Sonnet of Sonnets"* (twenty-eight sonnets), "The Thread of Life" (three sonnets), and "If Thou Sayest, Behold, We Knew It Not" (three sonnets).

In this chapter, I will discuss "The Thread of Life" and *"Monna Innominata"*—sequences that provide key examples of both "stated" and "semantic" silences. I will take Rossetti's insistence on reticence not as an impediment to understanding her poems but as a method of reading them. For by ignoring fixed context, contradictions, and supposed "singleness" of poetic voice, and by focusing instead only on the way words audibly and visually function, I will illustrate how Rossetti's sonnets cloak a ceaseless reiteration of her speaker's identity. Rather than simply "banqueting on bitterness" and burying herself "alive in a coffin of renunciation" as Gilbert and Gubar interpret Rossetti, I argue that she embeds in her sonnets an overpowering celebration of selfhood.[11] This celebration occurs through words that appear within other words (often without sound), those that cross between phrases, those suggested by implicit rhymes and those that serve as homophones of the printed text.

Through her repetitions of woman's selfhood, Rossetti seems to overwhelm references to masculinity altogether. Her sonnets pronounce a request for forgotten women's words. However, just like Charlotte Smith and Elizabeth Barrett, Rossetti does not limit her focus to women's silence. By purposefully obscuring her speaker's identity, she leaves open the possibility that this speaker could *also* be a man. The varying gender of Rossetti's lyric subject likens her to Smith, who uses many male speakers in her sonnets. But Rossetti pushes Smith's system to yet another level: while Smith directly states her speakers' different identities (at least in the context of her novels where the sonnets first appeared), Rossetti accomplishes the same motion through ambiguity and indirection.

Like Smith and Barrett, Rossetti suggests that irrespective of gender, lyric poetry stages an unsettling battle between blankness and music. As a prototypical lyric form, the Petrarchan sonnet occurs through limited lines, number of syllables per line, meter, rhyme scheme, and an imposed octave/sestet structure; like all lyric poems, sonnets elide, compress, and restrain. Through semantic ambiguity as well as through formal condensation, Rossetti's sonnets sing of their inability to make sounds. This process ironically gives rise to affirmations of the speaker's presence; read differently, references to speechlessness equate with declarations of selfhood. By constantly announcing the speaker's self-presence, Rossetti's sonnets escape silence. However, because the speaker's personality both takes the place of "stated"/"semantic" silence and also stays unspecified, the lyric subject becomes the equivalent of silence itself. Nameless, forgotten women therefore do reappear as speakers in Rossetti's sonnets, but they simultaneously sing and fail to sing. Because this double status does not distinguish women sonneteers from poets in general, Rossetti ultimately may define lyric poetry as the very music of voicelessness.

THE POETICS OF SECRECY

Isobel Armstrong's analysis of the nineteenth-century expressive tradition historicizes Rossetti's paradoxical relationship to silence and sound. For Armstrong, nineteenth-century "expressive theory is above all an aesthetics of the *secret,* the hidden experience."[12] This interpretation derives partly from the agreement between G. H. Lewes and John Stuart Mill about poetic language. In *Monthly Repository* of 1833, Mill posits a break between feelings and the way they are communicated. For Mill, poetic language comes as close as possible to representing feelings which themselves will always remain hidden: poetry "is the delineation of the deeper and more secret workings of human emotions"; it is "feeling confirming itself to itself in moments of solitude and embodying itself in symbols which are the nearest possible representations of the feeling."[13]

Because Victorians believed the mind could not be brought outwards into linguistic form, they separated feelings and representation. As Armstrong explains, representation becomes the obstacle that emotion is supposed to overcome. Since the representational symbol is both the method of articulation and the structure of its constraint, "*ex*pression and *re*pression, although in conflict with another, are interdependent. They constitute one another, so that expression is predicated upon repression" (341). But the main supposition of expressive theory is that language can never coincide with primal feeling. In other words, the theory "cannot account for language" (342).

Difficulties in the expressive tradition particularly troubled women writers. Armstrong observes that Dora Greenwell applies the language of secrecy to women in social life but then associates this reticence with the expressiveness of women's art. Greenwell affirms that in poetry the woman is able to write that which is camouflaged in interpersonal relationships. Somehow, though, a necessarily unknown identity is what poetry supposedly makes apparent: "the secret is an open secret—and a closed one" (Armstrong 342). Greenwell writes: "It is surely singular that woman, bound, as she is, no less by the laws of society than by the immutable instincts of her nature, to a certain suppression of all that relates to personal feelings, should attain . . . a voice so sad, so truthful, so earnest, that we have felt as if some intimate secret were at once communicated and withheld,—an Open Secret, free to all who could find its key—the secret of a woman's heart, with all its needs, its struggles, and its aspirations."[14] In sum, expressive models of language approve the projection of emotions outwards and also the unreachable dimension of these emotions. Communication, therefore, involves "struggle and limit, transgression and boundary, silence and language" (Armstrong 344). As Armstrong makes clear, Christina Rossetti's work illustrates these tensions in the expressive tradition. Joseph Phelan observes a link between Armstrong's discussion of expression and repression and nineteenth-century women's attraction to the sonnet form: "What Isobel Armstrong calls the 'aesthetics of the *secret*' which dominates women's poetry during the early nineteenth century gives rise not only to various forms of masking and displacement (such as the dramatic monologue), but also to the retention of a privileged site of encoded personal utterance in the sonnet" (47).

Before I discuss Rossetti's sonnets, I would first like to foreground her general approach to silence through an analysis of "Winter: My Secret," a poem that plays with the same Petrarchan tradition that we will see many of her sonnets dismantle. In Hassett's words, "Winter: My Secret" may "stand as a singularly representative piece" (62). Tonally, the poem casts the reader as a bothersome male lover who makes demands that the speaker—his "beloved"—does not want to obey. Serving as "almost a summa of [Rossetti's] work," "Winter: My Secret" begins with a self-defiant, mocking resistance to reveal its subject (Armstrong 357):

> I tell my secret? No indeed, not I:
> Perhaps some day, who knows?
> But not today; it froze, and blows, and snows,
> And you're too curious: fie!
> You want to hear it? well:
> Only, my secret's mine, and I won't tell.[15]

This refusal to resolve an enigma, the poet's unwillingness to disclose a secret, serves as the poem's theme. Characteristically, Rossetti obscures what is concealed to such a degree that the reader has difficulty knowing whether or not the secret even exists. Her second stanza thus begins:

> Or, after all, perhaps there's none:
> Suppose there is no secret after all,
> But only just my fun.

The poem goes on to associate the revelation of its secret with an unwanted openness to sexual violence. Clarifying that because it is winter she needs "a shawl, / A veil, a cloak, and other wraps," the speaker tells us she wears her "mask for warmth." Her account of what would happen if she opened her protective clothing closely echoes images of sexual aggression in Rossetti's much longer poem, *Goblin Market.* In "Winter: My Secret," the speaker describes winds that will come "whistling thro' [her] hall; / Come bounding and surrounding [her], / Come buffeting, astounding [her], / Nipping and clipping thro' [her] wraps and all." Similarly, in *Goblin Market*'s allegorical rape scene, the goblin men approach Lizzie, "hobbling, / Flying, running, leaping, / Puffing and blowing, / Chuckling, clapping, crowing, / Clucking and gobbling, / Mopping and mowing," and then "Barking, mewing, hissing, mocking, / Tore her gown and soiled her stocking" (1:2, 19–21).[16] Because of the threat of sexual violence in "Winter: My Secret," the speaker's reluctance to reveal her secret connects to her preservation of virginity. Even if the reader/listener "would not peck," the speaker does not risk believing this assurance; rather, she will not "be pecked at by every wind that blows." Even in spring, she does not trust "March with its peck of dust." The phallic references here are obvious; to protect herself from sexual aggressions, the speaker must maintain secrecy so as to keep her virginity safe.

The poem closes with a depiction of summer, when the speaker's secret might either be told or surmised. With another echo of *Goblin Market,* the speaker ties the unveiling of her secret to "golden fruit . . . ripening to excess." But in *Goblin Market,* the mythical male figures who sell what men could not sell "in any town" do manage to corrupt Laura almost to the point of her death; in "Winter: My Secret," we are given no reason to believe the speaker will ever share her secret (1:1, 13). The "drowsy birds" that "sing less and less" hardly seem to correspond to the speaker's vocalization (in poetry) of the secret she hides. The rhyme between "less" and "excess" posits an antithesis that in a sense negates the meaning of both terms. And the word "guess," which rhymes with this opposition ("Or you may guess") thereby becomes compromised, too. Furthermore, in a good example of a "semantic" silence, we learn that there must be "not too much sun nor too much cloud," and that "the warm wind" must be "neither still nor loud." The perfect balance between sun and cloud and the idea of wind moving but without noise all create circumstances in which the speaker *might* tell her secret. Hassett concludes, "Ending with a fantasy that holds the probabilities of disclosure and nondisclosure in ambiguous suspension, Rossetti has the fun of her poem while emphatically maintaining her distance" (62). Even if her unimaginable conditions are met, the speaker still does not agree to resolve the puzzle (of which, we know, there might be none) since she finally asserts, "*Perhaps* my secret I may say" (my italics). As Armstrong illustrates, the poem "turns on the refusal of expression. It is about and is itself a barrier" (357).

What is the secret in Rossetti's poem? Alison Chapman reads "Winter: My Secret" as playfully resisting the sentimental tradition, which "insists that women's poetry is confessional and personal" (*Afterlife of Christina Rossetti* 6). Chapman postulates that Rossetti's "resistance to that ideology of female poetic creativity, from within the sentimental tradition, signifies a 'secret' that is precisely the rhetorical vacillation between disclosure and confession" (6). For this reason, Rossetti's "secret" seems to involve "the very absence of the feminine subject that the sentimental tradition is predicated upon and, furthermore, the subject is captured in the process of fading from the text, or oscillating between presence and absence. The 'secret' is that there might be no subject to disclose" (6). Ultimately, if "Winter: My Secret" serves in Chapman's words as "the paradigmatic Rossettian resistance to self-representation from within the sentimental tradition," it reveals how Rossetti's poetry in general "circulates around the illusion that there might be no fully present subject that speaks" (9). According to Chapman, Rossetti's resistance to inscribing the personal opens up the possibility of an alternative mode of subjectivity: "Withholding the personal secret—and, indeed, deleting subjectivity itself—in Rossetti's writings is not merely a form of protest against the gender ideology that insists women's writing is autobiographical, nor is it merely an implicit critique of Victorian amatory and social values. It is, rather, the very provisional and tentative gesturing towards a new process of subjectivity [. . .] Perhaps this is Christina Rossetti's secret" (15).

I agree with Chapman that Rossetti complicates or blocks her readers' ability to equate the speaking subject in her poems with her biographical self. However, as I will show in this chapter, I do not agree that Rossetti's resistance to autobiographical writing results in a deletion of subjectivity. Instead of reading Rossetti as dancing around the possibility that "there might be no fully present subject that speaks," I perceive a different phenomenon: rather than deleting subjectivity, Rossetti creates an overabundance of speaking selves; rather than hinting that no subject exists, she implies that more speakers exist than easily can be comprehended.[17] At times her repeated personal pronouns seem to condense into a single subject that reiterates its presence, supplanting other levels of meaning (a dynamic I will explore in "The Thread of Life"); at other times, her speakers and addressees shift and multiply so fluidly that it becomes difficult or impossible for us to confidently pin them down (the pattern I will elucidate in *"Monna Innominata"*).

DOMINANT SELFHOOD IN "THE THREAD OF LIFE"

While both "Winter: My Secret" and *Goblin Market* thematize resistance (the refusal to tell a secret, to buy the fruit of goblin men), they demonstrate this point through content rather than form. For all its repudiations of a voyeuristic intruder, "Winter: My Secret" might continue indefinitely to entangle the reader in its own denials and contradictions, without ever giving away what it hides. Similarly, the seduction that Lizzie resists in *Goblin Market,* far from alienating us from the fruits proffered by dangerous, otherworldly men, enmeshes us in highly sensual, extravagant chains of description. Rossetti's sonnets, on the other hand, approach the same topic of withholding but in a much more constrained structure. Thus the paradox Armstrong highlights between expression and repression—a dilemma that was especially intense for nineteenth-century women writers—plays itself out both thematically and formally in the sonnet frame.

In her 1881 collection, *A Pageant and Other Poems,* Christina Rossetti published, among others, the sonnet sequences *"Monna Innominata: A Sonnet of Sonnets"* and "The Thread of Life." I will preface my exploration of *"Monna Innominata"* by first taking a look at the three sonnets in the shorter "The Thread of Life." The first poem of this three-sonnet sequence accentuates the tension that persists throughout Rossetti's poetry as a whole:

THE THREAD OF LIFE
1.

The irresponsive silence of the land,
The irresponsive sounding of the sea,
Speak both one message of one sense to me:—
Aloof, aloof, we stand aloof, so stand
Thou too aloof bound with the flawless band
Of inner solitude; we bind not thee;
But who from thy self-chain shall set thee free?
What heart shall touch thy heart? what hand thy hand?—
And I am sometimes proud and sometimes meek,
And sometimes I remember days of old
When fellowship seemed not so far to seek
And all the world and I seemed much less cold,
And at the rainbow's foot lay surely gold,
And hope felt strong and life itself not weak.[18]

The first sonnet begins with an anaphoric description of silence and sound; both are "irresponsive" and both emanate from natural sources—the land and the sea. These two indifferent powers "speak" the same message: a four-time repetition of the word "aloof." The poem then presents two possible readings. On the one hand, it seems the land and the sea are speaking the words "Aloof, aloof." Referring to themselves as "we," they address the speaker as "thou" and "thee." On the other hand, because the expression "Aloof, aloof" does not appear in quotation marks, it seems that Rossetti herself speaks the words. In this way, "we" would refer to all humanity. Because she distinguishes "thou" from humanity, Rossetti suggests that she refers to a higher power, perhaps even Christ himself. Bound in perfect inner solitude, the Christ figure cannot be freed (or does not choose to be) from his "self-chain." Consequently, just as we have seen in Barrett's sonnets, where "my hand" and "this heart" remain untouchable, no heart can touch "thy heart," no "hand thy hand."

The start of the sestet, however, makes a striking turn. Beginning, "And I am," Rossetti echoes "hand thy hand." As "hand" contains the word "and," "I" rhymes with "thy," and "am" recalls the repeated "hand," the speaker appears, without warning, to take the place of Christ. Furthermore, unlike the previous eight lines, this line contains five different references to the word "me": "so-*me*-ti-*me*-s proud and so-*me*-ti-me-s *me*-ek" (and the last word, of course, also sounds like "me"). The only line from the octave with a similar structure is the third: "Speak both one *me*-ssage of one sense to *me*." The lines are set up to resemble each other, we might observe, as the first begins with a word that rhymes with the final word in the second. In this way, "speak" also simulates "me"—the same word that appears in "*me*ssage" and as the ending of the line. To continue through the sestet, line 10 contains four references to the speaker's identity: "And so-*me*-ti-*me*-s I re-*me*-mber." Line 11 holds "me" in "see-*me*-d" (which echoes "me," as does "seek"). Line 12 has the word "I" and a repetition of "see-*me*-d." Finally, the last two lines of the sonnet contain no references to the speaker's self at all.

For the duration of the sestet, the speaker moves through a series of contradictions: she or he is "sometimes proud and sometimes meek"; she or he remembers when "hope felt strong and life itself not weak." Rereading the octave, we notice that "me" forms an end-rhyme with "thee," reinforcing the identification between speaker and addressee that the internal rhyme scheme suggests. (And according to my first reading, these two terms are indistinguishable.) The self-chained me/thee figure contrasts with the word "free," thematically set in opposition to self-entrapment but audibly merged with it.

This distinction between liberty and confinement relates to the discrepancy between noise and silence. By rhyming "me," "thee," and "sea," the speaker builds a curious arch between the self, the auditor and sound; Rossetti ties all three terms to "irresponsive sounding." At the same time, the "irresponsive silence of the land" connects, through rhyme, both to the auditor's "hand" and to the speaker's own person: "And I am."[19] The speaker, then, not only blends with (or even appropriates) the auditor's personality but the two figures become paradoxically associated with both freedom and constraint, both sound and silence.

The second sonnet directly states that the speaker is imprisoned:

2.

Thus am I mine own prison. Everything
Around me free and sunny and at ease:
Or if in shadow, in a shade of trees
Which the sun kisses, where the gay birds sing
And where all winds make various murmuring;
Where bees are found, with honey for the bees;
Where sounds are music, and where silences
Are music of an unlike fashioning.
Then gaze I at the merrymaking crew,
And smile a moment and a moment sigh
Thinking: Why can I not rejoice with you?
But soon I put the foolish fancy by:
I am not what I have nor what I do;
But what I was I am, I am even I.

(2:3, 123)

The speaker distinguishes him- or herself from nature (we recall the silence of the land, the sound of the sea)—a world of music where "the gay birds sing" and "all winds make various murmuring." Just as both silence and sound speak *one* message in the first sonnet, so do they now equally produce song: "Where sounds are music, and where silences / Are music of an unlike fashioning." With this dual reference to music, then, the octave concludes. The sestet depicts the speaker, in contrast, as excluded from both silence and sound; because of this exclusion, the speaker cannot produce music, and is thus unable to "rejoice" with the "merrymaking crew." This thought causes the speaker to "smile a moment and a moment sigh"—a typical Rossettian contradiction (another example of a "semantic" silence) that appears to tell us nothing about the speaker's sentiments.

The entire sestet unfolds through echoes of the words "I" and "you." The ninth line contains the word "I" and ends with "crew," which serves as a rhyme with "you" two lines down. The tenth line retrieves the same sound from "I" in "smile" and also in "sigh," which rhymes with "I" four lines later. The eleventh line repeats "I" but ends with "you"; the twelfth line echoes "you" in "soon" and in "foolish," again repeats the word "I" and concludes with its rhyme, "by." Finally, the last two lines erupt with immoderate quantities of the word "I": it occurs seven times in twenty syllables. The word "you" is recalled at the end of the second to last line, "do," but "I" overtakes it both in number and because it constitutes the final word of the sonnet.

The speaker claims that his or her identity is neither equivalent to what he or she has, nor to what he or she does, but rather is equal to a state of being itself. The last words of this sonnet, however, are difficult to understand: "I am, I am even I." In order to grasp the expression, we must read it as a formal and thematic intensification of the speaker's state of being. Phelan reads this sonnet as showing how "solitude has become a limiting and debilitating distance from the possibility of earthly pleasure" (97). While Phelan does not notice Rossetti's elaborate wordplay, which makes such words as "I," "my," and "me" visible in other words, he comments about Sonnet 2 that the "repetition of the personal pronoun in this poem, and especially the forest of 'I's in the last two lines, succeeds in objectifying and even reifying it so that it seems no longer a mere cipher for the self but a mould into which the self must fit" (97); consequently, "it is precisely the 'I' she has created for herself through her poetry that has become her 'prison'" (97). I think the sonnet calls for an even closer reading. I will go on to show that throughout "The Thread of Life" Rossetti ultimately associates her speaker's identity not with prison but with freedom. The last line of Sonnet 2 not only repeats "I am"; it also strikingly contains 1) the word "my" ("I a-[*my*]-am even I") and 2) the word "me" ("I a-[*me*]-ven I"). Looking back at earlier parts of the sonnet, we begin to see this same kind of wordplay throughout the poem. The word "me" appears in "*me*rrymaking" and just afterwards in "mo*me*nt," repeated twice. Even the frustrating self-contradictory line, "And smile a moment and a moment sigh" takes on an altogether new meaning when it is read as a reiteration of the speaker's identity: "And s-[*my*]-le / sm-[*I*]-le a *m*-o-*me*-nt and a *m*-o-*me*-nt s-*I*-gh."[20] The poem therefore progresses by stating and restating the speaker's all-encompassing selfhood.

In the second sonnet we witness a similar pattern to what we saw in the first, when the speaker's identity usurps that of the auditor. But the addressees are not the same from sonnet to sonnet: in the first case the speaker addresses "thou"—a self-chained, nonhuman figure—and in the second case "you"—"everything around," seemingly all a part of nature. I illustrated how the rhyme scheme in the first sonnet not only incorporated "thou" into "I" but also related this joint entity to silence as well as to sound. Yet in the second sonnet the speaker is only able to gaze at, rather than participate in, silence and sound. How might we make sense of this contradiction?

We must turn to Rossetti's third sonnet before we can solve this puzzle:

3.

Therefore myself is that one only thing
I hold to use or waste, to keep or give;
My sole possession every day I live,
And still mine own despite Time's winnowing.
Ever mine own, while moons and seasons bring
From crudeness ripeness mellow and sanative;
Ever mine own, till Death shall ply his sieve;
And still mine own, when saints break grave and sing.
And this myself as king unto my King
I give, to Him Who gave Himself for me;
Who gives Himself to me, and bids me sing
A sweet new song of His redeemed set free:
He bids me sing: O death, where is thy sting?
And sing: O grave, where is thy victory?

(2:3, 123)

This poem begins by reinforcing the dominance of selfhood that the previous two sonnets have established: "Therefore myself is that one only thing." Even more so than the former sonnets, this poem stresses the speaker's possession of self. References to selfhood occur in every line of the sonnet except for the final line. The first line contains "myself"; the second, "I" (and an echo of "me" in "keep"); the third, "my" and "I"; the fourth, "mine"; the fifth, "mine"; the sixth, the word "me" in "*me*llow" (the same number of letters as "myself"); the seventh, "mine"; the eighth, "mine"; the ninth, "myself"; the tenth, "I" and "me"; the eleventh, "me" and "me"; the twelfth, "me" in "redee-*me*-d"; the thirteenth, "me" (echoed in "He").

Over the course of the sonnet we learn that the speaker's self remains all that belongs to him or her—throughout life, no matter what changes time brings, and until death; the speaker even retains his or her identity after death. This continued ownership of identity involves music: "when saints break grave and sing." We now recall the speaker's inability to sing in the previous sonnet; here, all she or he can do, just as before, is hold onto one "sole possession"—the self. The sestet begins not with a discovered capacity to make music but instead with the act of giving oneself to God. This divine figure also gave Himself for the speaker ("Who gave Himself for me") and continues to give Himself ("Who gives Himself to me"). The divine self-sacrifice, however, demands a corresponding sacrifice on the speaker's part: "and bids me sing." But the speaker already does give the self as a substitute for the music that she or he will never be able to put out. It is as though the speaker gives the self to the divinity who gave Himself for the speaker; the repetition, here, "Who gives Himself to me," introduces a new requirement.

My reading of "The Thread of Life" complicates Arseneau's analysis of its culmination. She reads the third sonnet as articulating an anticipation "of a new song beyond earthly mutability" in such a way that "the eternal self is offered to Christ in reciprocal sacrifice and love" (184). In Arseneau's view, "The lament for vanished song that dominated in previous poems in the volume is now inverted" (184). As I see it, on the other hand, while the speaker is asked to sing a "sweet new song of His redeemed set free," this request is not fulfilled. The Lord bids the speaker to sing three times in four lines: "and bids me sing . . . He bids me sing . . . And sing." Yet we are never told that the speaker *does* sing. Rather, we only hear what the speaker is supposed to sing: a "sweet new song of His redeemed set free," "O death, where is thy sting?," "O grave, where is thy victory?"

The way in which the speaker assumes the auditor's role in the first two sonnets sheds light on how we might read the sequence's conclusion. Here, perhaps as a result of the appropriative maneuvers of the first sonnets, there is no auditor at all, only an objectified third party, "Him." The speaker's remarks about "Him" resemble the earlier gestures of identity exchange. The speaker says, "And this myself as king unto my King / I give to Him Who gave Himself for me; / Who gives Himself to me." Rossetti's choice of homophones—"king" and "King"—confuses the line that separates the two. Noticing that in the sestet "me" rhymes once with "free" and once with "victory," we remember the opening rhymes from the first sonnet, where "me" rhymes with "sea," "thee," and "free." Furthermore, we might recognize that Rossetti juxtaposes "me" with "free" in Sonnet 2: "Around *me free* and sunny and at ease" (my italics). Therefore, although her speaker's explicit claim is that she or he is *not* free ("Thus am I mine own prison"), in all three sonnets Rossetti persistently affiliates her speaker's identity with liberation. We return to the same question posed by the first sonnet: how is it possible for the speaker to be at once self-chained and free, at once ostracized from silence and sound and aligned with them, at once asked to sing by another whose identity the speaker seems to incorporate and incapable of singing at all?

It is important to comment here that Rossetti placed much weight on biblical texts, which describe heaven as a place of song. When discussing Revelations 14:2–3 ("I heard the voice of harpers harping with their harps: And they sung as it were a new song before the Throne"), Rossetti writes: "Heaven is revealed to earth as the homeland of music: of music, thus remote from what is gross or carnal; exhibiting like-wise an incalculable range of variety, which rebukes and silences perverse suggestions of monotonous tedium in the final beatitude."[21] Rossetti infers from Rev. 8:1, a work that recounts a half-hour "silence in heaven," that this form of silence came about because one "may have been looking or preparing to look earthwards" (*The Face of the Deep* 241). Quite clearly, she excludes silence from heaven altogether: "Silence seems unnatural, incongruous, in heaven. On this occasion [Rev. 8:1] and remotely we may surmise it to be a result of the Fall, for when earth first saw the light in panoply of beauty the morning stars sang together and all the sons of God shouted for joy; sinless earth, for sinless it then seems to have been whether or not inhabited, called forth instead of silencing an outburst of celestial music" (*The Face of the Deep* 241). As Diane D'Amico puts it, "For Rossetti, as 'Golden Silences' suggests, silence was a characteristic of a fallen earth."[22]

Given that Rossetti equates music and heaven, it makes sense for the divine figure in the third sonnet of "The Thread of Life" to continue demanding that the speaker produce song about "His redeemed" and the afterlife. The "Him" who "bids" the speaker to "sing" presumably casts his request in song. Because of the combination of identities that the poem brings about ("And this myself . . . I give, to Him"; "Who gave Himself for me"; "Who gives Himself to me") we might see the speaker as asking in a divine voice (that is, quite possibly singing) for music. But she or he refuses to bring forth the commanded song. It is in this way that the speaker remains trapped in "prison": all this speaker can do is give the self to the self, at once sing an entreaty for song and repudiate song. The speaker's "stated" silence, like that of the land, is "irresponsive" because it does not on any level reply to the request for music. And like the sounding of the sea, the voice in which the speaker "bids" herself to sing is "irresponsive" because it never stops making the same demand, regardless of the question's unanswerability ("and bids me sing . . . bids me sing . . . And sing"). In the association with the sea/sound and perhaps in a broader sense with poetry itself, the speaker finds freedom and access to the divine—"sea," "me," "thee," "free"; "me," "free," "victory." However, in the simultaneous resistance to music, the speaker remains silenced and imprisoned: "[silent] land," "stand," "band," "hand"; "sing"/"sting." What emerges is the music of this split identity: Rossetti's concurrent admittance to sonority and her soundlessness, her own supplication for music (in song) and her refusal/inability to sing.

DONNE INNOMINATE

My reading of "The Thread of Life" will help me to clarify Rossetti's difficult use of stated and semantic silences in her macrosonnet or "sonnet of sonnets." Rossetti wrote *"Monna Innominata,"* according to the sequence's preface, in order to retrieve from traditional sonnet sequences early heroines or "unnamed ladies"—"donne innominate"—who have "come down to us resplendent with charms, but

[. . .] scant of attractiveness" (2:3, 86). Sung by less conspicuous poets than Dante and Petrarch, these female love objects might nevertheless have shared their lovers' "poetic aptitude"; therefore, had "such a lady spoken for herself," she would have painted a "more tender, if less dignified" portrait than her male admirers (2:3, 86). Rossetti distinguishes her own work from that of her most celebrated female poetic rival: "Or had the Great Poetess of our own day and nation [Elizabeth Barrett] only been unhappy instead of happy, her circumstances would have invited her to bequeath to us, in lieu of the 'Portuguese Sonnets,' an inimitable 'donna innominata' drawn not from fancy but from feeling, and worthy to occupy a niche beside Beatrice and Laura" (2:3, 86). Rossetti's words about her successful precursor reflect some competitiveness, for she implies that Barrett's happiness may have prevented her from 1) writing with feeling rather than fact and 2) creating a speaker of the same stature as Beatrice or Laura. In response to this criticism, Rossetti later insisted that she had not meant Barrett failed to equal the poetic grandeur of Dante and Petrarch but simply that she had not spoken with the unhappy voice of a "donna innominata." With this ambivalent preface the sequence begins, inspiring many feminist critiques about whether or not Rossetti manages to reclaim the voice of a nameless forgotten woman. Writing in an overtly anti-Petrarchan style, Rossetti may, in Margaret Homans's view, write "love lyrics from the position of the silent object in the complete awareness that she is attempting to reverse centuries of tradition when she does so, but in the end tradition writes her perhaps as much as she rewrites tradition."[23] In Mary Finn's words, "Rossetti cannot force language to restore the voice of silenced women."[24] The sequence contains so many ambiguities that it becomes difficult to follow its narrative line.

In his book *Christina Rossetti in Context,* Antony Harrison provides a useful summary of *"Monna Innominata."*[25] He observes that in the first four sonnets—the "quatrain" of this "sonnet of sonnets"—we hear the speaker express a need for her beloved's presence; next, she wishes to remember their first meeting; thirdly, she envisions perfect union between herself and her beloved only in her dreams; fourthly, the lovers come suddenly together, apparently with unity between them. The second "quatrain" shifts to the subject of religion. The speaker "renounces the service proffered by her lover in favor of his granting it to God" (Harrison 153). Subsequently, the speaker softens her recent renunciations. She explains that she cannot love her own beloved if she does not love God, and she cannot love God if she does not love him. She imagines a complete union with her lover as "happy equals" in the afterlife. The eighth sonnet strengthens the speaker's hope for such a union by drawing a parallel with the book of Esther. With her turn to the sestet, the speaker completely deprives herself of any physical realization of her love. The twelfth sonnet restates the speaker's opinion that she is spiritually united with her beloved, regardless of whether or not he finds another lover. And finally, the last sonnet gives even greater force to the speaker's resignation, loss, and her inability to sing.

With Harrison's helpful summary in mind, I think it is essential to assess the relation between "Rossetti"'s own voice and that of the sequence's forgotten historical woman.[26] In the preface to *"Monna Innominata,"* Rossetti never states that she will write her sequence from the point of view of a nameless woman from the past. Instead, she asserts that Beatrice and Laura lack attractiveness, that unnamed ladies did not speak for themselves and that Elizabeth Barrett was happy and thus did not give us a "donna innominata." Rossetti merely implies that an unhappy Barrett might have *played* the role of a "donna innominata," instead of the happy persona she wrote into her sonnets.

As we have already seen in the case of Charlotte Smith, overly personalized or biographical readings of sonnets may still impede our critical understanding of women's work. However, nineteenth-century critics did align writers' lives with the subject of their poems. It was for this reason that Robert Browning described Barrett's decision to call her sonnets "Portuguese" as a "mask" designed to cover their autobiographical nature. William Michael Rossetti similarly discounted Rossetti's preface to *"Monna Innominata"* as a ruse to discourage readers from probing into his sister's private life:

> To any one to whom it was granted to be behind the scenes of Christina Rossetti's life—and to how few was this granted—it is not merely probable but certain that this "sonnet of sonnets" was a personal utterance—an intensely personal one. The introductory prose-note, about "many a lady sharing her lover's poetic aptitude," etc., is a blind—not an untruthful blind, for it alleges nothing that is not

> reasonable, and on the surface correct, but still a blind interposed to draw off attention from the writer in her proper person.[27]

William Rossetti's remarks only encouraged later critics to advance biographically oriented speculations about what might have driven Rossetti to write *"Monna Innominata."*[28] Some conjectured that it was Rossetti's relationship with the scholar Charles Bagot Cayley, who proposed to her in 1866 and whom she rejected. Others think she might have been motivated by her earlier courtship with the Pre-Raphaelite Brotherhood member, James Collinson, who also proposed to her but whom she rejected for religious reasons. Lona Mosk Packer even hypothesizes that Rossetti was in love with the married painter William Bell Scott—a theory that has since been discredited (Whitla 84).

Of course, we do not want to limit our reading of Rossetti's poetry to a reconstruction of her biography or to a repetition of nineteenth-century interpretations of her work. But as I have shown through "The Thread of Life," pronouns have a way of coalescing in Rossetti's sonnets, which alerts us to the possibility that the "I" and "you" figures in *"Monna Innominata"* might not always remain the same. In fact, at crucial moments, Rossetti's same-tense poetic counterpart seems to address nameless forgotten women from history rather than her own perhaps nonexistent beloved.

We might certainly read the first line of the sequence this way, as though Rossetti's poetic persona speaks to "donne innominate": "Come back to me, who wait and watch for you:—" (2:3, 86). And the third sonnet also works well when read from this angle. It is as if Rossetti writes poetry to a "donna innominata," and although she grieves that this writing cannot bring the woman back to life, she also wishes that she could continue writing this way indefinitely. The sequence's premise is that the poems are themselves fictional; Rossetti says, "*had* such a lady spoken for herself," reminding us that she never did (2:3, 86; my italics).[29] Later, she writes, "only in a dream we are at one." Given this explicit fictionality, Rossetti implies that she and the "donna innominata" merge and separate throughout the sonnets (2:3, 87). It is almost as if we must read "I" as changing between present- and past-tense writer and "you" as shifting from man to woman and back again.[30] The sequence's goal, which seems akin to that of "The Thread of Life," would be to bring all of these figures into one single entity, simultaneously self-chained, silent, and capable of producing song.

Like many other sonnets in *"Monna Innominata,"* Sonnet 4 complicates the fusion between speaker and addressee:

4.

I loved you first: but afterwards your love
Outsoaring mine, sang such a loftier song
As drowned the friendly cooings of my dove.
Which owes the other most? my love was long,
And yours one moment seemed to wax more strong;
I loved and guessed at you, you construed me
And loved me for what might or might not be—
Nay, weights and measures do us both a wrong.
For verily love knows not "mine" or "thine;"
With separate "I" and "thou" free love has done,
For one is both and both are one in love:
Rich love knows nought of "thine that is not mine;"
Both have the strength and both the length thereof,
Both of us, of the love which makes us one.

(2:3, 88)

This sonnet can be read as if written from *any* of the multiple characters' points of view. If understood as spoken in Rossetti's own voice, the poem works on two levels. Most obviously (through a kind of "stated" silence), she is speaking to a male beloved whose "loftier song" drowned out "the friendly cooings of [her] dove." This position is hard to understand in a sequence that aims to construct a speaker "worthy to occupy a niche beside Beatrice and Laura." Rossetti cannot be suggesting that "friendly cooings" would earn her speaker such a niche. Not only in his poetry but also in his love this beloved "construed [her] / And loved [her] for what might or might not be—." With the turn to the sestet, Rossetti tells us that, in love, we should not attempt to weigh and measure or to separate between "mine" and "thine," "I" and "thou." In other words, the speaker believes her identity cannot be distinguished from that of her beloved. Here she seems to undo the self-deprecation of the octave, for at this point she proposes that no distinction exists between her beloved's "loftier song" and her own "friendly cooings," thereby removing her previous "stated" silence.

On the other hand, if speaking to the "donna innominata" of history rather than to a lover, Rossetti's poetic persona offers us a radically different construct. This mysterious woman from history could have responded to Rossetti's overtures by singing "such a loftier song" than the "friendly cooings of [Rossetti's own] dove." The love between speaker and addressee derives from conjecture since the women exist in two different centuries: "I loved and guessed at you, you construed me / And loved me for what might or might not be—." Rather than weighing and measuring each other, however, the two women need no longer differentiate between their identities but might share a single role. Their reciprocal love makes them "one," which suggests that the sequence should be read both in terms of identity separation, as the octave implies, and also in terms of character amalgamation, according to the law advanced by the sestet.

If the poem is supposedly pronounced by the "donna innominata," it follows that she would describe Rossetti as producing "loftier song" in comparison to her own "friendly cooings," which have since been drowned out. Her request that she and Rossetti be united works to ameliorate and revive her own lost words. And if written from the perspective of this nameless woman from history to a male beloved, the lines sound like what Rossetti herself would say, recognizing the female poet's inadequacy but appealing for unification with the force that produces "loftier song."

Other possible readings suggest that Rossetti is speaking not only to a beloved but also to a poet.[31] As the preface alerts us, she might in this and in many other sonnets in *"Monna Innominata"* contemplate Elizabeth Barrett's "loftier song." Alternatively, she might be speaking in Barrett's voice—the "unhappy" Barrett—whose "friendly cooings" were "drowned out" by a male poet-lover's (possibly even Christina Rossetti's own) song. Or she might be addressing her own brother, who, being a poet himself, threatened to suffocate her words not only in his role as her editor but through his accomplished poetry as well.

Finally, the sonnet can be read from the point of view of a male poet/beloved (perhaps even Dante Gabriel himself). In this case, speaking to either Rossetti or to the "donna innominata," he laments that she sang "such a loftier song" than his own "friendly cooings." While he loved her consistently (and this point does seem justified by the entire sequence), she loved him at times more and at times less. In the end, both people need to realize that they speak as one single individual. Chapman asserts that "[t]he sonnet emerges as a key space in which to engage Dante Gabriel Rossetti's aesthetics: the space, as *'Monna Innominata'* makes clear, for the unnamed lady, the beloved of the Petrarchan tradition (epitomised by Laura to whom Christina claims a direct genealogical link). It is a space which renders her the absent and mute beloved, and a space within which the silenced projects her voice" (*The Afterlife of Christina Rossetti* 100). Yet Chapman does not consider the possibility that Dante Gabriel Rossetti may also exchange roles with "the unnamed lady." Reading the sonnet as spoken by a number of different speakers, as I propose to do, causes us to recognize that throughout the sequence Rossetti, the "donna innominata," and even the male beloved play interchangeable roles. Furthermore, *any* of these characters' poetry can perform simultaneously as "song" and as "cooings" (which have since been drowned out).

Because the speaker's persona is so variable, the sequence provides us with entirely different conclusions about the status of writing. Any of the potential speakers might be muted, and any might be able to achieve song. The double status of writing as drowned out "friendly cooings" ("stated" silence) and "loftier song" might be reconciled if we examine the references to selfhood that pervade Rossetti's sequence. This extreme focus on the self might also clarify seemingly inexplicable aspects of the sonnets. For example, the second sonnet is especially hard to interpret; it disrupts the Petrarchan tradition (a convention also followed by Elizabeth Barrett) of writing in response to cherished memories of the past. Whereas the Petrarchan quotation that precedes the sonnet reads "Ricorro al tempo ch'io vi vidi prima" ("I recur to the time when I first saw thee"), Rossetti inverts his claim in her first line: "I wish I could remember; that first day" (2:3, 87).[32] The entire second sonnet concerns the impossibility of remembering any details of the lovers' first acquaintance. Hassett relates this sonnet to Rossetti's emphasis on amnesia as opposed to remembrance: "Instead of providing a passage about the fabled first sight of the beloved, Rossetti arranges for a sort of amnesia to afflict her speaker and creates from the absence of memory a new experience of erotic yearning. Her speaker longs to recall the forgotten glance that must have preceded the forgotten first touch" (170). We learn that the speaker cannot remember the "first day" or the "first hour" or the "first moment" of the meeting, whether the season was "bright or dim," "Summer or Winter." Beginning, "I wish I could remember" the speaker restates this regret even at the start of the sestet, which introduces no variation into the sonnet's structure—"If only I could recollect it"—and in the poem's second to last line—"If only now I could recall." All this sonnet finally tells us is that the first meeting slipped away "unrecorded" and "traceless" and that the speaker was too "blind" and too "dull" not to hold it in her mind.

Through "semantic" silence, Rossetti underscores a familiar contradiction in line 12: "It seemed to mean so little, meant so much." Why in fact *did* the first meeting mean "so much"? In other words, if in her sequence Rossetti aims to rewrite the amatory poetic tradition, why here does she merely repeat the importance of a Petrarchan convention that she fails (because she is "so blind" and "so dull") to uphold successfully? Hassett juxtaposes this sonnet with Sonnet 20 from *Sonnets from the Portuguese.* There, Barrett remembers her life prior to meeting her beloved—a time when she had no idea that he existed—and concludes "Atheists are as dull, / Who cannot guess God's presence out of sight." Hassett astutely points out that Rossetti uses the word "dull" as a reminder of Barrett's sonnet. In this way, Rossetti emphasizes the difference between her poetic project and Barrett's happier one. Reading the line, "It seemed to mean so little, meant so much" as an example of "mild diction and extraordinarily deft compression," Hassett concludes: "The understated style of *Monna Innominata* tells us, with a regret that is all the lovelier for its patient candor, that love's arrival was not epiphanic, that the precious moment lost in the fog of the commonplace was not after all, a moment, and that true love doesn't need (or need to invent) such a valorizing episode. The scrupulous restraint and honesty of Rossetti's style allows us to believe in the profundity of her speaker's love. The wondering inflation of Barrett Browning's strives to prove the strength of hers" (174). While Hassett's reading may be true on a literal level, a closer reading of Rossetti's perplexing line "It seemed to mean so little, meant so much" permits a more textured understanding. In this context, my interpretation of "The Thread of Life" is useful because it suggests that we look very closely at the way Rossetti structures her self-contradictory lines. Just as in the line I broke down previously, "And s-*m*-*I*-le / s-*my*-le a *m*-o-*me*-nt and a *m*-o-*me*-nt sigh [which rhymes with 'I']," this line might read "It see-*me*-d to *me*-an so little, *me*-ant so *m*-uch." Not only does the word "me" occur three times in the space of ten syllables, it is echoed by both the words "seemed" and "mean," and the letter "m" appears four times. Furthermore, as in "The Thread of Life," the first two lines of the second sonnet begin with multiple references to the speaker's identity. The first line, for example, starts "*I* wish *I*" and is followed by "re-*me*-*m*-ber" (in which "re" echoes "me"); the second line ends "mo-*me*-nt of your *me*-eting *me*" (in which "meeting" echoes the "me" that follows it). Therefore, the speaker's apparent emphasis on her blindness disguises the assertiveness of her claim: a persistent reminder of her presence.

Like Sonnet 2, Sonnet 5 disturbs contemporary critics because its self-deprecating sestet seems to reach a patriarchal conclusion:

5.

O my heart's heart, and you who are to me
More than myself myself, God be with you,
Keep you in strong obedience leal and true
To Him whose noble service setteth free,
Give you all good we see or can foresee,
Make your joys many and your sorrows few,
Bless you in what you bear and what you do,
Yea, perfect you as He would have you be.
So much for you; but what for me, dear friend?
To love you without stint and all I can
Today, tomorrow, world without an end;
To love you much and yet to love you more,
As Jordan at his flood sweeps either shore;
Since woman is the helpmeet made for man.
(2:3, 88–89)

Repetition reads strangely in the first two lines: "heart's heart" seems as if it could be altered simply to "love." And would anything be lost if "myself myself" were reduced to "myself"? (88). Sonnet 4 gives us a new way of reading these seemingly gratuitous anaphors. For example, the division between "heart's heart" and "you" by means of a conjunction suggests that the poem involves two separate sets of individuals. As "heart's heart" parallels "myself myself," we are again led to construct a double persona: Victorian woman speaker/ past-tense woman poet. "O my heart's heart" might be read as spoken by *either* the Victorian woman or her nameless counterpart. Because of the word duplication here, the phrase could even be interpreted as "O my heart's clone." The conjunction "and," then, introduces another entity: presumably the masculine love object of either present or past-tense poets. We might read the phrase "and you who are to me / More than myself myself" to mean that the male beloved is more to the speaker than herself paired (i.e., more than past and present selves together). The prayer, then, that God give "you all good *we* see or can foresee" might also be read according to this principle of the speaker's dual identity (88; my italics). Moreover, we hear echoes of the word "me" three times in this line: "we," "see," "foresee" (88). It is important that the sonnet's initial end-rhyme is the word "me" because it alerts us to the recurrence of this sound in line 5 ("we"; "see"; "foresee"). The sestet, which begins "So much for you, but what for me, dear friend?" answers this unsettling question by becoming almost a satire of one of Barrett's *Sonnets from the Portuguese:* "To love you without stint and all I can / Today, tomorrow, world without an end / To love you much and yet to love you more / . . . Since woman is the helpmeet made for man" (88–89). It seems nothing can be done with these lines except to read them as painful self-caricatures.

The beginning of the sixth sonnet might help us put into perspective the last poem's sestet. Sonnet 6 begins with an apology, though it is not at first clear from the sequence what the speaker is apologizing for: "Trust me, I have not earned your dear rebuke" (2:3, 89). Although the "Trust me" with which the sonnet opens suggests that there has been an exchange between speaker and addressee, the nature of this dispute remains unexplained. There has been no occasion for a "rebuke." The last two sonnets, after all, have 1) proclaimed the oneness of poet and beloved and 2) prayed for the beloved to receive "all good we see or can foresee" while at the same time acknowledging the speaker's duty to remain a "helpmeet made for man." Given our own troubled reaction to the ending of Sonnet 5, the timing might be appropriate for a reprimand to be made. In fact, the line "Since woman is the helpmeet made for man" may have provoked friendly condemnation. The speaker thus can go on to justify her love for God—greater than her love for her beloved—at the same time that she claims she cannot love God at all without also loving a mortal man.

This sonnet, like the third sonnet in "The Thread of Life," contains an excessive number of references to the speaker's identity. In the first line, we see "me" and "I"; in the second, "I" and "me"; in the fifth, "I"; in the sixth, "I"; in the seventh, "I." With the turn to the sestet, the speaker's selfhood entirely takes over the poem. Line 9 has "I," "my," and "I" again (furthermore, it holds the word "while," which echoes "I" as well as "my," "*m*ost" and "deem," which recalls, and even contains, inverted, the word "me.") The tenth line has "I"; the eleventh, "I" and "me"; the twelfth, "I"; the thirteenth, "I" two times, and the fourteenth line also has "I" two times. The stress placed on the speaker's identity here—an emphasis that, while increasing, ends in a paradox ("I cannot love you if I love not Him, / I cannot love Him if I love not you"), reads as a corrective to the seemingly powerless resignation of Sonnet 5's conclusion. It is as if, by rebuking the speaker for her perhaps false submission, the beloved inspires her true desire: to possess an identity that resounds everywhere, taking over more and more space, her wish to love both God and man to the fullest.

The speaker's desire to possess an omnipresent identity helps to account for Sonnet 12, which goes so far as to approve the beloved's choice of another woman. This sonnet recalls earlier poems in the sequence because it reiterates the speaker's selfhood. In fact, every line of the poem except for the octave's final line contains "I," "my," "me," or "mine." I have italicized these references to make them more apparent:

12.

If there be any one can take *my* place
And make you happy whom *I* grieve to grieve,
Think not that *I* can grudge it, but believe
I do commend you to that nobler grace,
That readier wit than *mine,* that sweeter face;
Yea, since your riches make *me* rich, conceive
I too am crowned, while bridal crowns *I* weave,
And thread the bridal dance with jocund pace.
For if *I* did not love you, it might be
That *I* should grudge you some one dear delight;
But since the heart is yours that was *mine* own,
Your pleasure is *my* pleasure, right *my* right,
Your honorable freedom makes *me* free,
And you companioned *I* am not alone.

(2:3, 92)

If we pursue these references further, we observe sound repetitions of "I" and "me" in other words that echo throughout the poem: "be," "sweeter," "conceive," "bridal," "weave," "bridal," "be," "freedom," and "free." The word "bridal" occurs not only between "I" and "I" in line 7, but it recurs in line 8, meaning that Rossetti stresses the speaker's identity in *every* line of the sonnet. Furthermore, her rhymes "be" and "free" reappear throughout the sequence as end-rhymes with "me" (this structure occurs four times in just fourteen sonnets, and in one additional case "me" rhymes with "liberty," a variation of "free"). Rossetti's audible emphasis on her speaker's identity throughout the sequence parallels this sonnet's theme; she states, "But since the heart is yours that was mine own," ending, "And you companioned I am not alone." It is not so unusual for the speaker to equate her heart with that of her beloved, but it seems curious that she would thereby feel benefited by his involvement with another woman.

The enthusiastic ending of Sonnet 12 falls apart with the start of Sonnet 13: "If I could trust mine own self with your fate / Shall I not rather trust it in God's hand?" (2:3, 92–93). The opening lines conflict with Sonnet 8: "If I might take my life so in my hand." The rest of Sonnet 13 further confuses the speaker's beginning wish. The image of sparrows falling at their "appointed date" is disconcerting, and the idea of numbering the "innumerable sand" in addition to weighing "the wind and water with a weight" contradicts the speaker's earlier emphasis on weightlessness: in Sonnet 4, she says, "Nay, weights and measures do us both a wrong . . . For one is both and both are one in love." Furthermore, the end of the octave, "Whose knowledge *foreknew* every plan we planned" opposes certain elements in the sequence's rhyme scheme (my italics). The speaker uses "me" and "foresee" as end-rhymes in Sonnet 2 as well as in Sonnet 5. In Sonnet 7, she rhymes "me" with "sea," which in "The Thread of Life" had connected to sound; here, we might also read "sea" as the homophone of "see"—a rhyme that will recur in Sonnet 9: "see"/"me." Therefore the speaker undermines the Lord in whose power she trusts her beloved's fate. With the turn to the sestet, she searches her heart for "all that touches" her beloved. What she finds, there, however, is "love's goodwill" that is both "impotent" and "helpless to help." This love's understanding is "dull" and its sight "most dim," which explains the need for her beloved to go somewhere else with his own "love's capacity." As a whole, then, the thirteenth sonnet 1) undercuts the Lord's abilities and 2) describes the speaker's love for her beloved as "helpless," "impotent," "dull," and "dim."

These self-deprecating remarks, which, in fact, do not reflect badly on the speaker but only on her love for the other person, finally destroy the sequence's attempts to communicate the speaker's hopeless love for a man. It is here that Sonnet 14 begins:

14.

Youth gone, and beauty gone if ever there
Dwelt beauty in so poor a face as this;
Youth gone and beauty, what remains of bliss?
I will not bind fresh roses in my hair,
To shame a cheek at best but little fair,—
Leave youth his roses, who can bear a thorn,—
I will not seek for blossoms anywhere,
Except such common flowers as blow with corn.
Youth gone and beauty gone, what doth remain?
The longing of a heart pent up forlorn,
A silent heart whose silence loves and longs;
The silence of a heart which sang its songs
While youth and beauty made a summer morn,
Silence of love that cannot sing again.

(2:3, 93)

Lacking youth, beauty, and bliss, the speaker refuses to follow Barrett's example of holding out her poems to her beloved like flowers. I agree with Marjorie Stone that Rossetti plays against Sonnet 44 in *Sonnets from the Portuguese* here: "Rossetti, for her part, forcibly repudiates such flowers in her concluding sonnet: 'I will not seek for blossoms anywhere.'"[33] She wishes, instead, to leave these flowers to youth. The tercet poses the question of what remains and answers, finally, with the "stated" silence "of love that cannot sing again." In this last sonnet of her sequence, Rossetti seems to silence her speaker completely: now that youth and beauty have vanished, no music remains.

Repetitions dominate the fourteenth sonnet more than any other. The first phrase, "Youth gone, and beauty gone," recurs two lines later as "Youth gone and beauty," at the start of the sestet, "Youth gone and beauty gone" and in the second to last line as "While youth and beauty." Her question, "what remains of bliss," reappears as "what doth remain?" In its last five lines, the sestet includes both "longing" and "longs"; "heart" appears three times; "silent"/"silence" occurs four times. These recurring phrases and terms lend a musical quality to the final sonnet. Although Rossetti speaks of silence, of an inability to sing, she seems to communicate this powerlessness in song itself.

In her double emphasis on silence and song, Rossetti draws an important allusion to Dante's work. Because Dante married in spite of his spiritual attachment to Beatrice, Piccarda—also forced to marry—lifts his idea of love by singing the *Ave Maria,* and, as she sings, she disappears into song. This image of Piccarda melting into music might correspond to the situation of Rossetti's persona, who fades away at the end of her sequence, leaving only her song "to echo in the ear" (Whitla 108–9). Surely this kind of departure works well if read in relation to a "donna innominata," who left nothing behind except for the music of her silence. However, the lines work equally well as Rossetti's own utterances—she who contrasted her poetic project with Elizabeth Barrett's in her preface seems consciously to reject Barrett's equation of poems with flowers in *Sonnets from the Portuguese.*

The sequence's "I" references culminate in this final sonnet—regardless of who the speaker is—even after she or he claims no longer to be able to sing. The sonnet provides the following answer to the question "what doth remain?":

> A s-*I*-lent heart whose s-*I*-lence loves and longs;
> The s-*I*-lence of a heart which sang its songs
> Wh-*I*-le youth and beauty *m*ade a su*m*-*me*-r morn,
> S-*I*-lence of love that cannot sing again.

In other words, read literally, what remains in the end is only silence—the speaker's inability to recover her songs from youth and the suffocation of a longing heart. However, I think it is imperative that we open our ears and eyes to Rossetti's fourfold repetition of "s-*I*-lent"/"s-*I*-lence," together with other echoes of "I" and "me" in her final quatrain. No other reader of Rossetti's poetry has noticed this surprising reiteration of selfhood. In his reading of Sonnet 14, Phelan concludes: "As so often in Christina Rossetti's work, there is a kind of Pyrrhic victory in this complete self-abnegation, a sublimity in a self-denial so absolute that it ends up effacing the speaker's very existence" (123). In fact, Rossetti answers her question "what doth remain?" very differently than with the silence of self denial. What remains may only be the speaker itself. This speaker doubles as silence, or as an inability to sing.

"The Thread of Life" altogether reinforces my reading of Sonnet 14. There, the speaker claimed to be unable to sing, reasoning that this incapacity in no way changes her or his identity: "*I* am not what *I* have nor what *I* do; / But what *I* was *I* am, *I* a-me-ven *I*." It is this self, and not song, that the speaker chooses to give us; however, the Lord asks her to sing a "sweet new song of His redeemed set free." As we have seen, because of the speaker's unification with and even usurpation of her auditor—whether Christ, nature or the Lord—Rossetti encourages us to read the request for song as pronounced in the speaker's own musical voice. Separating from itself, the speaker both sings a request for song and then refuses to fulfill this request.

The same dynamic occurs in *"Monna Innominata"*; if the speaker is female, she on one level persistently dominates her male auditor. And Rossetti merges with her "donna innominata" to such a point that it becomes impossible for the reader to distinguish between them. Her final question, "what doth remain?", yields the speaker's own self as an answer, a self doomed to eternal silence; however, we realize from earlier sonnets (just as in Sonnet 2 of "The Thread of Life") that she has not been able to sing since the beginning of the sequence, for the very first sonnet concludes with a question, "Ah me, but where are now the songs I sang / When life was sweet because you called them sweet?" And we are told in Sonnet 4 that "the friendly cooings" of the speaker's dove have been drowned out. Just as the speaker in "The Thread of Life" must sing both of death's impotence and of its redemptive power, the speaker in *"Monna Innominata"* must explain where her songs have gone. Her response corresponds to the speaker's in "The Thread of Life"; what remains is simply silence—the unspeaking presence of the speaker herself. Yet clearly it is the speaker who asks herself what remains. In fact, it is the speaker herself who "sings" this question—the musical climax of the entire sequence. Her question, which ends, "doth remain?" correlates syllabically with the sonnet's final words, "sing again." And this sonnet does "sing again" term after term, phrase after phrase, sound after sound.

In spite of this woman-oriented reading, we have seen that the speaker's gender does not remain constant in the sequence. Male as well as female characters ask themselves "what doth remain?" and all of them conclude that "silence" is the only possible outcome. This silence not only refers to the absence of women poets from distant history; it suppresses the words of every possible speaker. By ironically defining these speakers' identities, the word "silence" creates a resounding chorus of unidentifiable voices.

The sequence as a whole possesses the very musical qualities that Curran and others have noticed in Rossetti's work: "the ease of the poet's rhymes," the "not inconsiderable gift of felicitous music" (Curran, "The Lyric Voice of Christina Rossetti" 297–99). In her "true lyric voice," Rossetti asks herself (and all of her imagined speakers) the following questions from sonnet to sonnet (299): "Ah me, but where are now the songs I sang?"; "So much for you; but what for me, dear friend?"; "And who hath found love's citadel unmanned?"; "And who hath held in bonds love's liberty?"; "Shall I not rather trust it in God's hand?"; "what remains of bliss?"; "what doth remain?" But our sense of her "quiet voice," our feeling that Rossetti "has so little to say," emerges when we take seriously her claim that silence is all she has left (297–98). Without noticing Rossetti's persistent references to selfhood in *"Monna Innominata,"* critics fall for her sad retreat into silence at the end of the sequence. Whitla concludes, "The poem ends with an expression of a much darker heart where art fades into silence. At that point nothing more can be said" (113). Betty Flowers hypothesizes, "Perhaps it is only love that cannot sing again, and the Lady will sing of other themes. More likely, though, to judge from the valedictory quality of these last lines, the Lady whose heart is pent up will not sing again at all."[34] Arseneau sees the poet's song as having been silenced by more than mutability or the passage of time; instead, the concluding silence of the sequence results from the "nexus of literary, gender, and spiritual relations that Rossetti invokes" (184). And while Hassett points out that Rossetti will go on to write other poems, she nevertheless concludes about the sonnet of sonnets: "Though the interval in *Monna Innominata* is uncertain, time and loss leave their mark on Rossetti's speaker [. . .] A discerningly intelligent woman with a distinctive voice and considerable 'poetic aptitude' has reached an impasse as a lover" (186–87). Yet, it is important that we reread the speaker's answer to the question "What doth remain," as I have shown that Rossetti equates selfhood with "stated" as well as with "semantic" silences. This selfhood encompasses every identity: Rossetti speaking to her own beloved or to the "donna innominata"; the "donna innominata" speaking to her beloved or to Rossetti; at times it can even be the male beloved speaking to Rossetti or to the "donna innominata." Just as in "The Thread of Life," the speaker's all-encompassing identity even comes to rival the authority of God. It is for this reason, perhaps, that Rossetti calls her sequence *"Monna Innominata."* For "Monna" reads as "*my* lady" instead of simply as "lady." Inverted, it contains the word "no," and this word reappears in "In-*no*-minata" as well. And the final word contains another reference to the self: in fact, we could read the entire title as *"My* d-*on*-na In-*no*-*me*-nata." The sequence's title therefore both conflates Rossetti's personality with that of the nameless lady from history and annuls this identification. We are left with "me" and "no-me"—the same sort of split personification that we saw in "The Thread of Life."

In the most highly structured possible lyrical form—a "sonnet of sonnets"—Rossetti requests that dead, unremembered women sing. She renders her request unanswerable; but at the same time she answers it by blessing these women with the very music that they will always be denied. Nameless women do reappear, as silence, but they also separate into time-traveling selves that will forever sing a lament for their own impossible song. This divided identity appropriates every kind of subjectivity, undercutting everyone's ability to speak at the same time that it forces each individual to sing and sing the desire for his or her own unattainable music.

Christina Rossetti criticism remains disparate—scholars simultaneously assert that she is quiet and musical, that she revives lost women's voices and that she fails to do so—because these contradictions all apply: Rossetti gives sound to music and to silence, to women's voices and to their absence. In so doing, she uses the sonnet or the "little song" to prove that she (and all of her unknown female precursors) cannot, at the same time that they assuredly will, "sing again" and again.

CHAPTER FOUR

"Silence, 'Tis More Cruel than the Grave!"

Isabella Southern and the Turn to the Twentieth Century

By charting a pathway from Charlotte Smith's late-eighteenth-century efforts to Elizabeth Barrett's and Christina Rossetti's contributions in the nineteenth century, I have highlighted female sonneteers' progressive acceptance of silence both as a thematic emphasis and as a structural refusal to reveal information. This gravitation to silence reflects women poets' struggle to call attention to the impossibility of speech (both by women historically and also specifically within the long nineteenth century), but it also serves as a means of expression itself. In chapter 1, I stressed the pull to excessive articulation in Charlotte Smith's sonnets (written from many points of view and across different genres) at the same time that I underscored Smith's tendency to align her poetic persona with characters whose power to speak has been taken from them. In chapter 2, I investigated Elizabeth Barrett's decision to enlist a non-recuperative version of negativity as a critique of William Wordsworth, and I demonstrated how, through this critique, Barrett accentuates the "silence of [her] womanhood"—a kind of speechlessness that she equates both with her feminized grief and with the productive limits of poetry in general. In chapter 3, I illustrated how for Christina Rossetti silence operates on both "stated" and "semantic" levels—that is, in her sonnets silences either declare themselves explicitly or else they disrupt communication through contradictions and ambiguity within her style.

In addition to using silence both thematically and structurally, nineteenth-century female poets also suppressed other women's poetic work. Elizabeth Barrett probably never read Charlotte Smith, and in her preface to *"Monna Innominata"* Christina Rossetti overtly dismisses Elizabeth Barrett, declining to imitate her "happy" tone. At the end of the first chapter I examined other Romantic women sonneteers—Charlotte Smith's contemporaries and early successors. While these female sonneteers all proposed revisions to Smith's approach to silence, they remained bound to their own forms of wordlessness. Helen Maria Williams closely paralleled Charlotte Smith, though the sorrow in Williams's work appears considerably milder than Smith's "blank despair." And Anna Maria Smallpiece used vagueness and omission to seem to tell a different (and more socially acceptable) story than the tale of betrayed homosexual love.

In this chapter, I would like to explore how the contemporaries and the first successors to Elizabeth Barrett and Christina Rossetti reformulated the claims made by their most famous female counterparts. I will begin by discussing work by Maria Norris, Dora Greenwell, and Michael Field, all of whom in their sonnets refer to Barrett and Rossetti by name. At first glance, Norris, Greenwell, and Field appear to write sonnets that do nothing but praise their poetic heroines. Upon closer scrutiny, however, these poems reveal conflicting aims. After a brief discussion of Norris, Greenwell, and Field, I will devote my attention to an analysis of Isabella J. Southern. Southern's book, *Sonnets and Other Poems,* which appeared in 1891, dramatically rewrites Barrett's and Rossetti's work.[1] Although she mentions neither of them by name, Southern persistently echoes and reworks their poems. In particular, Isabella Southern uses her sonnets to illustrate a passage from past to future tense, suggesting that as time progresses, silence proves itself to be the opposite of golden.

MARIA NORRIS AND DORA GREENWELL: IN "PRAISE" OF ELIZABETH BARRETT

Maria Norris's sonnet "On Mrs. Browning" was published in *The Ladies' Companion* on August 1, 1851. At the time, Barrett was still alive; she had already married Robert Browning, and she had published the *Sonnets from the Portuguese* in 1850. The sonnet reads as follows:[2]

ON MRS. BROWNING

There is a fancied shape that haunts my dreams
Large-eyed and pensive, wearing on the brow
A starry circlet, whose clear radiance seems
Serenely from the light within to flow.
Serious yet sweet the expression of the face
Answering the modulations of the lyre,
Which 'neath her hands gives out with mournful grace
Songs brimming o'er with tenderness and fire.
These lyrics oft have moved my inmost heart;
Like minor music fall they on the ear,
With dying cadence lingering while they part,
As loath to leave me to the silence drear.
Still be that Unknown Friend about my way,
Her Songs my dreams by night, my spirit-food by day.

Initially, "On Mrs. Browning" reads as an expression of unmitigated admiration for Barrett's poetry. Norris tells us that Barrett wears a "starry circlet" on her brow, and her poems double as "minor music"—songs "brimming o'er with tenderness and fire." Barrett's "lyrics" have moved the speaker's "inmost heart." And Norris's sonnet ends with the desire for Barrett to continue to serve as an "Unknown Friend," whose "Songs" will constitute (as they did when this sonnet was written) the speaker's "dreams by night" and "spirit-food by day."

Even though "On Mrs. Browning" undeniably praises Elizabeth Barrett, together with her poetry, Norris's sonnet takes on new meaning when it is juxtaposed with Barrett's own writing. First, "On Mrs. Browning" is a Shakespearean sonnet (abab / cdcd / efef / gg). Barrett's sonnets, on the other hand, follow Wordsworth, Milton, and Petrarch in their use of Italian form. Second, Norris's sonnet begins, "There is a *fancied shape* that haunts my dreams" (my italics). In other words, Barrett exists as a figment of Norris's imagination. Third, in Norris's last quatrain, she explains that Barrett's lyrics (like "minor music") seem "loath to leave [her] to the silence drear." However true this line may be, it resonates oddly with many of Barrett's sonnets, which gravitate thematically toward silence—a point that I underscored in chapter 2. Referring to "Mrs. Browning" as an "Unknown Friend," the sonnet implies, too, that Barrett plays the role of a muse, whose Songs may actually be composed by Norris, as they function first as her "dreams by night" and only second as her "spirit-food by day." These observations do not mean that Norris's sonnet is critical rather than laudatory. But it is important to keep our ears open to the sonnet's strange notes, for similar tensions more forcefully trouble the other eulogies that I will go on to examine.

Like Maria Norris, Dora Greenwell dedicated a sonnet of apparent praise to Elizabeth Barrett in 1851. This sonnet, "To Elizabeth Barrett Browning, in 1851," forms part of a pendant with Greenwell's "To Elizabeth Barrett Browning, in 1861."[3] The first sonnet reads as follows:

TO ELIZABETH BARRETT BROWNING, IN 1851

I lose myself within thy mind—from room
To goodly room thou leadest me, and still
Dost show me of thy glory more, until
My soul, like Sheba's Queen, faints, overcome,
And all my spirit dies within me, numb,
Sucked in by thine, a larger star, at will;
And hasting like thy bee, my hive to fill,
I 'swoon for very joy' amid thy bloom;
Till—not like that poor bird (as poets feign)
That tried against the Lutanist's her skill,
Crowding her thick precipitate notes, until
Her weak heart break above the contest vain—
Did not thy strength a nobler thought instil,
I feel as if I ne'er could sing again!

In her first sonnet to Barrett, Greenwell compares Barrett's skill as a poet with her own. Unlike Norris, who refers to Barrett in the third rather than in the first person, Greenwell addresses Barrett directly. Greenwell's first lines associate the spaciousness of Barrett's mind with the greatness of her poetry. The rooms of Barrett's mind double as stanzas of poetic verse. As sonnets often appear printed as single stanzas, Greenwell hints that she may be lost in a sonnet sequence.

And indeed Barrett's *Sonnets from the Portuguese* had come out the year before Greenwell composed her poem of praise. Unlike Norris's sonnet, Greenwell's is Petrarchan rather than Shakespearean (abba / abba / cbb / c*BC*). For this reason, it resonates with Barrett's own work and indeed her pendant recalls *Sonnets from the Portuguese.* Here, however, Greenwell adopts Barrett's position as a weak, "overcome" lover and Barrett assumes the position of the beloved as "a larger star." If Barrett did not instill "a nobler thought" with her strength, Greenwell would feel (and yet grammatically it seems she nevertheless *does* feel) "as if I ne'er could sing again!" The sonnet's rhyme structure emphasizes its thematic closure. As the *b* rhymes repeat through the sonnet ("still," "until," "will," "fill," "skill," "until," "instil"), the rhyme scheme seems to demand an additional *b* rhyme after "instil"; appropriately, however, the sonnet is forced to break off with the line, "I feel as if I ne'er could sing again!" Greenwell's failure to complete the fourth *b* couplet reinforces her statement of inadequacy at the end of the sonnet.

While Greenwell's first sonnet uses a date from Barrett's lifetime as part of its title, the second sonnet refers to a time just after her death. In her article, "Entombing the Woman Poet: Tributes to Elizabeth Barrett Browning," Samantha Matthews discusses nineteenth-century poets' obsessive interest in other writers' graves: "In the nineteenth century this ritual of creative renewal is often rhetorically structured in elegiac tribute poems located at the grave."[4] As a specialized form of elegy, Matthews explains, tribute poems tended to be written about well-known poets by younger or less famous ones. In general, these poems were written by male poets and not by women. Women poets did write elegies for famous dead poets; however, instead of traveling to visit these poets' graves, women generally used "the conventional elegiac rhetoric of self-silencing and transcendence, shifting the site of mourning from the external, material world (the grave) to an interior, imaginative realm" (32). Unlike the male authors who wrote tribute poems after Barrett's death (Matthews discusses James Thomson's "E.B.B." and Alfred Austin's "At Her Grave"), Greenwell makes no mention of Barrett's physical grave in her elegiac sonnet:

TO ELIZABETH BARRETT BROWNING, IN 1861

I praised thee not while living; what to thee
Was praise of mine? I mourned thee not when dead;

I only loved thee,—love thee! oh thou fled
Fair spirit, free at last where all are free,
I only love thee, bless thee, that to me
For ever thou hast made the rose more red,
More sweet each word by olden singers said
In sadness, or by children in their glee;
Once, only once in life I heard thee speak,
Once, only once I kissed thee on the cheek,
And met thy kiss and blessing; scarce I knew
Thy smile, I only loved thee, only grew,
Through wealth, through strength of thine, less poor, less weak;
Oh, what hath death with souls like thine to do?

Greenwell's first sonnet creates a sense of inadequacy by incorporating within it three couplets that use the b rhyme (still / until, will / fill, skill / until) and then cutting the fourth couplet short (instil); her second sonnet, by contrast, does not suffer from any such problem. While, like the first sonnet, the second one follows an Italian rhyme scheme (abba / abba / ccd / dcd), it does not generate the misleading impression that a couplet will appear when one will not. This second sonnet resembles Barrett's *Sonnets from the Portuguese* even more closely than the first one. In particular, it recalls Barrett's Sonnet XXI, which begins, "Say over again, and yet once over again, / That thou dost love me."[5] Barrett continues to repeat her request that her beloved will reiterate his love for her: "Say thou dost love me, love me, love me—toll / The silver iterance!" Barrett's sonnet reads abba / abba / cdc / dcd; Greenwell's sonnet reads identically despite its reversal of two syllables in its first tercet: abba / abba / ccd / dcd. When Greenwell's sonnet reverses Barrett's rhyme structure, it also contradicts Barrett's on the level of content. In her first tercet, Barrett asks, "Who can fear / Too many stars, though each in heaven shall roll— / Too many flowers, though each shall crown the year?" In Greenwell's first tercet, on the other hand, singularity is stressed over multiplicity: "Once, only once in life I heard thee speak, / Once, only once I kissed thee on the cheek, / And met thy kiss and blessing." Singularity here corresponds to the reticence that Greenwell makes apparent in the first lines of her sonnet: "I praised thee not while living; what to thee / Was praise of mine?" Matthews concludes about this kind of silence: "Dora Greenwell's sonnet 'To Elizabeth Barrett Browning in 1861' articulates reticence as the type of true feeling, not elegy or eulogy" (32). Consequently, Greenwell links her lack of praise to her lack of mourning, which she relates to her love: "I mourned thee not when dead; / I only loved thee,—love thee!" As a result, the dead body is not referred to in Greenwell's sonnet: "This insistence on present, continuing love is independent of the susceptible material body, and aims to transcend the poet's grave, keeping her memory alive by talking to the spirit" (32). Beyond this, Matthews speculates that Greenwell's focus on the immaterial "is partly attributable to her generation's unwillingness to be defined in the same terms as preceding generations of women poets (Greenwell was only fifteen years younger than Barrett Browning)" (32).

While in the first sonnet Greenwell plays the role of Barrett herself and Barrett takes on the part of the glorified beloved, in the second sonnet Greenwell's speaker assumes the character of Barrett's beloved and writes in response to Barrett's own requests of her suitor. As Barrett begged, "Say thou dost love me, love me, love me—toll / The silver iterance!," Greenwell echoes in her third line, "I only loved thee,—love thee!" and again in the fifth, "I only love thee" and again in the twelfth, "I only loved thee." Here, Greenwell moves from the past tense, "loved thee," to the present, "love thee!" and then continues in the present, "love thee," finally ending in the past, "loved thee." While in the first sonnet Greenwell's speaker exclaims, "I feel as if I ne'er could sing again!," the second sonnet shows no evidence of similar feelings of inadequacy. Instead, the second sonnet only communicates the speaker's strength as a result of her love for Barrett. Moreover, we learn that the speaker "only grew / Through wealth, through strength of thine, less poor, less weak." This is strikingly different from the first sonnet, where the speaker begins, "I lose myself within thy mind" and where she goes on to state, "all my spirit dies within me, numb, / Sucked in by thine, a larger star" and finally, "I feel as if I ne'er could sing again!" Rather than communicating "hopeless grief," Dora Greenwell's two sonnets to Barrett reveal that she has benefited from Barrett's poems, that she envied her, and that she feels stronger and more capable now that Barrett has died.

DORA GREENWELL AND MICHAEL FIELD: IN "PRAISE" OF CHRISTINA ROSSETTI

Overall, both Maria Norris and Dora Greenwell treat Elizabeth Barrett as a muse figure. While their sonnets do eulogize Barrett, they celebrate the poets inspired by Barrett (that is to say, Norris and Greenwell themselves) to an even greater degree. I will now take a look at two poems written in apparent applause of Christina Rossetti. Both are addressed *to* Rossetti herself; the first is by Dora Greenwell and the second is by Michael Field. Greenwell's poem reads as follows:[6]

TO CHRISTINA ROSSETTI

I have mingled my grapes and my wine.
The Song of Songs

Thou hast filled me a golden cup
With a drink divine that glows,
With the bloom that is flowing up
From the heart of the folded rose.
The grapes in their amber glow,
And the strength of the blood-red wine
All mingle and change and flow
In this golden cup of thine.
With the scent of the curling wine
With the balm of the rose's breath,—
For the voice of love is thine,
And thine is the Song of Death!

Greenwell's poem to Rossetti looks like a sonnet, yet it falls short in various ways; first, each line only contains eight syllables instead of ten; second, the poem only has twelve lines instead of fourteen. I am including the poem here, however, because it seems to call attention to its shortcomings as a failed sonnet. As I noted in chapter 3, sonnets make up almost one-fifth of Christina Rossetti's total work. And Greenwell's poems addressed to Elizabeth Barrett do appear in sonnet form. Even though Greenwell praises Rossetti's poetry, calling it "a golden cup" that "glows" with "a drink divine," her poem ends morbidly: "For the voice of love is thine, / And thine is the Song of Death!" The poem progresses in its rhyme scheme from abab to cdcd to dede; similarly it progresses thematically from the "golden cup" to the "grapes in their amber glow" to the "voice of love" to the "Song of Death!" While Greenwell's pendant to Barrett reads more as love sonnets than as poems of admiration, "To Christina Rossetti" focuses only on Rossetti's poetry.

Angela Leighton discusses Greenwell's friendship with Rossetti in *Victorian Women Poets: Writing Against the Heart*. Of Rossetti's female contemporaries, Greenwell became, in Leighton's words, "probably her closest confidante" (124). Like Rossetti, Greenwell "was also single, lived with her beloved mother and was something of a religious mystic and recluse" (124). While Greenwell's poem at least in the opening eight lines expresses great admiration for Rossetti, Rossetti sent Greenwell in reply "a characteristically aloof and impersonal lyric, 'Autumn Violets,' which makes no obvious reference to her friend" (124). Using *The Songs of Songs* as a preface to her poem (together with biblical imagery throughout) and thanking Rossetti for filling a golden cup with a glowing "drink divine," Greenwell relates Rossetti's poetry to spiritual inspiration. At the same time, by replacing "breath" with "Death" at her poem's close, Greenwell calls attention to life-denying qualities in Rossetti's work.

Michael Field's sonnet, which is also called "To Christina Rossetti," shows similarities with Greenwell's poem of the same title.[7] Like Greenwell's, Field's sonnet associates Rossetti with death:[8]

TO CHRISTINA ROSSETTI

Lady, we would behold thee moving bright
As Beatrice or Matilda 'mid the trees,
Alas! thy moan was as a moan for ease
And passage through cool shadows to the night:
Fleeing from love, hadst thou not poet's right
To slip into the universe? The seas
Are fathomless to rivers drowned in these,
And sorrow is secure in leafy light.
Ah, had this secret touched thee, in a tomb
Thou hadst not buried thy enchanting self,
As happy Syrinx murmuring with the wind,
Or Daphne thrilled through all her mystic bloom,
From safe recess as genius or as elf,
Thou hadst breathed joy in earth and in thy kind.

Beginning the sonnet, "Lady, *we* would behold thee," Michael Field calls attention to "his" own dual identity (my italics)—aunt and niece, Katherine Bradley and Edith Cooper (who were involved in a lesbian relationship) wrote their poems together under a single pseudonym. "To Christina Rossetti" is a Petrarchan sonnet: abba / abba / cde / cde. And Field begins by relating Rossetti to the female beloveds from famous sonnet sequences written by men. But Rossetti does not fulfill this wish.[9] Instead of "moving bright," she longs for "passage through cool shadows to the night." Field asks her, "Fleeing from love, hadst thou not poet's right / To slip into the universe?"

Apparently, Rossetti was not touched by "this secret"; in other words, she seems not to have known that she had "poet's right / To slip into the universe" nor that "sorrow is secure in leafy light." Because she did not know this secret, she "buried" her "enchanting self" in a tomb. Consequently, Rossetti did not do what Field desires in the last two lines of the sonnet: "From safe recess as genius or as elf, / Thou hadst breathed joy in earth and in thy kind." The phrase "thy kind" has several possible meanings, one of which is simply "female poets," which Katherine Bradley and Edith Cooper also were. Although they long to see Christina Rossetti "moving bright," Rossetti disappoints them. This is because Michael Field is privy to a "secret" that Rossetti does not know—women (in particular, perhaps, women who flee from heterosexual love or who admit to lesbian love) are not obligated to bury themselves in tombs (of silence and grief).

While "To Christina Rossetti" serves as an elegy, Susan Conley agrees that it "adopts a markedly ambivalent, even critical stance towards its subject."[10] For this reason, the elegiac mood of the sonnet does not derive so much from Rossetti's death as from Field's disapproval of her writing. Ultimately, Field thinks of Rossetti as "an unfit subject for pastoral elegy and—partly in consequence—an unfit muse for future poets. The poem thus becomes a kind of pastoral elegy *manqué*" (Conley 365). As Leighton points out, Field lacks Rossetti's "explosive self-repression" (*Victorian Women Poets* 227). Finding in homosexual meanings "an inspiration for a love poetry which seemed never to have been written before," Field created a new style of writing that challenged the assumptions not only of Rossetti but of all of their female precursors and contemporaries (211). Thus, Leighton concludes that "Michael Field, in many ways, belongs altogether outside the tradition of Victorian women's verse" (204). Writing their best poems about and to each other, while at the same time cloaking their biographical identities through the use of a male pseudonym, Katherine Bradley and Edith Cooper escaped the constraints by which other Victorian women poets were bound. The revelation of their biographical identities, which happened inadvertently (though perhaps inevitably) after their first book had garnered favorable reviews, caused them to be neglected and dismissed by critics for the rest of their lives—a silence that would pursue them for most of the twentieth century. In Marion Thain's words, "After the successful reception of *Callirrhoë* in 1884, Michael Field was never to be so joyously received again."[11]

In spite of their varying status with the critics, Bradley and Cooper passed their lives "in the more open climate of the rebellious Nineties and in communication with many of their famous contemporaries"; consequently, they enjoyed a security and confidence which distinguished them from their precursors (Leighton, *Victorian Women Poets* 204). As a result, Field's poetry lacks "the sense of language itself as a forbidden fruit snatched from the world of punishing experience" (226). In summary, regardless of an apparent overall intention to praise them, Norris, Greenwell, and Field found a certain degree of fault in their most famous female counterparts; their sonnets partially critique the very women that they seem to praise. In so doing, Barrett's and Rossetti's contemporaries and immediate successors anticipated twentieth-century developments—a modern outlook that is especially pronounced in sonnets by Isabella Southern.

ISABELLA SOUTHERN: THE RETURN TO PERSONIFICATIONS

In 1891, Isabella J. Southern responded to both Barrett and Rossetti in *Sonnets and Other Poems*. Southern's work is quite modern in its rejection of Barrett's and Rossetti's more affectionate approach to silence. However, Southern's sonnets recollect Charlotte Smith's in the number of personifications that the speaker invokes. It is perhaps for this reason—the unusually extravagant use of eighteenth-century personification techniques at the brink of the twentieth century—that Southern's poetry has faded into obscurity. Southern personifies a wide variety of abstractions. Like Smith, Southern genders most abstractions feminine: Liberty, Dawn, Nature, the Past, the Present, the Future, Sin, Duty, Pain, Decay, Autumn, Winter, Fate, Spring, Order, Peace, Rest, Oblivion, Sincerity, and Hope. The main abstraction that Southern genders masculine—Death—takes on some weight, however, both because it is gendered masculine in two different sonnets and because it is the first gendered personification that appears in the sequence: "I lay and looked at Death. His face was mild" (2).

While Charlotte Smith courts a series of conflicting, feminized terms—Melancholy, Hope, Friendship, Solitude, etc.—the objects of Southern's affection do not oppose one another in the same way. The list of Southern's praised/courted entities might run as follows: Language, Nature, the Sun, Love, Liberty, Wisdom, Dawn, Time, Sympathy, Martyrdom, Production, Life, Purity, Duty, Evolution, Preparation/Inspiration, Speech, the "Worlds" inside of us, Patience, Maturity/Growth, Pity, Mother Earth, Hope, the Nineteenth Century, Tears, Genius, Joy, Pain, Repentance, Sincerity, and Resignation. As opposed to what happens in Smith's sonnets, none of these terms contradict each other. Whereas Smith sets up mute echo chambers of conflicting ideas that permit no progression forward, Southern is more interested in what can be *produced* over a period of time. As Southern says in "Life's Justification," "Production only can decide / If man, or tree, to live is justified; / For life has either blossomed or decayed" (16). Even the pain that such production requires is given validity in her writing.

"PAST AND FUTURE": SOUTHERN, BARRETT, AUTOBIOGRAPHY, AND WOMEN'S WRITING

Of all of the praised/courted abstractions in Southern's sonnets, the most pivotal ones involve the passage of time. Southern's comments about her relationship to the Past, the Present, and the Future help her at once to revise Elizabeth Barrett's writing and to fashion her own approach to silence. Before I turn in detail to Southern's critique of Barrett (and in particular to her critique of Barrett's "Past and Future," together with its revision, "Future and Past") I will first provide some background about these earlier poems and their implication for the relationship between Barrett's authorship and autobiography. In 1845, Robert Browning informed Elizabeth Barrett that her sonnet "Past and Future" was the most moving poem that he had ever seen: "I have been reading among other poems that sonnet—'Past and Future'—which affects me more than any poem I ever read"(*BC* 11:174). Browning used this poem to support his argument that Barrett's poems (unlike his more dramatic verse) were wholly autobiographical. He continues his praise of "Past and Future" by identifying the sonnet with Barrett's own *self*: "How can I put your poetry away from you, even in these ineffectual attempts to concentrate myself upon, and better apply myself to, what remains?" (*BC* 11:174). As he explains in another 1845 letter, her poetry means infinitely more to him than his ever could mean to her, for she does what he always wanted to do—she speaks in her poems with her own voice: "you speak out, *you*,—I only make men & women speak,—give you truth broken into prismatic hues, and fear the pure white light, even if it is in me" (*BC* 10:22).

Barrett disagrees; she insists that she values Browning's work more than he values hers. The superiority of his work over hers is, in her terms, a *gendered* one:

> In one thing, however, you are wrong—Why should you deny the full measure of my delight & benefit from your writings? I could tell you why you should not—You have in your vision two worlds—or to use the language of the schools of the day, you are both subjective & objective in the habits of your mind—You can deal both with abstract thought, & with human passion in the most passionate sense. Thus, you have an immense grasp in Art; & no one at all accustomed to consider the usual forms of it, could help regarding with reverence & gladness the gradual expansion of your powers. Then you are "masculine" to the height—and I, as a woman, have studied some of your gestures of language & intonation wistfully, as a thing beyond me far! & the more admirable for being beyond. (*BC* 10:26)

Barrett's choice to gender the opposition between strictly personal poetry and poetry that is both "subjective and objective" will be important when I examine Southern's revision of "Future and Past." The gendered distinction between private and public writing has its origins in the history of spiritual autobiography. As Felicity Nussbaum explains, autobiography "was first conceptualized as a genre toward the end of the eighteenth century, and its definition has been applied retrospectively to the preceding age."[12] While the editor of a German collection entitled *Selfbiographies of Famous Men* claimed he owed his inspiration for this idea to Johann Gottfried Herder, Nussbaum notes that Herder did not use the term "selfbi-ograhy" himself. She specifies that the English term is usually linked to Robert Southey's usage in the *Quarterly Review* of 1809, although Issac D'Israeli did use both the terms "self-biography" and "self-character" in a 1796 essay. By the third decade of the nineteenth century, the word "autobiography" was so common that it attracted little attention. And from 1826 to 1833, thirty-four volumes of earlier works appeared, published under the title *Autobiography: A Collection of the Most Instructive and Amusing Lives Ever Published, Written by the Parties Themselves* (the first series of its kind to call attention to the freshly named genre of autobiography). (2)

Historically "self-biographies" originate in spiritual autobiographies. As Nussbaum asserts, the most celebrated and "most unified of seventeenth- and eighteenth- century spiritual autobiographies, Bunyan's *Grace Abounding* (1666), created a prototype for generations of readers and writers in its shaping of an ideal Dissenting self within the context of religious injunctions for self-examination" (64). Like men, women also wrote spiritual autobiographies, but in England the conditions required for such a practice—the existence of a body of women who could write and also read autobiographical texts—took place "when Quaker women's journals and testimonies were disseminated in the latter half of the seventeenth century, and in the later publication of scandalous memoirs in the mid eighteenth century" (133). Nussbaum finds it "especially remarkable" how female spiritual autobiographers express "their record of turmoil over whether to speak publicly, often involving their conflict with scriptural, church, and domestic authority over public preaching" (167). Many worried about the threat that public speaking posed for their sexual identity. It was, after all, considered improper for women publicly to engage in preaching. Nussbaum explains that women often mentioned a childish desire to be ministers, which they were forced to dismiss because womanhood meant they must hide "their ambition to speak through public disavowal" (167).

While Nussbaum argues that female spiritual autobiographers struggled to come to terms with their ability to speak publicly, she also points out that some "feminist theorists have come close to claiming that women's experience intrinsically lends itself to private autobiographical writing in diaries and journals" (133). When this sort of private writing was made public in the shape of "serial autobiographical forms," women ended up "mimicking the dominant ideologies of themselves." In other words, women could not separate themselves entirely from the culturally prescribed gender roles that had become ingrained in their consciousnesses (133). In keeping with the prescribed gender roles of her time, Elizabeth Barrett slightly reformulates the public/private distinction. Whereas, earlier in history, female spiritual autobiographers were afraid of speaking publicly, Barrett maintained that women poets could not speak publicly about *public* life; or, at the very least, they could not speak as well as men could about the public world. Women could, however, speak publicly about the *private* dimension to their lives. Consequently, women's poetry might be seen as more autobiographical than men's.

Barrett's insistence on the autobiographical nature of women's writing in general, and of her own in particular, resonates with the times in which she lived. As Joanne Shattock points out, "The polarization of the 'public' (male) and the 'private' (female) sphere is part of Victorian ideology, but, as historians remind us, it was a very real part of nineteenth-century experience."[13] Essays in Shattock's volume make evident that while work eventually moved out of the private space and into a public workplace, writing remained one kind of employment that could be enacted from within the domestic realm. As a result, women's writing became doubly private: it was pursued both on and about domestic territory. Edgar Allen Poe agrees with Barrett's argument to Robert Browning in his review of one of her early collections of poetry: "A woman and her book are identical."[14]

As a genre of its own, women's autobiography first became popular during the Victorian period. Linda Peterson explains that in the initial advertisement to the 1826 series, *Autobiography: A Collection of the Most Instructive and Amusing Lives Ever Published, Written by the Parties Themselves,* the publishers John Hunt and Cowden Clarke featured no women's self-writing.[15] However, within a year, Hunt and Clarke decided to include two samples of women's autobiography—both in the subgenre of *chroniques scandaleuses:* the memoirs of Mary Robinson (known as the mistress of the Prince of Wales) and the *Life* of Charlotte Clarke, the daughter of an actress famous for cross-dressing, off- as well as onstage. But when Margaret Oliphant began to write a series of critical essays on autobiography for *Blackwood's Edinburgh Magazine* in 1881, she used women's self-writing in three of her seven installments. Peterson stresses that in "the fifty-five years between Hunt and Clarke's series . . . and Oliphant's essays in *Blackwood's,* the literary status of, and public knowledge about, women's self-writing had dramatically changed" (210). What had appeared to be a lesser genre at the start of the century, consisting mainly of spiritual confessions or scandalous chronicles, had become a prevalent, and even a highly respected genre by the late nineteenth century. In contrast to the scandalous memoirs that had been popular examples of women's autobiography during the eighteenth century, the Victorian period saw the rise of domestic memoirs—accounts transcribing the day-to-day lives of conventional wives and daughters. Barrett's interest in autobiography sheds light on Southern's critique—the two poets specifically position themselves at different moments in history.

Barrett's "Past and Future" is a perfect example of a sonnet that contrasts the condition of the speaker's self in the past and the present and then confidently predicts the direction that the future will take:[16]

PAST AND FUTURE

My future will not copy fair my past
On any leaf but Heaven's. Be fully done,
Supernal Will! I would not fain be one
Who, satisfying thirst and breaking fast
Upon the fulness of the heart at last
Says no grace after meat. My wine has run
Indeed out of my cup, and there is none
To gather up the bread of my repast
Scattered and trampled; yet I find some good
In earth's green herbs, and streams that bubble up
Clear from the darkling ground,—content until
I sit with angels before better food:
Dear Christ! when Thy new vintage fills my cup,
This hand shall shake no more, nor that wine spill.
(Barrett, *The Complete Works,* Vol. 2, 228)

By personalizing the temporal progression that she discusses—"*My* future will not copy fair *my* past"—Barrett the living poet brings her readers into her poetic world (my italics). If Robert Browning were to write to her and court her and eventually convince her to marry him, he might change the sad certainty with which Barrett writes. And Browning does not hesitate explicitly to enter the poem in his description of how much he liked it: "may God bless me, as you pray, by letting that beloved hand shake *the less* . . . I will only ask, *the less* . . . for being laid on mine thro' this life!" (*BC* 11:174). Barrett alludes to her absent reader at the turn from octave to sestet—"My wine has run / Indeed out of my cup, and there is none / To gather up the bread of my repast / Scattered and trampled." By rhyming "repast" with "past," Barrett contradicts the first line of the sonnet—"My future will not copy fair my past." Were the future to copy the past, the past would occur again; "repast" both indicates the meal for which one hungers and the repetition of the speaker's past. It is just after the sonnet's volta that we see how this "repast" has become "scattered and trampled." The speaker's distress has to do with the fact that "there is none / To gather up" her fallen bread. But what if the absent reader should appear and gather up the speaker's bread? Or what if the reader could make the speaker's hand shake less so that her wine does not run out of her cup? This is what Browning proposes to do. Because he succeeds, the poem ceases to be true. Barrett was then obligated to rewrite the poem, which she did in *Sonnets from the Portuguese.*

Poem XLII in *Sonnets from the Portuguese*, a reversal of "Past and Future," was probably XVII, now missing, in the Morgan sequence. It was removed from the sequence for the printer's copy (the Houghton manuscript) and resurfaced in 1850 and in 1853 on p. 362 of Volume I as a separate sonnet entitled "Future and Past." The sonnet was reintroduced into *Sonnets from the Portuguese* in 1856, but as XLII, not XVII, which makes sense given the speaker's slow decision to return her suitor's love in the sequence:

XLII

'My future will not copy fair my past'—
I wrote that once; and thinking at my side
My ministering life-angel justified
The word by his appealing look upcast
To the white throne of God, I turned at last,
And there, instead, saw thee, not unallied
To angels in thy soul! Then I, long tried

By natural ills, received the comfort fast,
While budding, at thy sight, my pilgrim's staff
Gave out green leaves with morning dews impearled.
I seek no copy now of life's first half:
Leave here the pages with long musing curled,
And write me new my future's epigraph,
New angel mine, unhoped for in the world!
(Barrett, *A Variorum Edition* 147)

Using the same first line as "Past and Future," this sonnet keeps a similar rhyme scheme. While the first line of the 1844 sonnet rhymes with "fast," "last," and "repast," the first line of the 1850 sonnet rhymes with "upcast," "last," and "fast." In effect, the 1850 sonnet reverses the "ast" rhyme structure from 1844: the two-syllable "repast" from 1844 begins the rhyme sequence (following "past") in 1850, this time reformulated as "upcast." And the next two rhymes read as "last" and "fast," which occur in reverse order from 1844. From these rhymes alone, it is as if in 1844, the speaker's "fast" will "last" as the bread from her "repast" is scattered and trampled, with no one to pick it up for her. In 1850, conversely, the speaker's eyes are now "upcast"—yet rather than seeing the Christ who will fill her cup in the afterlife, she turns to view her suitor, who is "not unallied" to angels in his soul. Consequently, she has had her last fast, which explains the reordering of these two words. However, none of this means that her future will copy her past (even in a good way)—"I seek no copy now of life's first half"; her miraculously original future, though, hasn't happened yet.

Because Robert Browning interfered with the truth claims she made in her 1844 sonnet, Elizabeth Barrett will no longer make any. Instead, she asks him to take over the writing process.[17] While the 1850 sonnet's last lines *could* be read to mean "[*I*] leave here the pages with long musing curled, / And [*I*] write me new my future's epigraph," and I am saying this to *you,* "New angel mine, unhoped for in the world!," it is much more likely that the speaker is telling her suitor to leave here the pages on which she has written (which would include this sonnet as well) and to write her future down for her, to invent it, not as a copy of her past but as some new, budding, unhoped-for phenomenon.[18] At the same time, as Thomas Gray made clear, we might want to read the word "morning" as a double for "mourning"—even though the speaker receives "comfort fast" after being "long tried / By natural ills," her "pilgrim's staff" gives out "green leaves" that are "impearled" with the dews (the tears) of grief. No matter what richness the suitor will bring to the speaker, her grief will not disappear as a result of his love. The speaker treasures her grief, as the word "impearled" implies, and she knows that the budding green leaves of love will bring the signs of her sadness (like dew) with them. Furthermore, the dews of grief will appear on these leaves regardless of how many buds grow at the sight of the suitor and also regardless of the speaker's own silence.

Barrett personalizes the passage of time in her two "Past and Future" sonnets, beginning each one "*My* future will not copy fair my past" (my italics). As we have seen, it was the intensely autobiographical nature of "Past and Future" that drew Robert Browning more intimately to the poem than to any he had ever read. Barrett agreed with him that her poems were autobiographical, and she gendered this aspect of her work, arguing that her poetry was more private than his because she was a woman and was therefore blind to the public dimension of life. In "Past and Future," she says that her "repast" has become "scattered and trampled" because "there is none" to gather up her fallen bread. For this reason, she awaits the afterlife—the time when her problems will be miraculously solved. Once Browning has interfered with her life plan, she gives up speech altogether in her revision of "Past and Future," insisting that what she wrote before was wrong and that her suitor (who plays the role of an "angel") must "write" her "future's epigraph."

While Barrett personalizes the past, the present, and the future ("My future will not copy fair my past"; "my repast"; "my future's epigraph"), Southern distances herself from moments in time by personifying them. As a response to Barrett's "Past and Future" (together with its revision in *Sonnets from the Portuguese*), Southern prints two poems next to one another: "Past and Present" and "The Future" (17–18):

PAST AND PRESENT

The Past with fixéd features lies behind,
No mantling blush endears her visage cold,

Her form is cast in monumental mould,
The hands are still, the sculptured eyes are blind,
Strange hieroglyphs upon her robes I find
And seek some clue to priceless tales, untold
Since living youth and beauty round her rolled.
And loving hearts her secret lore divined.

Both Past and Future must abide for aye;
The Present wanes, e'en as her name I speak,
She waits not till I stoop to kiss her cheek,
But slips from my embrace; and where she lay,
The Past, unchangeable, mocks my lips' play
And laughs to scorn, my cry for her I seek.

THE FUTURE

The Future flits before me, while I race
To catch her scented garments as she flies.
Ah! she disdains my eager, urgent cries,
That she should slacken her aerial pace,
Permit me but one glance at her fair face.
She flits and flits; my ardour never dies,
"Did I possess thee, I were good and wise,"
Yet unrelentingly she veils her grace.

Shall I e'er hold that lovely flutt'ring thing
Within my hand, and kiss her bloom away?
Shall she elude me ever, and for aye,
While I my love-sick praises to her sing?
'Twere better so; no present hour can bring
A gift so glorious as the Future may!

One key difference between Barrett's "Past and Future" sonnets and Southern's "Past and Present" / "The Future" has to do with the two poets' *knowledge* of the time frames they discuss. Barrett knows both the past and the future in her first sonnet; she is certain that "My future will not copy fair my past," and she has faith that when Christ's "new vintage fills my cup, / This hand shall shake no more, nor that wine spill." In Barrett's own revision of "Past and Future," she is equally aware of the past. The poem begins, "'*My future will not copy fair my past'*— / I wrote that once. . . ." And she knows that her future will involve "green leaves" of love, "morning dews" of grief, and whatever happy ending her Beloved chooses to "write" as her future's epigraph. Writing on the cusp of the twentieth century, Southern, on the other hand, laments that she cannot understand how to read the past: "The Past with fixéd features lies behind, / No mantling blush endears her visage cold, / Her form is cast in monumental mould, / The hands are still. . . ." Interestingly, Southern picks up here on Barrett's own reference to the future in "Past and Future": when Christ's "new vintage" will fill her cup, Barrett tells us that "This hand shall shake no more, nor that wine spill." Browning also highlights these lines in his response to Barrett's sonnet, and begs that her "beloved hand" will shake the less, "I will only ask *the less* . . . for being laid on mine through this life!" (*BC* 11:174).

In Southern's sonnet, the past seems to be not only personified as a woman but as a *dead* woman. When Southern published her sonnets, Barrett had been dead for thirty years. By mentioning the way that the Past's "hands are still," after Barrett in a similarly titled sonnet, "Past and Future," insisted her own hands would "shake no more" in the afterlife, Southern implies that when she speaks to the Past she addresses none other than the dead Elizabeth Barrett herself. Barrett's "Past and Future" has turned into Southern's "Past and Present" for Barrett's "Future" is literally Southern's "Present." Southern's criticism of the Past—her judgment that the Past is wholly unresponsive—might be read as her disapproval of Barrett's poetry in general. Words like "fixéd features" and "form" ("cast in monumental mould") recollect the regular, measured style in which Barrett wrote. These features particularly apply to sonnets, with their fixed rhyme schemes, meter, line count, and syllable count per line. By the time that Southern published her work, Dante Gabriel Rossetti had already described the sonnet as a "moment's monument," which would further relate the idea of the Past's "form" being "cast in monumental mould" to Barrett's use of the sonnet structure. Dante Gabriel Rossetti makes the point at the end of his self-reflexive sonnet that in Charon's hand the sonnet pays the toll to death. Here, Barrett—her sonnets, the whole past itself—appears with "fixéd features," no "blush" upon a "cold" face, still hands and "blind" eyes. To "read" this past is to find bizarre "hieroglyphs" and through these to "seek some clue to priceless tales," which nevertheless cannot be discovered. And yet Isabella Southern responds to this deceased, insensible past by *repeating* it; just like Barrett, Southern, too, writes sonnets. It is for this reason that the Present in Southern's sonnet "wanes, e'en as her name I speak, / She waits not till I stoop to kiss her cheek, / But slips from my embrace." The Present becomes the Past that Southern initially reproves. Like the Past, the Present is not kissable. Slipping from the speaker's embrace, the Present turns into the "unchangeable" Past who mocks the speaker and laughs at her. Specifically, the Past/Present mocks and laughs at the speaker's "lips' play" and her "cry." In other words, Southern's own declaration (uttered either as "lips' play" or as a "cry") that she cannot read the Past instantly has become part of the very Past that lacks life. Like Barrett's sonnets, Southern's words also have "fixéd features" and a "form" that is "cast in monumental mould."

While Southern's speaker "seek[s] some clue" to the Past and "speak[s]" the name of the waning Present, endeavoring to "kiss" the Present's "cheek," her pursuit of the Future is more active. Instead of only stooping to kiss the Future's cheek, she "race[s] / To catch her scented garments as she [the Future] flies." And instead of simply speaking her name, she utters "eager, urgent cries." But like the Past and the Present, the Future "disdains" her pleas. The speaker cannot manage to grab hold of or even to catch a glimpse of the Future: "She flits and flits; my ardour never dies." The speaker is more in love with the Future than with the dead, unattractive Past or with the Present, whose cheek she stoops to kiss. Hence, she asks, "Shall I e'er hold that lovely flutt'ring thing / Within my hand, and kiss her bloom away? / Shall she elude me ever, and for aye, / While I my love-sick praises to her sing?" The answer to this question is of course yes, but we are told that "'Twere better so." If the speaker could hold the future in her hand, this would make the future a part of the present, which would bring it closer to the lifeless form of the Past.

Southern echoes Barrett's revision of "Past and Future" when she argues that the Future will necessarily surpass both Present and Past: "no present hour can bring / A gift so glorious as the Future may!" Her frustration that she cannot see the Future repeats throughout her collection of sonnets, however. Because the Future remains invisible, it is *possible* that the Future will not be glorious at all. This fear of the Future resounds throughout Southern's sonnets, although she tries to explain her fear away with assertions about how evolution works.

One of the problems that Southern has with the Future has to do with her reaction against the way that earlier female sonneteers clung to silence as the only or even as the most correct means of expression.

SOUTHERN'S CRITIQUE OF BARRETT'S "HOPELESS GRIEF"

The main point of Barrett's 1844 sonnet "Grief" is that sorrow for what has been lost needs to resemble death itself. This turns the mourner into a kind of "monumental statue set / In everlasting watch and moveless woe / Till itself crumble to the dust beneath." Southern recollects Barrett's use of the word "monumental" in her revision of the "Past and Future" sonnets. The Past in Southern's "Past and Present" not only mirrors Barrett's vision of herself in the future, but it also mirrors Barrett's vision of "hopeless grief." Barrett's model of the true mourner who stands "like a monumental statue set" parallels Southern's Past with its "cold" visage" and its "form" that "is cast in monumental mould." When Southern tells us that "The hands are still, the sculptured eyes are blind," she does not simply recall Barrett's image of herself in the afterlife. She also recalls Barrett's sonnet "Grief" where the true griever stands in "moveless woe." Unable to "arise and go," Barrett's mourner also has still hands. Furthermore, Barrett makes a point in her sonnet that she reiterates throughout her other poems as well as her letters—for Barrett, the person caught in "hopeless grief" cannot even cry. After her brother Edward's death, Barrett wrote to Mary Russell Mitford:

> Oh my dearest friend! That was a very near escape from madness, absolute hopeless madness—For more than three months I could not read—could understand little that was said to me. The mind seemed to myself broken up into fragments. And even after the long dark spectral trains, the staring infantine faces, had gone back from my bed,—to *understand,* to hold on to one thought for more than a moment, remained impossible. That was, in part, because I never could cry. Never! The tears ran scalding hot into my brain instead of down my cheeks—That was how it happened. (*BC* 5:83)

Like Barrett, in the agony of grief, and also like Barrett's depiction of what a true griever most resembles—"a monumental statue" with "marble eyes" that will never be "wet" to the touch—Southern's personified Past has "sculptured eyes" that are also "blind." It is as if Barrett's early image of herself in the future has merged with her view of the true griever—like the "monumental statue set," Barrett the griever will never cry and will never again be able to move in space due to the extent of her woe.[19] Perhaps this is why Barrett repeats her reference to her grief even in her amatory revision of "Past and Future" in 1850. As we have seen, in Southern's "Past and Present," Barrett's future has become personified as the Past—one with "fixéd features," no "mantling blush," a "visage cold," still hands, blind eyes, with strange "hieroglyphs upon her robes" and a "form" that is "cast in monumental mould." Southern leaves the Past behind—the first line of her sonnet tells us this: "The Past with fixéd features lies behind . . . ." It is the future that she races after. Although the future "flits and flits," the speaker's "ardour never dies."

In effect, Southern makes Barrett's perception of perfect mourning a vision of the past. There are two interrelated aspects to Barrett's definition of "hopeless grief"—the lack of tears and silence.[20] Southern takes issue with both of these failures: to cry and to speak. As we have seen, Barrett's poems often treat her inability to weep. In another 1844 grieving sonnet, "Tears," Barrett places little value on the capacity to cry:

TEARS

Thank God, bless God, all ye who suffer not
More grief than ye can weep for. That is well—
That is light grieving! lighter, none befell
Since Adam forfeited the primal lot.
Tears! what are tears? The babe weeps in its cot,
The mother singing; at her marriage-bell
The bride weeps, and before the oracle
Of high-faned hills the poet has forgot
Such moisture on his cheeks. Thank God for grace,
Ye who weep only! If, as some have done,
Ye grope tear-blinded in a desert place
And touch but tombs,—look up! those tears will run
Soon in long rivers down the lifted face,
And leave the vision clear for stars and sun.
(Barrett, *The Complete Works,* Vol. 2, 229)

Here, Barrett refers to the kind of grief that produces tears as "light grieving!" She tells those who "suffer not / More grief than ye can weep for" to thank and bless God for the gift of tears. For the rest of the octave, Barrett produces a list of others who are able to cry, including the "babe" who "weeps in its cot" and the "bride." The opening of the sestet, then, simply repeats the claims made at the start of the octave. While the octave begins "Thank God, bless God, all ye who suffer not / More grief than ye can weep for," the sestet proclaims, "Thank God for grace, / Ye who weep only!" The sestet then shifts slightly, explaining that if readers cry but also feel desolate, all they have to do is to look up and the tears will depart from their faces, leaving their "vision clear for stars and sun." In other words, even the worst possible grief (as long as it produces tears) will "soon" evaporate.

At the same time, by instructing those who "grope tear-blinded in a desert place / And touch but tombs" to "look *up,*" Barrett contradicts the point she makes in "Grief" (my italics). In "Grief," she says that "only men, incredulous of despair, / Half-taught in anguish," choose to "beat *upward* to God's throne in loud access / Of shrieking and reproach" (my italics). This is because "Full desertness, / In souls as countries, lieth silent-bare." The people who "grope tear-blinded in a desert place / And touch but tombs" have already proven themselves to be "Half-taught in anguish" if, as Barrett tells us at the start of "Tears," "That is well— / That is light grieving!" Angela Leighton summarizes the "alternative message" in Barrett's "Tears": "What the poem finely but not quite inaudibly leaves in silence is that other message of despair. The speaker is calm and philosophical, and does not pretend to confide any personal feeling. She tells of Christian redemption and of visionary revelation. But neither of these is for the ones who cannot weep" (*Elizabeth Barrett Browning* 85). The true griever—the "monumental statue set"—is not capable of groping or touching. The reason it cannot move is *because* it cannot cry: "If it could weep, it could arise and go."

Two of Isabella Southern's sonnets radically revise Barrett's understanding of what it means to cry: "After Rain" (81) and "Tears" (114). "After Rain" reads as follows:

AFTER RAIN

How pure the air when ceases summer rain,
And day's bright atmosphere is crystal clear;

The birds in ecstasy arise again
On quiv'ring wings, that almost still appear.
Each living thing lifts up its head anew,
The sun shines out, and clouds pass quickly by;
Our tears are shed, and hope springs up to sue
For life and love, where sorrow longed to die.

Thank God for tears! It is the silent grief
That eats like rust into a sullen soul,
Or flashes swift, dry fire, to devastate
With dangerous lightning of despair and hate.
When torrents fall, away the storm-clouds roll
And sunshine gilds each shining, rain-washed leaf.

Southern begins "After Rain" as a metaphoric continuation of the ending to Barrett's "Tears." Barrett instructs those who "grope tear-blinded in a desert place" to "look up" so that their "tears will run / Soon in long rivers down the lifted face, / And leave the vision clear for stars and sun." And Southern begins "After Rain," "HOW pure the air when ceases summer rain, / And day's bright atmosphere is crystal *clear.*" Just as Barrett declares that the "tear-blinded" vision will soon become "*clear,*" Southern relates how after the rain ceases, "day's bright atmosphere" will become "crystal *clear*" (my italics). In Barrett's sonnet, clarity of vision permits the view of "stars and sun." Southern, too, describes how the "sun shines out" after the rain. Southern makes the connection between the summer rain and tears at the end of the octave: "Our tears are shed, and hope springs up to sue / For life and love, where sorrow longed to die."

At the start of the sestet, Southern repeats Barrett, who in "Tears" said at the beginning of the octave, "Thank God, bless God, all ye who suffer not / More grief than ye can weep for" and at the beginning of the sestet, "Thank God for grace, / Ye who weep only!" Southern, too, introduces her sestet with the line "Thank God for tears!" But the difference between Barrett's sonnet and Southern's becomes glaringly apparent in the next lines of "After Rain": "It is the *silent* grief / That eats like rust into a sullen soul, / Or flashes swift, dry fire, to devastate / With dangerous lightning of despair and hate" (my italics). Therefore, Southern heatedly rejects the model of genuine grief put forth by Barrett in "Grief" and "Tears." Leighton recapitulates Barrett's position in her grieving sonnets:

"The silence of Elizabeth's unspoken grief runs like a strong undertow to these poems, which are won from its current with evident effort. This silence is not a superior form of expressiveness, which gives to language a reach beyond itself; it is simply a negation. The real 'desert place' of grief makes the poet's 'high-faned hills' distant and irrelevant. Grief, for Elizabeth Barrett, is the blank side of writing, which shames and contradicts the high revelations of poetry" (*Elizabeth Barrett Browning* 89). Instead of agreeing that "hopeless grief is passionless" and that it needs to be expressed in "silence like to death," Southern proclaims that "silent grief" is dangerous, generated by "a sullen soul." Southern returns to her metaphor for tears in the last two lines of her sonnet: "When torrents fall, away the storm-clouds roll / And sunshine gilds each shining, rain-washed leaf." In Barrett's "Tears," the fact that the "tear-blinded" vision will soon become "clear for stars and sun" does not mean crying is the best way to communicate "hopeless grief." Rather, Barrett suggests that if a mourner can cry in the first place (no matter how serious the grief *feels*), that person is experiencing only "light grieving." In Southern's "After Rain," it would appear that true grieving does produce tears, and we should be grateful for them because everything will be fine once the "tears are shed." The problem, in Southern's view, is with "silent grief" for such sorrow is inauthentic and treacherous.

In terms of its rhyme scheme, "After Rain" stands alone in Southern's collection of 136 sonnets: abab / cdcd / efg / gfe. No other sonnet in the volume uses this rhyme structure. And the rhyme pattern that Southern has chosen for "After Rain" brilliantly mirrors what takes place on the content level. The interweaving rhymes in the first quatrain effectively reveal the speaker's interconnected observations. Because the second quatrain begins, "Each living thing lifts up its head anew," Southern needs here a completely fresh rhyme that will "lift up its head anew." Therefore, instead of repeating the *a* or the *b* rhyme from the first quatrain here (as she does in 121 of her 136 sonnets), Southern begins her second quatrain with a new rhyme—literally, with the word "anew." She then follows the same rhyme scheme with *c* and *d* as she did with *a* and *b* in the first quatrain. Just as each "living thing lifts up its head anew," our "tears are shed, and hope brings up to sue / For life and love" and just as "The sun shines out, and clouds pass quickly by," we learn that hope springs up "where sorrow longed to die."

As in the second quatrain, the sestet introduces a new idea when it refers to "silent grief." In keeping with this thematic deviation, Southern begins the sestet with a new rhyme. But the sestet works differently from the octave. Instead of using the interweaving rhyme scheme that dominated the first eight lines, Southern ends the sonnet efg / gfe. What is interesting here is that the first tercet, efg, reverses itself in the second tercet, which reads as its mirror image: gfe. And this reversal is exactly what happens thematically. The first tercet describes "silent grief," which "eats like rust into a sullen soul." Because of the unsettling impact of silent grief, it makes sense that in the first tercet our ears would be soothed by no rhymes at all. On the level of sonority, the first line of the second tercet reverses the impact of what has just been said. The twelfth line in fact forms a couplet with the eleventh. By the end of the first tercet, we crave rhyme, and so the second tercet begins by completing a rhyming couplet. From this point on, Southern stops talking about "silent grief" and instead speaks about the healing aftermath of tears. Even more obviously than in her revision in "After Rain," Southern rewrites Barrett's "Tears" in her own sonnet, "Tears":

TEARS

Spring showers are tears of childhood, soon they pass,
And leave the sweet forget-me-nots more pure;
They freshen every tender blade of grass,
The little griefs they quickly, surely cure.
But tears of stern maturity, alas!
Are wild destructive torrents, hard to endure,
And gather sullenly, a leaden mass,
With scanty power to soften, or allure.
Old age forgets the fiercer thunder rain,
As spirit cleanses off each earthly stain;
The bliss and agony for it are past,
An even hue o'er joy and grief are cast:
Though gentle tears of memory may fall,
The light and shade of life no more appal.

As "Tears" appears at a later point in Southern's collection than "After Rain," it also reads as a revision of this earlier sonnet. Indeed, the sonnets in Southern's book move progressively forward in time, so that toward the end of the book she prints "A Retrospect," which begins, "THE end is drawing near; I seem to know / That what I had to say is almost said; / That one prepares to sever from my head / The lock that binds to life" (122). While "After Rain" begins, "How pure the air when ceases summer rain," "Tears" changes "summer rain" to "spring showers." And while "After Rain" describes the way that "day's bright atmosphere" becomes "crystal clear," with "birds in ecstasy" arising, the sun shining, clouds passing by, our tears being shed and "hope spring[ing] up to sue / For life and love," "Tears" paints the same picture, but explains that this sort of scenario only occurs in "childhood" and early youth. "Tears" repeats many of the images from "After Rain." For example, in "Tears," Southern describes how after spring showers, "the sweet forget-me-nots" become "more *pure*" in the same way that in "After Rain" she exclaims, "HOW *pure* the air when ceases summer rain" (my italics). Southern's "Tears" switches after the first four lines; the second quatrain opens, "But tears of stern maturity, alas!" When Southern comments on these mature tears, she calls them "wild destructive torrents, hard to endure" that "gather sullenly, a leaden mass." Here, she recalls the word "sullenly" from "After Rain." However, in "After Rain," it is the absence rather than the presence of tears that accompanies sullenness. Furthermore, when Southern calls the "tears of stern maturity" "wild *destructive* torrents," she reminds us of the absence of tears in "After Rain"; there, words like "devastate" and "dangerous" illustrate the influence of "silent grief." Unlike tears in both Barrett's poems and in "After Rain," the "tears of stern maturity" have "scanty power to soften, or allure." In this later poem, it is not a question of silence, which still seems for Southern to feed "like rust" upon a "sullen soul" or else "to devastate / With dangerous lightning of despair and hate." Nevertheless, even tears have ceased to provide any comfort.

Southern uses the opening rhyme scheme to show the progression from the "tears of childhood" to those "of stern maturity." The first rhyme in the initial quatrain reads as "pass"/"grass." Both words have positive connotations. Tears in early life "pass," Southern tells us, and they also "freshen every tender blade of grass." This rhyme evolves in the second quatrain into "alas!"/"mass." Unfortunately ("alas!"), the tears of "stern maturity" gather in the fashion of "a leaden mass." The image of "a leaden mass" recalls Barrett's version of what it means to suffer from "hopeless grief." Southern picks up on another key word from Barrett's "Tears"—the word "light." Barrett's goal in "Tears" was to contrast "*light* grieving" with serious grief—"More grief than ye can weep for" (my italics). Barrett repeats the word "light" in her third line: "That is *light* grieving! *lighter,* none befell / Since Adam forfeited the primal lot" (my italics). She then enumerates all of the "light" occasions on which tears appear: "The babe weeps in its cot, / The mother singing, at her marriage-bell / The bride weeps. . . ." This leads her to exclaim at the start of the sestet "Thank God for grace, / Ye who weep only!" The groping and the touching of those who find themselves "tear-blinded in a desert place" also reflect a kind of lightness for Barrett—the physical levity made possible by tears. Furthermore, those who grope and touch are able to "look up!" at which point their tears soon depart and their vision becomes "clear for stars and sun." That is to say, those who can cry ultimately find access not only to stars but to the *light* of day.

In the final line of her sonnet "Tears," Southern plays with the word "light": "The *light* and shade of life no more appal" (my italics). The word "light" clearly has three meanings in Barrett's sonnets: light as in light from the sun at the end of "Tears" when "those tears will run / Soon in long rivers down the lifted face, / And leave the vision clear for stars and sun"; light as in light in weight when those who do not suffer more grief than they can weep for manage to "grope" and "touch" and "look up" (in contrast to the "monumental statue set" that remains in "moveless woe"); and light as in the opposite of serious when Barrett says, "That is light grieving!" and goes on to describe instances where tears in no way represent tragic grief. In Barrett's version there may be two kinds of tears—the "light" tears of the "babe in cot," "bride," "mother," and "poet" in the hills on the one hand and the seemingly more serious tears of those who "grope tear-blinded in a desert place / And touch but tombs." These two forms of weeping have the same result in Barrett's sonnet, however: both represent forms of "light grieving."

As opposed to what happens in Barrett's "Tears," in Southern's "Tears" the two types of weeping are quite distinct. In the first case, "tears of childhood" quickly pass and "freshen every tender blade of grass"; the "tears of stern maturity," by contrast, are "wild destructive torrents, hard to endure." The difference between Barrett's second, apparently more serious example of weeping and Southern's "tears of stern maturity" relies on the extent to which these two forms of grief find relief. In Barrett's case, the most awful instances of tear-producing sorrow nevertheless soon terminate in consolation. For Southern, the "tears of stern maturity" have a much more difficult, if not impossible, chance of generating comfort. People in old age cannot achieve "lightness" by crying because, as Southern explains, they have lost their recollection of what levity is. Bliss, agony, joy, and grief all appear to share the same "hue." For this reason, Southern takes issue with Barrett's argument against "light grieving." The "tears of stern maturity" are anything but light for Southern (related instead to a "leaden mass"). Given Southern's exclamation in "After Rain," "Thank God for tears! It is the silent grief / That eats like rust into a sullen soul," we can infer that in both sonnets she critiques Barrett's equation between "hopeless grief" and "silence like to death."

SOUTHERN'S CELEBRATION OF LANGUAGE

Southern not only argues against Barrett's equation of silence with true grieving; she celebrates the power of language itself. Her sonnet "Of Language" (3) is worthy to be printed here because of the strong case it makes in favor of the supremacy of speech:

OF LANGUAGE

In words, as in a clinging drapery,
Men clothe an evanescent, shrinking thought,
And send it forth. By passing breezes caught
Upon its errand swiftly doth it flee
From home to home, from land to land, to be
A guest most gladly welcomed, and full fraught
With inspiration from its fountain brought.
It whispers hope and peace to misery,
And breathes upon a frost-bound heart to thaw
Its icy bands, that it may run and sing,
To other souls reviving water bring:
Then wakes a sleeping fancy to explore
A magic land it never saw before
The world within, which there lay slumbering.

As I proposed in chapter 2, Barrett revises Wordsworth's "Composed Upon Westminster Bridge" in her 1844 sonnet "Grief." Southern provides her own revision of Barrett's critique of Wordsworth in "Of Language." Southern begins the sonnet by relating words to clothes—"a clinging drapery." Here, men clothe their thoughts in words because without words thought lacks substance. While Barrett depicts "hopeless grief" as eternal, placing her authentic griever in the same position as the "monumental statue set," Southern conceptualizes thoughts and feelings very differently. For Southern, thought is "evanescent" and "shrinking"; only language gives thought weight. In Wordsworth's sonnet, the City wears the beauty of the morning the same way that it wears nakedness; in Southern's sonnet, by contrast, men clothe thought in words "as in a *clinging* drapery" (3; my italics). This drapery does not risk falling off or ceasing to be; rather, it grips the object it clothes, setting language in opposition to Wordsworth's beautiful city and to Barrett's "monumental statue" of grief. Acting contrary to these variations on "silent, bare"/"silent-bare" phenomena, Southern's version of language brings nothing but good. Specifically, for Southern, language has the ability to move through space (which both Wordsworth's city and Barrett's griever lack); thoughts that have been clothed in "words, as in a clinging drapery" travel very quickly.

"Of Language" comes close to standing alone as far as its rhyme scheme goes in Southern's collection (abba / acca / dee / dde). Although it is similar to nine other sonnets, including "Of True Love," "The Spring-Time of Love," and "Robert Browning," it differs from all of these because of the similarity of its *b* and *c* rhymes. The sonnet begins the same way that 100 other sonnets in Southern's volume do, with an abba rhyme scheme. It then switches to an acca rhyme scheme in the second quatrain; however, while the *b* rhyme reads as "thought"/"caught," the *c* rhyme reads very similarly as "fraught"/"brought." It is not that the "thought" has been "caught" by language. On the contrary, the thought has been clothed in language so that it can be "caught" by "passing breezes." Through language, thought becomes personified for Southern. It wears words the way people do clothes, and when it visits homes it is received as a "guest most gladly welcomed." Moreover, it "*whispers* hope and peace to misery" and it "*breathes* upon a frost-bound heart to thaw / Its icy bands" (my italics). Language seems to provide even more than tears do. Once it has thawed the "icy bands" of a "frost-bound heart," language permits this heart to "run and sing, / To other souls reviving water bring." On some level, the "icy bands" turn into tears that, in Barrett's words, will soon run "in long rivers down the lifted face, / And leave the vision clear for stars and sun."

In "Composed Upon Westminster Bridge" and "Grief," Wordsworth and Barrett accentuate immobility. For Wordsworth, "Ships, towers, domes, theatres, and temples lie" motionless "in the smokeless air," the "very houses seem asleep," and "all that mighty heart is lying still!" For Barrett, the true griever resembles "a monumental statue set / In everlasting watch and moveless woe"—a being that *cannot* "arise and go." While nothing is able to move in "Grief," the one force that does travel in Wordsworth's sonnet is the river: "The river glideth at his own sweet will." In Southern's "Of Language," language-clothed thought resembles a river with its gliding motion—it flees "swiftly," "whispers," "breathes," permits others to "run and sing," as well as to bring "reviving water" to "other souls." Southern's sonnet also makes reference to Wordsworth's comment about how the "very houses seem asleep." In "Of Language" it is language that wakes these houses up. As thought that has been clothed in words flees swiftly from "home to home," it also "*wakes* a sleeping fancy to explore / A magic land it never saw before / The world within, which there lay *slumbering*" (3; my italics). In chapter 2, I suggested that the slumbering houses in Wordsworth's sonnet evoked a prescience of death, especially considering the concluding line, "And all that mighty heart is lying still!" Wordsworth's city resembles Barrett's "monumental statue set"—a figure that will eventually crumble to the dust beneath, even though Barrett nevertheless still asks us to touch it. In "Of Language," it would appear that language has the capacity to wake up the past. In many ways language bears a resemblance to the future—if nothing else, language extends into the future while mortality prevents human beings from continuing to live in this world. For this reason, after men "clothe an evanescent, shrinking thought," they "send it forth." Language, then, gives inspired people the ability to bring the past to life in the same way that it brings them into dialogue with the future.

Southern furthers this idea in "Of Silence and Speech" (30), where she exposes the horror of silence in spite of its alleged merits:

OF SILENCE AND SPEECH

Silence—'tis said—is golden! yet it seems
To some the parchèd gold of desert sands,
Dreary and desolate, where mirage stands
Luring the thirsty traveller, who deems
That he shall drink, for he afar caught gleams
As of a shining lake beneath the sun,
Yet sadly is deceived, for he hath won
But phantoms bodiless as are his dreams.

Ah, when an eager, longing, lonely soul
Athirst for sympathy, companionship,
Meets Silence, 'tis more cruel than the grave!
But Speech, like summer thunder's passing roll,
Relieves the air and cools the fevered lip,
While its soft showers the drooping flowers lave.

"Of Silence and Speech" shares its rhyme scheme with only one other sonnet in the 136-sonnet volume, a later poem called "Disuse and Decay" (77): abba / acca / def / def. And the pairing between these two sonnets makes thematic sense. "Of Silence and Speech" is about the negative consequences that follow from silence—the unused or inaccessible faculty of speech—while "Disuse and Decay" discusses what will become of the "unused limb" as well as the "neglected soul." In "Disuse and Decay," the unused limb "must shrivel and decay" while the neglected soul "as surely pines, / Contracts, grows dim, no longer clearly shines, / Then flickers, and fades out." The same could be said of what happens when speech is unused or abandoned in "Of Silence and Speech." The sonnet begins by contrasting the misleading status of silence as "golden" with its reality as "the parchèd gold of desert sands." Here, we are again reminded of Elizabeth Barrett's two references to silence in the desert. The octave does not limit itself to an abba rhyme pattern but instead introduces a third rhyme so as to emphasize the difference between what the "thirsty traveller" *thinks* will be found in the desert and what turns out to be the case. Southern links the "phantoms" or hallucinations that trouble the traveler to the way his dreams are "bodiless."[21]

Southern's traveler ultimately thirsts for "sympathy" and "companionship." When the traveler's "eager, longing, lonely soul" meets silence instead, this fate is "more cruel than the grave!" While Barrett claims grief should embrace silence and thus resemble death, Southern exclaims that silence is *more cruel* than death itself. In the concluding lines to "Of Silence and Speech," speech is shown to have the exact same effect as tears. We saw a similar use of metaphor in Southern's "Of Language" where words bring "inspiration" from their "fountain" and additionally allow people to bring "reviving water" to "other souls." In "Of Silence and Speech," language resembles "summer thunder's passing roll," which ties speech to the "summer rain" imagery in "After Rain" (imagery that also relates falling "torrents" to tears). Similarly, speech relieves "the air and cools the fevered lip, / While its soft showers the drooping flowers lave." In summary, Southern's approach to silence and speech is not simply different from Barrett's, but, in fact, opposite; in Southern's work, whatever benefits silence may appear to bestow prove to be ultimately groundless. Southern takes issue with earlier nineteenth-century women poets' appreciation for silence—only language has the ability to guide us into the future tense.[22]

SOUTHERN'S CRITIQUE OF CHRISTINA ROSSETTI

As we have seen, Isabella Southern refers in her sonnets both to Wordsworth's "Composed Upon Westminster Bridge" and to Barrett's critique of Wordsworth, formulating, as it were, a third level of critique. Southern performs the same gesture with respect to Christina Rossetti and Rossetti's response to her brother, Dante Gabriel. In Southern's sonnet "Look Upward," we can see a distinct connection to Christina Rossetti's "An Echo from Willowwood," which was Rossetti's own revision of her brother's "Willowwood" sequence. Dante Gabriel Rossetti published the four-sonnet "Willowwood" sequence along with twelve other sonnets in *The Forthnightly Review* in 1869. His wife Elizabeth Eleanor Siddal had died six years before—in 1862—due to a likely suicide because of his infidelity to her.[23] Christina Rossetti, in turn, composed "An Echo from Willowwood" in 1870; it was published in 1890, seven years after her brother's death:

AN ECHO FROM WILLOWWOOD
"O ye, all ye that walk in Willowwood."
D. G. Rossetti

Two gazed into a pool, he gazed and she,
Not hand in hand, yet heart in heart, I think,
Pale and reluctant on the water's brink,
As on the brink of parting which must be.
Each eyed the other's aspect, she and he,
Each felt one hungering heart leap up and sink,
Each tasted bitterness which both must drink,
There on the brink of life's dividing sea.
Lilies upon the surface, deep below
Two wistful faces craving each for each,
Resolute and reluctant without speech:—
A sudden ripple made the faces flow
One moment joined, to vanish out of reach:
So those hearts joined, and ah! were parted so.

The main difference between Christina Rossetti's "Echo from Willowwood" and Dante Gabriel Rossetti's "Willowwood" sequence (not printed here) involves a shift in point of view. As we observed in chapter 3, Christina Rossetti's voice often migrates from place to place in her sonnets, even if any one given stance contradicts another. On its most obvious level, Rossetti's sonnet could be about two lovers who must part and whose parting is witnessed by the authorial persona, who takes the place of the god of Love from Dante Gabriel's sonnet. However, if we read the first-person speaker as corresponding to Love, this would permit Christina Rossetti to play the part of one of the lovers. "An Echo from Willowwood" might, then, tell the story of two people (any people) who most likely love each other but who are forced to part. And Rossetti could play the role of either of the two lovers or simply the part of the onlooker.

In "Look Upward" (123), Isabella Southern corrects Christina Rossetti's revision of her brother:

LOOK UPWARD

They walked one day together, he and she,
Along a rough field-path; a silent pair.
He inwardly repined, "There's naught to see
Upon a road like this, that leads nowhere."
While she, with beaming eyes, looked lovingly
At budding trees and hedgerows passing fair,

And higher yet, where on an azure sea
The cloudlets sailed without a shadowing care.

Was that one universe these creatures saw?
His gloomy brows were gathered to a frown,
While she forgot the beaten track worn brown,
And saw on every side a bounteous store
Of beauty, that transfigured earth's dull floor;
For she gazed up, while he looked ever down!

The alternating structure of Southern's first eight lines finds its impulse in the "he and she," which echoes Rossetti's "Two gazed into a pool, he gazed and she" and "Each eyed the other's aspect, she and he." Southern also repeats Rossetti's emphasis on silence. In Rossetti's case, the man and the woman gaze into a pool "without speech." In Southern's "Look Upward," the man and the woman are "a silent pair." Southern juxtaposes the attributes of her male and female wanderer with the abab rhyme scheme in the octave. For example, "he and she" rhymes with "naught to see" (the man's point of view) as well as with "looked lovingly" (the woman's perspective) and "azure sea" (part of the woman's viewpoint yet reminiscent of "the water" from both of the Rossettis' sonnets). Furthermore, "a silent pair" rhymes with "that leads nowhere" (the man's point of view) as well as with "passing fair" (the woman's perspective) and "shadowing care" (which seems at first glance to represent the man's standpoint but that reads in full "*without* a shadowing care" and therefore reflects the woman's angle of vision) (my italics).

In the last tercet of "Look Upward," the man that Southern describes looks down while the woman looks up. Southern relates what the woman in her sonnet sees as she looks up and contrasts this perspective with that of her male companion. Because Southern calls her sonnet "Look Upward," she compels us to sympathize with the woman in her sonnet and to take issue with the man. As her sonnet echoes Christina Rossetti's more closely than her brother's on the level of content, Southern leaves us with a puzzle. Who is the man and who is the woman described in "Look Upward"? An initial reading might suggest that the "silent pair" represents Dante Gabriel and Christina Rossetti. If we could safely say that Christina Rossetti looks upward while Dante Gabriel Rossetti does not, this reading might be plausible. And yet, as we have seen, Christina Rossetti criticizes Elizabeth Barrett in the preface to *"Monna Innominata"*; Barrett's problem as Rossetti articulates it, is that she is too happy. Indeed, if anything, Christina Rossetti looks down rather than up in her poems.

Then again, if we interpret Christina Rossetti's "An Echo from Willowwood" as a revision of her brother's "Willowwood" sequence, there are ways that she does "look upward" in comparison to him. His sequence stresses the fact that a wronged, narcissistic male lover looks down into the water and sees (in his own reflection) the reincarnation of a dead woman, who falls "back drowned" once Love stops singing. In Christina Rossetti's sonnet, on the other hand, both man and woman gaze *together* "into a pool"; both are alive and even though they long to unite, their faces join only for a moment before vanishing "out of reach." In *The Nineteenth-Century Sonnet,* Joseph Phelan suggests that by personifying Love, Dante Gabriel Rossetti directly imitates Dante's practice in *Vita Nuova.* As Phelan sees it, "One manifestation of this archaism is a renewed objectification of the beloved, something against which Barrett Browning and to a certain extent Meredith had struggled in their respective sequences" (118). Looking at Christina Rossetti's revision of "Willowwood," it appears that she, too, struggles against her brother's objectification of his beloved. Southern follows Christina Rossetti's lead: "Two gazed into a pool, he gazed and she" becomes, for Southern, "THEY walked one day together, he and she." Yet in both of the Rossettis' sonnets, an act of looking down occurs. It is this image that Southern counters. Her man and woman do not gaze into the water but instead walk along "a rough field-path." The sonnet is about different kinds of vision.

While the man in "Look Upward" believes there is "naught to see" and that the road "leads nowhere," the woman looks "lovingly" at "budding trees and hedgerows passing fair, / And higher yet." The woman forgets all about "the beaten track worn brown." Southern repeats Christina Rossetti's introductory word in her last line: "gazed." The first line of Christina Rossetti's sonnet reads "Two gazed into a pool, he gazed and she"; Southern takes issue with this claim in the last line of her sonnet: "For she gazed up, while he looked ever down!" Because the title of the sonnet is "Look Upward," it seems the woman in the sonnet plays the role of Isabella Southern herself. Gazing up, she abandons introspective reflections as well as narcissistic reflections, instead embracing the beauty of the natural world, which leads her "higher yet"—to divine as opposed to worldly sights and sound. The man in the sonnet speaks pessimistically inside himself—"He inwardly repined, 'There's naught to see / Upon a road like this, that leads nowhere.'" On the other hand, Southern implies that the woman who gazes around and upward at the natural and divine world is best prepared to break the silence of the pair.

"UPON THE PAST AND FUTURE": IN PRAISE OF ROBERT BROWNING

Without ever invoking them by name, Isabella Southern argues with Elizabeth Barrett and Christina Rossetti in her sonnets. Those to whom she explicitly gives positive attention in her poems are all men. Despite the fact that Dante Gabriel Rossetti receives negative treatment in "Look Upward," four men have sonnets written to them in Southern's collection: Shakespeare, John Milton, Robert Browning, and Leo Tolstoy. I would like to conclude this chapter by briefly examining Southern's sonnet, "Robert Browning" (63):

ROBERT BROWNING

Unmusical, grotesque sometimes thy lays,
And yet how deeply dost thou probe the heart!
Thou lay'st thy finger on its inmost smart
With healing magic; and the soul arrays
Reformèd forces in more subtile ways,
Upon more elemental, stronger lines;
Deep down into life's less exhausted mines
Thou darest, winning ore for future days.

Thy thoughts now saturate the minds of those
Who read them not: from thy deep well they drink,
Although of thee they never pause to think,
Nay, deem themselves perchance, thy bitter foes!
Upon the past and future thy hands close,
And *that* to *this* most firmly dost thou link.

This sonnet uses the following rhyme scheme, a pattern employed by nine other sonnets in Southern's collection: abba / acca / dee / dde. Significantly, Robert Browning is the only poet on Southern's list who did not write sonnets. Shakespeare and Milton excel in two different schools of sonnet writing. And Tolstoy, of course, wrote fiction. Consequently, Southern begins her sonnet by apologizing for the "unmusical" nature of Browning's work. However, Browning's poetry moves "deeply" into the heart, even in spite of its seemingly "grotesque" makeup. Southern repeats the word "deep" in the second, seventh, and tenth lines of her sonnet. Southern's primary interest in "Robert Browning" rests on her preoccupation with the passage of time. It seems from Southern's sonnet that Robert Browning dares to probe deep "down into life's less exhausted mines"; in so doing he wins "ore for future days." As his "hands close" upon the past and future, Browning binds the two firmly together: "And *that* to *this* most firmly dost thou link." Even though "Look Upward" encourages readers to follow the example of the woman in the sonnet—that is, readers are urged to look around and "upward" at the natural world—in "Robert Browning" Southern makes a different suggestion. Instead of writing musical sonnets about nature, the way that she has done, it might be better to follow Browning's example—to "probe the heart" and to dare deep "down into life's less exhausted mines." In Isabella Southern's opinion, while the rest of the world looks down rather than up, at the very least it will be able to drink from the "deep well" of healing, prophetic poetry, even if such verse has nothing to do with silence-centered sonnets or with any of the nineteenth-century women who gave birth to them.

As I have shown in this chapter, later nineteenth-century women poets struggled to invent a new kind of poetry—one that stood in contrast to the reticent work of their female precursors and contemporaries. While not exactly presenting a critique of Elizabeth Barrett, Maria Norris stresses aspects of Barrett's work that have nothing to do with the silence that Barrett pinpointed and cherished in many of her sonnets. Instead, Norris speaks of Barrett's poems as "minor music" possessing "dying cadence" that linger so as to counteract "the silence drear." Ultimately Norris sees Barrett as a muse figure, the dream of whom will inspire and facilitate future poetry. Dora Greenwell takes Norris's subtle revision of Barrett one step further. Placing her own sonnet "To Elizabeth Barrett Browning, in 1851" as part of a pendant, which concludes after Barrett's death in 1861, Greenwell illustrates a progression from feelings of inadequacy next to the living poet to a sense of strength after her death. Instead of being paralyzed by "hopeless grief," Greenwell discovers new powers in Barrett's absence.

Christina Rossetti incurs the same kinds of criticisms as those directed against Barrett. Dedicating an incomplete sonnet to Rossetti, Greenwell concludes her poem by reminding us that Rossetti's poetry functions as "the Song of Death." Regardless of the biblical references in Greenwell's poem, which stress the "divine" qualities of Rossetti's writing, we are not allowed to forget the morbid impulses that drive Rossetti's work. Michael Field pushes Greenwell's critique to a more complex level. Rossetti fails in Field's sonnet to occupy the role of Beatrice or Matilda in earlier sonnet sequences by male poets and to "slip into the universe" as a renowned female poet. Instead, Rossetti chose to bury herself "in a tomb." While Rossetti could have "breathed joy in earth and in [her] kind," she instead hid herself away in sadness, darkness, and silence. Field attempted to do something radically different—to write a daring new poetry that had never been written before. Indeed, it appears that we have only become able to embrace Field's revolutionary poetic goals in the late twentieth and the early twenty-first century.

Finally, in sonnets that bear witness to the sprit of her time, Isabella Southern explicitly rejects the silence-embracing sonnets of her female precursors as she breathlessly races into the twentieth century: an era when differences between male and female poets would begin to fall away.[24] Southern's sonnets reflect how Robert Browning came to replace Barrett in the literary canon and also how nineteenth-century women's sonnets (her own included) would strangely silence themselves and be supplanted by masculinized "elemental, stronger lines." However accurate Southern's predictions were, I think the time has come for us to look backwards once again to the very women poets who climbed either consciously or unconsciously into the "silent-bare" tombs of obscurity or grief. In these sonnets, the nearly invisible lines, the haunting gender reversals, the subtle intersections between the blank despair of death and the life of language and love, the persistent changes in address, the ambiguities that cloak potent and omnipresent references to the self, and the beseeching reactions against these retreats into indistinctness, will, I am sure, thoroughly surprise and enlighten us.

CONCLUSION

Women's Renunciation of the Sonnet Form

While male poets moved from amatory to political, social, and religious subjects in their sonnets, nineteenth-century British women mainly turned to sonnet writing as a means of confronting "hopeless grief." Charlotte Smith's *Elegiac Sonnets* of 1784, Helen Maria Williams's gentler sonnets of 1785, Anna Maria Smallpiece's sonnets in *Poems, Moral, Elegant and Pathetic* of 1796, Elizabeth Barrett's grieving sonnets of 1844 (together with her *Sonnets from the Portuguese* in 1850), and Christina Rossetti's later poetics of renunciation all thematize inconsolable sadness. Yet, a turning point occurs during the second half of the nineteenth century. As I have shown, Maria Norris, Dora Greenwell, and Michael Field refer to Barrett and Rossetti by name in sonnets that appear to praise their poetic heroines but that also offer subtle critiques of the very poets they seem to eulogize. Likewise, Isabella J. Southern, who published *Sonnets and Other Poems* in 1891, puts forth a dramatic revision of Smith, Barrett, and Rossetti. By explicitly rejecting silence, Southern enthusiastically leads us into the twentieth century.

For the women poets I analyze in my first three chapters, grief originates from unnamed sources. In the *Elegiac Sonnets,* Charlotte Smith varies her reason for bereavement from sonnet to sonnet (or else fails to specify any cause at all). Helen Maria Williams follows Smith's direction, although she introduces a more optimistic approach. Anna Maria Smallpiece confuses grief due to sickness with betrayal by a faithless friend with sadness because of a friend's death.

Elizabeth Barrett never provides a motivation for her despair (though biography and evidence in her poems point to her beloved brother's tragic death). Christina Rossetti writes of forgotten women from history whose indistinct grief she seems cryptically to share.

Described by a century of women sonneteers, grief is inextricably intertwined with silence. Smith equates her suffering with the "blank despair" of an unhappy exile; Barrett believes "full desertness" must be expressed "in silence like to death"; Rossetti ties the culmination of sadness to the "silence of love that cannot sing again." Not only do these poets claim that the justification behind their grief is untellable; they also presume the communication of their sadness can never fully occur. The figures beset by misery in these women's sonnets have no listening audience: the drowning mariner who utters inaudible cries, the "statue set / in everlasting watch and moveless woe," the "donna innominata" who did *not* speak "for herself."

Women do not simply liken their grief to wordlessness; rather, they suggest that this anguish may itself rise from the impossibility of speech. Smith's exiled wanderers cannot make their pain known, and the speaker, whose distress seems to have no derivation, identifies her predicament with their own. For Barrett, "irreparableness" combines incurable grief with her inability to incarnate nature in poems. And Rossetti troublingly reminds the reader that her "donna innominata" "cannot sing again."

I have suggested that women poets gravitated toward the sonnet form because, with its exigent rules of meter, syllable count, rhyme scheme, and structural shifts, it offered them a ready-made metaphor for the difficulties of articulation. Highly compressed and restrained, the sonnet helped to make inexpressibility visible. Yet the sonnet had always occupied an ambivalent ground: positioned between brevity and music, the "little song" ostensibly both can and cannot sing. It thus presented nineteenth-century women writers with a paradox that reflected their situation: their gestures of assertion were ultimately accomplished through rhetorical constructions that insisted on the stifling of assertion.

On the one hand, women poets needed to take the form away from the male sonneteers who had owned it for centuries. In so doing, women initiated what amounted to the first clearly recognizable female lyric tradition in Britain. On the other hand, the sonnet had not only been disparaged for a century prior to Smith's revival of the form, but it also continued to be critiqued after Smith by master sonneteers such as William Wordsworth and John Keats. Negatively contrasted with the epic, the sonnet makes Wordsworth think of nuns in "their convent's narrow room," while Keats feels uncomfortable that English must be chained by "dull rhymes." The swiftness with which sonnets must take place, the limits placed on what they can expose and their lack of inherent musicality (which Dante criticizes) all call this lyric form into question. Male poets resolve these dilemmas through the comfort of the sonnet's fixed shape and through its sharp, potentially revelatory turns. Revelation, however, is precisely what nineteenth-century women poets refuse to dramatize. They consequently do not follow the consolatory framework of elegiac sonnets by Thomas Gray and William Lisle Bowles; nor do they recapitulate Petrarch's amatory sonnet structure or implant something akin to Wordsworth's poetic encounters with the sublime.

Women sonneteers therefore blatantly violate the strategies of compensation and redemption that were often used by their male counterparts. As we have seen, Charlotte Smith's sonnets fall into two categories: they either court the feminized personifications that make speech possible or else they describe absolute wordlessness. This second category distinguishes Smith's work from that of her male precursors and contemporaries. Furthermore, Barrett's sonnets oppose Wordsworth's treatment of the sublime; while his sonnets move upwards and outwards with the turn from octave to sestet, hers burrow further inwards in order to create a more pronounced sense of voicelessness. And Rossetti rewrites not only the male-authored amatory sonnet tradition but even Barrett's own *Sonnets from the Portuguese,* when she attempts to draw a "more tender, if less dignified" portrait "than any drawn even by a devoted friend" (2:3, 86). For Isabella Southern, on the other hand, the appeal of silence is illusory; what seems golden to others reveals itself to be "the parchèd gold of desert sands / Dreary and desolate."

I have argued that famous nineteenth-century women poets such as Charlotte Smith, Elizabeth Barrett, and Christina Rossetti perform a four-step motion in their sonnets. They begin by confirming women's voicelessness; next they show how women's silence culminates in poetic speech; to illustrate this, they banish men from language altogether; finally, they struggle to eliminate gender through their poetry's double attraction to muteness and sound. For Charlotte Smith, neither male nor female personifications can speak; however, it is the feminine rather than the masculine incarnations that stimulate poetic language. Despite this gender reversal, Smith continually relates her speaker to the despondent male personifications whose expulsion from language is absolute. Yet, poetry lends both genders equal access to silence and voice. The writer (whether male or female, as Smith's sequence displays) achieves boundless poetic speech and also fails to translate emotions into words; this inaudibility (revealed in gaps, compression, elision, broken syntax) informs lyric poetry as a genre.

Like Smith, Elizabeth Barrett attests to women's silence—the "silent-bare" blankness of grief—and she also overturns conventional gender roles. Barrett at times mocks Wordsworth, with his "humble-lidded eyes, as one inclined / Before the sovran thought of his own mind," and even indirectly challenges him—"I tell you"—as being "incredulous of despair, half-taught in anguish." And she repeatedly undermines the male beloved's laurels in *Sonnets from the Portuguese* by depriving the man of the language he desires from her: "I drop it at thy feet." Rather, it is woman's silence (as opposed to man's speech) that makes up poetic language, for the lyric—as sonnets represent—occurs through pauses, confinement, and restraint: the "ren[t] garment of [the woman speaker's] life, in brief." Nevertheless, like Smith, Barrett eventually attempts to cancel out gender references, for she finally equates "the silence of [her] womanhood"—her divided position as "un[one]"; her torn words—with the trials of language: the act of splitting her "spirit so far off from myself. . . me. . . ." Just as the speech/silence opposition ceases to be a polarity for Barrett, so the male/female binary eventually fuses for her into the inseparable union required for the composition of true poetry.

Christina Rossetti counters Barrett by pushing her engagement with silence to another level. Both the premise and the conclusion of *"Monna Innominata"* acknowledge the unknown and nameless speaker's inability to sing. But Rossetti's sonnets closely resemble the project that Smith and Barrett undertake. To begin with, she hypothesizes that a silent woman—one who was merely written about at a distant point in history—might have shared her lover's "poetic aptitude." Then she writes a sonnet sequence that appears to confirm this woman's silence. Just like Smith and Barrett, however, Rossetti steadily inverts the gender alignments that her sequence presupposes. The female poetic speaker absorbs all other personae until it becomes unclear how to separate Rossetti from the "donna innominata" or the speaker from her addressee. And this speaker creates an echo chamber of self-references. Thus, not only does Rossetti mute masculinity by assimilating her male into her female persona, but she also excludes masculinity from her poetry's territory; her sonnets consist of ceaseless recitations of the speaker's silent but all-encompassing individuality. At the same time, the speaker's identity divides from itself, crossing over genders and historical periods. Because unrecalled women's sonnets both can and cannot "sing again," they must play a splintered role not unlike what poetry in general must perform. Simultaneously rupturing and consolidating personalities, *"Monna Innominata"* (or "M-on[no]-na In-no-mi[me]-nata") submits masculinity as well as femininity to poetry's divided status as silence and sound.

By uniting and disjoining gender and silence, nineteenth-century British women poets manipulated the very form that women of other nations avoided. Compellingly, twentieth- and twenty-first-century women poets in America as well as in England refuse to follow the example of their earlier British women counterparts. True, women poets such as Augusta Webster, Michael Field, and Edna St. Vincent Millay carried the sonnet from the end of the nineteenth century into the next.[1] Although contemporary women writers still draw energy from the form, "most women poets have shied away from the sonnet for decades."[2] In the end, the twentieth and twenty-first century "has brought a great flourishing of poetry by women, but most of that poetry has been free form" (Stout, "Fretting Not" 31). It seems that after taking the sonnet to the limits of renunciation, women began to rebel against the very social restraints that the sonnet permitted them to grieve.

Tracing a century of sonnets, I have shown how silence intensified in women's work; in the wake of this revival, women now revert back to the same freedom of form that seventeenth- and eighteenth-century British women poets claimed. Isabella Southern predicted this shift by rejecting Elizabeth Barrett in favor of Robert Browning (who did not write sonnets) as one who wins "ore for future days." Tightly holding the sonnet in their hands for one hundred years like "the essence sucked out of life," women finally drop the form at our feet.[3] Well-known twentieth-century male poets such as Robert Frost, W. H. Auden, and E. A. Robinson ardently embraced the sonnet, but women once again turned away, at last finding more unobstructed means to perform the lyric's complexly gendered dance between incoherence and clarity, brevity and wholeness, blankness and song.

NOTES

This book uses a consistent typographic format for the poems and their titles; this style may not reflect the poems' format as originally published: All lines align on the left (i.e., no lines have been indented), the titles are set in capital letters and without periods, and the first word of each poem begins with a capital letter, followed by lowercase.

NOTES TO INTRODUCTION

1. In *The Nineteenth-Century Sonnet* (New York: Palgrave, 2005), Joseph Phelan maintains that "[t]hanks to recent scholarship," critics now trace the sonnet revival back to Charlotte Smith, who developed "the 'elegiac sonnet' into a vehicle for the articulation of a certain type of intense and personal experience" (9). For earlier arguments about women's instrumental role in the sonnet revival, see Stuart Curran, *Poetic Form and British Romanticism* (Oxford: Oxford University Press, 1986), ch. 3, and Daniel Robinson, "Reviving the Sonnet: Women Romantic Poets and the Sonnet Claim," *European Romantic Review* 6 (1995): 98–127. When I speak of the "nineteenth century" in this book, I generally refer to the long nineteenth century, which, in the context of my study, begins with Smith's first publication of the *Elegiac Sonnets* in 1784 and ends with Isabella Southern's publication of *Sonnets and Other Poems* in 1891.
2. In *Eighteenth-Century Women Poets and Their Poetry: Inventing Agency, Inventing Genre* (Baltimore: The Johns Hopkins University Press, 2005), Paula R. Backsheider argues that "[w]ithout question, [Charlotte Smith] was a major contributor to the revival and is the poet associated with the rebirth of the sonnet as a popular form" (317). In *Desiring Voices: Women Sonneteers and*

Petrarchism (Carbondale: Southern Illinois University Press, 2000), Mary B. Moore explains that "Smith, not Wordsworth, is responsible for resurrecting the sonnet as a viable literary form after its neglect during the late seventeenth and most of the eighteenth centuries. Smith's book was the first in over a hundred years to use the sonnet form in sequence. Smith's sonnets are thus the originary text for the romantic sonnet" (152). And in "Charlotte Smith and British Romanticism," *South Central Review* 11 (1994), Curran suggests that Charlotte Smith is "the single most important voice that has been until quite recently suppressed from the historical record" (71).

3. See chapter 1 of Coleridge's *Biographia Literaria* (Clarendon, VT: Charles E. Tuttle Co., 1975) for an account of how Coleridge discovered Bowles's sonnets and why he admired them. See, for example, W. K. Wimsatt, "The Structure of Romantic Nature Imagery," in *The Verbal Icon* (Louisville: University Press of Kentucky, 1954), 103–16, and M. H. Abrams, "Structure and Style in the Greater Romantic Lyric," in *From Sensibility to Romanticism,* edited by F. W. Hilles and Harold Bloom (New York: Oxford University Press, 1965), 527–60.
4. For a discussion of Smith's changing reputation and Coleridge's shifting impression of Bowles, see Brent Raycroft, "From Charlotte Smith to Nehemiah Higginbottom: Revising the Genealogy of the Early Romantic Sonnet," *European Romantic Review* 9:3 (Summer 1998): 363–92.
5. Phelan makes this point about Coleridge's effort to remasculinize the sonnet through his admiration of the "'mild and manliest melancholy' of [Bowles's] poetry" (12).
6. Backsheider declares that "[t]oday, beside the slim output and mediocrity of the other revivalists (Thomas Edwards, Thomas Warton) Charlotte Smith seems a giant" (317).
7. Curran, *Poetic Form and British Romanticism,* 30. Note to "Stanzas suggested in a Steamboat off St. Bees' Heads" (1833).
8. Wordsworth's first published poem was a sonnet called "On Seeing Miss Helen Maria Williams Weep at a Tale of Distress." It was first published in the *European Magazine* XL (March 1787) under the pseudonym "Axiologus." Phelan argues that "[i]n aligning himself with Milton's 'manly and dignified' sonnets, Wordsworth is attempting to place some distance between himself and the female-dominated elegiac sonnet tradition of the late eighteenth century; and there is no doubt that part of his aim in returning to Milton was to 'remasculinise' the sonnet" (12). Jennifer Ann Wagner makes a similar claim about Wordsworth's turn to Milton in an effort to masculinize a female-dominated genre. See *A Moment's Monument: Revisionary Poetics and the Nineteenth-Century English Sonnet* (London: Associated University Presses, 1996), 13.
9. While Moore discusses Charlotte Smith's Elegiac Sonnets and Elizabeth

Barrett's Sonnets from the Portuguese in Desiring Voices, she does not focus on women's involvement in the nineteenth-century sonnet revival. Instead, Moore moves forward chronologically from Petrarch to Louise Labé, Lady Mary Wroth, Smith, Barrett, and Edna St. Vincent Millay.

10. Throughout *Little Songs* I will refer to EBB as Elizabeth Barrett instead of as Elizabeth Barrett Browning in part to distinguish her from Robert Browning and in part because she wrote all of the sonnets I discuss before she was married. When needed, I shorten Christina Rossetti to Rossetti; if I mention her brother I use his full name, Dante Gabriel Rossetti.
11. Paul Oppenheimer discusses the relationship between the sonnet and silence in *The Birth of the Modern Mind: Self, Consciousness, and the Invention of the Sonnet* (New York: Oxford University Press, 1989).
12. John Fuller, *The Sonnet*, No. 26 of the series *The Critical Idiom*, edited by John D. Jump (London: Methuen & Co., 1972), 3.
13. Gilbert and Gubar, *The Madwoman in the Attic* (New Haven, CT: Yale University Press, 1979), 546.
14. Rita Felski, *Literature after Feminism* (Chicago: University of Chicago Press, 2003). In *Little Songs,* I limit the geographical space of my study to England and the time period to the nineteenth century. In this way I remain aware of the limits of my sample and do not presume to extend my findings "into an all-encompassing theory of authorship" (88).
15. See Mellor, *Romanticism & Gender* (New York: Routledge, 1993), 7.
16. Lootens, *Lost Saints* (Charlottesville: University Press of Virginia, 1996), 2.
17. In Cheryl Glenn's words, "There is not one but rather many silences, and like the spoken or written, these silences are an integral part of the strategies that underlie and permeate rhetoric. Thus, silence is at once inside the spoken and on its near and far sides as well." See *Unspoken: A Rhetoric of Silence* (Carbondale: Southern Illinois University Press, 2004), 160.
18. For an intelligent and thought-provoking study of the relationship between Victorian women's writing, silence, and the literary canon, see Lootens, *Lost Saints*.
19. Barrett (Browning), *The Brownings' Correspondence,* edited by Philip Kelley, Ronald Hudson and Scott Lewis (Winfield, KS: Wedgestone Press, 1984–), Vol. 10: 14. From this point on, I will refer to *The Brownings' Correspondence* as *BC*.
20. Marjorie Stone devotes her book *Elizabeth Barrett Browning* (London: Macmillan, 1995) to an exploration of "how intersecting ideologies of gender and genre, sometimes compounded by the artificial barriers of historical periodization, have acted to obscure or conceal Barrett Browning's poetical achievement in a range of poetical or literary modes" (8). In Jerome J. McGann's words, "A number of books about Rossetti appeared in the early

1930s, several quite good, but after that she virtually disappeared from the academic scene for almost three decades; and even then she remained a marginal interest for another ten years or more." "The Religious Poetry of Christina Rossetti," in *Victorian Women Poets: Emily Bronte, Elizabeth Barrett Browning, Christina Rossetti,* edited by Joseph Bristow (New York: St. Martin's Press, 1995), fn 7, 185–86.

21. Alison Chapman, *The Afterlife of Christina Rossetti* (New York: St. Martin's Press, 2000), 36.
22. Felski, *Literature after Feminism,* 91.
23. Natalie M. Houston, "Affecting Authenticity: *Sonnets from the Portuguese* and *Modern Love," Studies in the Literary Imagination* 35:2 (Fall 2002): 103.
24. For this reason I am wary of arguments that depend too much on what Joan W. Scott calls "the evidence of 'experience'"; in Scott's words, "It is precisely this kind of appeal to experience as uncontestable evidence and as an originary point of explanation—as a foundation upon which analysis is based—that weakens the critical thrust of histories of difference." See Scott's "Experience" in *Feminists Theorize the Political,* edited by Judith Butler and Joan W. Scott (New York: Routledge, 1992), 24.
25. Butler acknowledges the importance of writing about women so as to combat the "pervasive cultural condition in which women's lives were either misrepresented or not represented at all." *Gender Trouble: Feminism and the Subversion of Identity* (London: Routledge, 1990), 4. However, she also urges us to abandon our attachment to the notion of prediscursive sex- or gender-specific identities. For Butler, "gender norms are finally phantasmatic, impossible to embody" (179). In *Gender Trouble,* Butler makes three important points: 1) the gendered self is produced through the stylized repetition of acts through time—that is, through performativity; 2) gender serves as the discursive/cultural means by which sexual difference is established as prediscursive; 3) ultimately, both gender and sex need to be thought of as culturally constructed categories.
26. Rather than relying on what many critics misperceive as the formulaic assuredness of her early work, Butler embraces uncertainty in her more recent studies. Instead of maintaining her earlier proposition that both sex and gender are culturally constructed categories, she explains that rather than being prior to discourse or enabled by discourse, sexual difference remains "*a question* that prompts a feminist inquiry, it is something that cannot quite be stated, that troubles the grammar of the statement, and that remains, more or less permanently, to interrogate." *Undoing Gender* (London: Routledge, 2004), 178. For this reason, Claire Colebrook is mistaken when, in proposing a revision to Judith Butler's interpretation of sex and gender, she writes, "As we have already noted, Butler's concept of gender as effected

through performance precludes the notion of positive sexual difference. Sex is produced as that which gender has always already named and stabilised." *Gender* (New York: Palgrave, 2004), 243.

27. Women's effort to silence resistance, when silence itself was the object of this resistance, resulted for nineteenth-century women sonneteers in what they term "blank despair" or "hopeless grief." As Juliana Schiesari shows in *The Gendering of Melancholia: Feminism, Psychoanalysis, and the Symbolics of Loss in Renaissance Literature* (Ithaca, NY: Cornell University Press, 1992), men alone were thought capable of melancholy during the Renaissance. Jahan Ramazani locates the shift from compensatory to non-consolatory poems of mourning in twentieth-century work. See, for example, *Poetry of Mourning: The Modern Elegy from Hardy to Heaney* (Chicago: The University of Chicago Press, 1994). In *Little Songs,* I propose a different model of literary history, showing how women sonneteers invented contemporary elegiac poetics a century in advance. Compelling recent studies of how mourning and melancholy operate (written about poetry, race, and politics, respectively) include David G. Riede's *Allegories of One's Own Mind: Melancholy in Victorian Poetry* (Columbus: The Ohio State University Press, 2005), Anne Anlin Cheng's *The Melancholy of Race* (Oxford: Oxford University Press, 2000), and Judith Butler's *Precarious Life: The Powers of Mourning and Violence* (New York: Verso, 2004).
28. The list of currently known and forgotten nineteenth-century female sonneteers that I provide in this book is necessarily selective. Discussing women sonneteers who appeared in sonnet anthologies and in criticism of the nineteenth century, Houston remarks, "The sonnets of Elizabeth Barrett Browning were especially praised, and Charlotte Smith, Anna Seward, Felicia Hemans, Christina Rossetti, Eliza Cook, Adelaide Procter, Dora Greenwell, Augusta Webster, Alice Thompson, Emily Pfeiffer and many others were frequently mentioned in accounts of important sonnet writers." "Towards a New History: Fin-de-siècle Women Poets and the Sonnet," in *Essays and Studies 2003: Victorian Women Poets,* edited by Alison Chapman (Cambridge: D. S. Brewer, 2003), 152. In her essay Houston chooses to examine sonnets by Mathilde Blind, Michael Field, and Rosamund Marriott Watson. Considering the large number of women poets who contributed to the nineteenth-century sonnet revival, exciting work still remains to be done in this field.

NOTES TO CHAPTER 1

1. Wordsworth's note to "Stanzas Suggested in a Steamboat off Saint Bees' Heads," from his "Poems Composed or Suggested during a Tour, in the Summer of 1833."

2. I will follow Smith's own English spelling of "Werther" as "Werter" throughout this chapter.
3. For background on Smith's life, see *The Collected Letters of Charlotte Smith,* edited by Judith Phillips Stanton (Bloomington: Indiana University Press, 2003).
4. The final two-volume edition of the *Elegiac Sonnets* contained ninety-two sonnets, together with other elegies. The poems continue to draw from more and more voices as the collection expands. Three Petrarchan translations from the first and second editions extend to four in the third edition; three sonnets taken from Goethe's Werter in the 1784 collection expand to five in the third and fourth editions. In the fifth edition, Smith adds three sonnets originally included in her first novel, *Emmeline,* and in the sixth edition she goes on to add five from her next novel, *Celestina.* When the collection had reached its final version it contained a total of thirty-six poems communicated by ventriloquized voices.
5. See Esther Schor, *Bearing the Dead: The British Culture of Mourning from the Enlightenment to Victoria* (Princeton, NJ: Princeton University Press, 1994), 61.
6. Bowles's *Fourteen Sonnets, Elegiac and Descriptive* (1789) was published in nine distinct editions in fifteen years. The difference in the effect of Bowles's and Smith's escalating prefaces, Schor argues, is that "Smith's sonnets come to indict the moral authority of her audience" while Bowles' sonnets "come to invoke the moral authority of God" (61).
7. See Daniel White, "Autobiography and Elegy: The Early Romantic Poetics of Thomas Gray and Charlotte Smith," in *Early Romantics: Perspectives in British Poetry from Pope to Wordsworth,* edited by Thomas Woodman (New York: St. Martin's Press, 1998), 65.
8. See Deborah Kennedy, "Thorns and Roses: The Sonnets of Charlotte Smith," *Women's Writing* 2:1 (1995): 49.
9. Charlotte Smith, *Elegiac Sonnets: 1789* (New York: Woodstock Books, 1992), 1.
10. Jerome McGann, *The Poetics of Sensibility: A Revolution in Literary Style* (Oxford: Clarendon Press, 1996), 157. In "*Elegiac Sonnets:* Charlotte Smith's Formal Paradoxy" (*Papers on Language and Literature: A Journal for Scholars and Critics of Language and Literature* 39: 2 [Spring 2003]: 185–220), Daniel Robinson reminds us that originally "the Greek elegy expressed grief; but the form broadened widely with Latin adaptations, such as Ovid's love elegies, *Amores,* to include almost any kind of subject" (186).
11. In her book *Romanticism, Lyricism, and History* (New York: State University of New York Press, 1999), Sarah Zimmerman reasons that Smith's "autobiographical poet's absorption in private sorrows operates with a theatrical dynamic," engaging audiences in an easy shift "between personal and social

dilemmas" (xv). Zimmerman backs up this argument with discerning studies of early editions of the poems ("the intensely autobiographical quality" of the single poems per page and the engravings that accompany several sonnets) (48). However, we might note that these eighteenth-century marketing features no longer apply to Smith's work; in Stuart Curran's 1993 edition, more than one poem is printed by page, with no illustrations.

12. Janet Todd, *Sensibility: An Introduction* (London: Methuen, 1986), 4.
13. Adela Pinch, *Strange Fits of Passion: Epistemologies of Emotion, Hume to Austen* (Stanford, CA: Stanford University Press, 1996), 66.
14. See also Labbe, "Selling One's Sorrows: Charlotte Smith, Mary Robinson and the Marketing of Poetry," *The Wordsworth Circle* 25:2 (1994): 68–71. Labbe and Sarah Zimmerman make similar points about Smith's techniques of self-presentation. See Zimmerman, *Romanticism, Lyricism, and History* and "Charlotte Smith's Letters and the Practice of Self-Presentation," *Princeton University Library Chronicle* 53 (1991): 50–77.
15. Labbe, *Charlotte Smith: Romanticism, Poetry and the Culture of Gender,* 166. Labbe's tendency to rely on assumptions about the autobiographical nature of Smith's sonnets betrays itself in various ways throughout her book. For example, in the introduction, "Embodying the Author," Labbe discusses Smith's "Sonnet LXII: Written on passing by moon-light through a village, while the ground was covered with snow." She theorizes that in this sonnet, "Smith simultaneously enacts her gender in her plea for help and her womanly despair, and rejects such a role in her wandering about" (13). However, to readers of Smith's novels (and during her lifetime Smith's readers were privy to details from her novels in a way that we no longer are today) it is clear that this sonnet first appeared in Smith's novel *The Old Manor House* (published in 1794, before its appearance in the seventh edition of the *Elegiac Sonnets,* Vol. 2 in 1795) and that it was supposedly written by the hero Mr. Orlando Somerive as he wanders the countryside searching for his lost love, Monimia. Labbe makes no mention of this novel in her introduction and does not refer to it for nearly 100 pages.
16. Phelan, *The Nineteenth-Century Sonnet,* 46–47.
17. Backsheider, *Eighteenth-Century Women Poets and Their Poetry,* 332. Backsheider views the "number of critics who have recognized a double voice" in Smith's sonnets as an improvement on purely autobiographical readings: "Adela Pinch and Mary Moore, for instance, both see Smith juxtaposing literary tropes and personal experience. Kathryn Pratt demonstrates that the speaker functions as both spectator and spectacle, and she uses individual sonnets as examples" (332).
18. The detailed footnotes in Curran's edition of Smith's *Elegiac Sonnets* provide the most basic information from her novels. For Sonnet 85, we learn only

that it was printed "in Smith's *The Young Philosopher: A Novel* (1798), where it is written by Mrs. Glenmorris to accompany the botanical drawings of her daughter Medora" (73). This explanation offers no evidence of the financial ruin to which the poem contextually alludes; nor does it set up Sonnets 85 and 86 as responding to one other. For Sonnet 86, we are merely told that it is "written by Delmont to his mother-in-law Mrs. Glenmorris as he awaits favorable winds for crossing from Wales to Ireland" (74). These insufficient details suggest that to achieve full understanding of Smith's sonnets, we must (like Smith's contemporaries) read the many novels in which her poems first appeared.

19. As we will see in Elizabeth Barrett's work, eighteenth- and nineteenth-century poets frequently correlated flowers with poetry itself. Thus, Smith begins the first poem of her collection, "The partial Muse has from my earliest hours / Smiled on the rugged path I'm doom'd to tread, / And still with sportive hand has snatch'd wild flowers, / To weave fantastic garlands for my head" (13). Read in this context, Sonnet 85's opening exclamation, "The fairest flowers are gone!," intimates that Smith's own "fair" poetry has been swept away—only Reason (masculine or feminine) commands her heart in the closing line.
20. For example, "The spot where pale Experience hangs *her* head" (44; my italics).
21. Smith was a strong supporter of Mary Wollstonecraft, who made a similar argument about detaching women from pure emotion and aligning them with reason through education.
22. See Edmund Burke, *A Philosophical Enquiry into the Origin of our Ideas of the Sublime and Beautiful,* edited by Adam Phillips (New York: Oxford University Press, 1990), 65.
23. Backsheider observes that Smith echoes earlier poems in this sonnet: "Again the poem echoes earlier poems, including Dryden's many meditations on Reason's wavering light" (335).
24. Smith quotes line 63 from "The Passions: An Ode to Music" in Sonnet 85, "The fairest flowers are gone!"—a sonnet that was printed first in her novel *The Young Philosopher*. See *The Young Philosopher* (Lexington: University Press of Kentucky, 1999), fn 32, p. 358.
25. James Thomson, *The Seasons* (London: Nonesuch Press, 1927), 126, 129, 136, 141–42, 147.
26. John Milton, *The Complete Poetry and Selected Prose of John Milton* (New York: The Modern Library, 1950), 33–34.
27. William Hayley, Esq., *Poems and Plays,* vol. 1 (London: T. Cadell, 1785), Epistle I: 3–4, 6, 8–10, 12, 14; Epistle II: 9, 33–34, 46–47, 52.
28. Moore comments about Sonnet 9: "Associating the erotic literary tradition

with shallow feeling and with masculinity, contrasting the rude pastoral shepherd with the feeling speaker, Smith seems to imply that male voices ignore or are ignorant of actual suffering" (158). As the "rude pastoral shepherd" is only one of two distinct types of silenced masculine personifications (and Smith persistently identifies her speaker with the opposing kind: the wanderer, mariner, exile, etc.), I only agree with Moore's reading in part.

29. See Curran, *Poetic Form and British Romanticism,* 30.
30. See *The Poems of Gray, Collins and Goldsmith,* edited by Roger Lonsdale (London: Longmans, 1969), 67–68.
31. See Wimsatt, "The Structure of Romantic Nature Imagery," 103–16, and Abrams, "Structure and Style in the Greater Romantic Lyric," 527–60.
32. Sylvia Mergenthal, "Charlotte Smith and the Romantic Sonnet Revival," in *Feminist Contributions to the Literary Canon: Setting Standards of Taste,* edited by Susanne Fendler (New York: The Edwin Mellen Press, 1997), 71.
33. Raycroft, "From Charlotte Smith to Nehemiah Higginbottom: Revising the Genealogy of the Early Romantic Sonnet," 375.
34. See Bowles, *Fourteen Sonnets, Elegiac and Descriptive,* 9. Robinson also uses this sonnet by Bowles to show how "Bowles's sonnet offers a sense of hope that Smith's lacks" as Bowles's sonnets in general "tend to lack the immediacy of grief that mark hers, affecting more of a grief-stricken pose than heartfelt sorrow." See "Reviving the Sonnet: Women Romantic Poets and the Sonnet Claim" (*European Romantic Review* 6: 1 [1995]: 98–127) (115).
35. Even though Bowles resembles Smith in his use of masculinized individuals and feminized abstractions, I am crediting Smith with this innovation as she published her sonnets before he did.
36. Steven Knapp, *Personification and the Sublime: Milton to Coleridge* (Cambridge, MA: Harvard University Press, 1985), 36.
37. In Book II of *Paradise Lost,* Milton describes Death as the "other shape, / If shape it might be call'd that shape had none / Distinguishable in member, joynt, or limb, / Or substance might be call'd that shadow seem'd" (133).
38. Immanuel Kant, *Critique of Judgment,* translated by Werner S. Pluhar (Indianapolis: Hackett, 1987), 135.
39. Wordsworth read these poems (his own first published poem in 1787 was a sonnet inspired by Williams, "On Seeing Miss Helen Maria Williams Weep at a Tale of Distress"), and surely drew inspiration from them, although he claimed he turned to sonnet writing because of Milton alone. Wordsworth's first published poem appeared in the *European Magazine* XL (March 1787) under the pseudonym "Axiologus."
40. See, for example, *Poems, Moral, Elegant and Pathetic: And Original Sonnets by Helen Maria Williams* (London, 1796), 213–20. I was able to examine at the British Library both an early copy of this manuscript and Anna Maria

Smallpiece's volume, *Original Sonnets, and Other Small Poems* (London: J. Johnson, 1805).

41. See *A Century of Sonnets: The Romantic-Era Revival,* edited by Paula R. Feldman and Daniel Robinson (New York: Oxford University Press, 1999), 42–44.
42. Smallpiece, *Original Sonnets, and Other Small Poems,* 40.
43. Williams, *Poems, Moral, Elegant and Pathetic,* 216.
44. Smallpiece, *Original Sonnets, and Other Small Poems,* 1–3, 6, 8–9, 33, 36.
45. Ibid., 4, 8, 37–38, 45.
46. For an account of the only three existing reviews of Smallpiece's poems, see Stephen C. Behrendt, "In Search of Anna Maria Smallpiece," *Women's Writing* 7:1 (2000): 55–73. Behrendt also discusses Smallpiece's sonnets in "Telling Secrets: The Sonnets of Anna Maria Smallpiece and Mary F. Johnson," *European Romantic Review* (Special Issue: The Romantic-Period Sonnet) 13 (2002): 393–410. He is not as convinced as I am about the strong homoerotic impulses that drive Smallpiece's work.
47. Smallpiece uses variations on the word "friend" such as "friend sincere" (2), "false friend" (10), "Friend belov'd" (20), "friendship faithful" (27), "distant friend" (32), and "faithless friends" (33) at least forty-two times in her collection of fifty-one sonnets.
48. It is important to note, too, that Smallpiece removes the male gender of some naturalized personifications such as the "fainting wretch" (24) reminiscent of Bowles, the "poor sailor" (24), and the "night trav'ller" (44). This further reinforces her implicit affiliation with them.
49. In "Wordsworth and Gray's Sonnet on the Death of West," Peter J. Manning points out that "the governing contrast between abounding nature and the withered speaker in the sonnet derives from the conventions of Italian Renaissance love poetry in which the lover mourns the loss of his beloved" (*SEL: Studies in English Literature* 22:3 [Summer 1982]: 515). Manning also calls our attention to other moments in Gray's sonnet that imply his love for West was sexual in nature. For example, Gray uses the word "fruitless" (which can mean "having no offspring") instead of "fruitlessly." Furthermore, the phrase "imperfect joys" in line 8 "echoes a Restoration sub-genre of erotic poetry concerned with sexual impotence and frustration" (515).

NOTES TO CHAPTER 2

1. After 1850, and after her marriage to Robert Browning, Barrett turned away from the sonnet form, working instead on alternate forms, such as the epic in her novel-in-verse, *Aurora Leigh* (1857). In *Elizabeth Barrett Browning, Woman*

and Artist (Chapel Hill: The University of North Carolina Press, 1988), Helen Cooper relates the "formal discipline" of the sonnet to "the speaker's imprisonment": "The decision to leave the 'close room' of the *Sonnets* was paralleled by Barrett's decision to leave her room in Wimpole Street" (109).

2. Although Barrett derived creative energy from her attraction to the constraints of the sonnet form, she also shielded her genius through these very constraints. For this reason, Barrett's brilliance is more apparent to the casual reader in her letters than it is in her poems. In his introduction to *The Letters of Elizabeth Barrett Browning to Her Sister Arabella,* Scott Lewis calls attention to the discrepancy between Barrett's epistolary and poetic accounts of the same events, concluding that the former is "in many ways more evocative" than the latter (xxxi).
3. See Esther Schor, *Bearing the Dead: The British Culture of Mourning from the Enlightenment to Victoria*. Schor argues that Wordsworth himself "would use [Gray's] Sonnet's central figure of thought, the elegiac topos of the failed response, as the motivating trope of the Intimations Ode" (57). In her critique of Wordsworth, Barrett may indirectly echo the elegiac sonnets that his work at once dismisses and embeds.
4. It would have been difficult for Barrett not to think of Wordsworth's "Elegiac Stanzas: Suggested by a Picture of Peele Castle" (1807) when her own brother drowned in 1840. As I will discuss later, it was at this point in her career that her relationship with Wordsworth became especially intense.
5. See Jonathan Culler, "On the Negativity of Modern Poetry: Friedrich, Baudelaire, and the Critical Tradition," in *Languages of the Unsayable: The Play of Negativity in Literature and Literary Theory,* edited by Sanford Budick and Wolfgang Iser (New York: Columbia University Press, 1989). Culler identifies two approaches to negativity in the Western tradition: a model that "prepare[s] for aesthetic recuperation" and a non-recuperative sort that he relates to Paul de Man's view of the "unpredictable play of the letter" as well as to Jacques Derrida's reading of the Platonic *khora* (205).
6. Elizabeth Barrett, "Sonnet XIII," *A Variorum Edition of Elizabeth Barrett Browning's* Sonnets from the Portuguese, edited by Miroslava Wein Dow (New York; The Whiston Publishing Company, 1980), 46. I will use the *Variorum Edition* to quote from Barrett's *Sonnets from the Portuguese:* when I cite Barrett's other poems, I will use *The Complete Works of Elizabeth Barrett Browning,* edited by Charlotte Porter and Helen Browning, 6 vols. (New York: Thomas Y. Crowell & Co., 1900, reprinted 1973 by New York: AMS Press).
7. See Mary Russell Mitford, *Recollections of a Literary Life* (New York: Harper and Brothers, 1852). As Mitford made public, "this tragedy [of her brother's drowning] nearly killed Elizabeth Barrett"; she had insisted against her father's will that Edward stay by her bedside in Torquay, therefore feeling

herself to be the cause of his nearby death (170–71).

8. Angela Leighton, *Elizabeth Barrett Browning* (Bloomington: Indiana University Press, 1986), 80.
9. *The Letters of Elizabeth Barrett Browning,* vol. 2, edited by Frederic G. Kenyon (New York: Macmillan, 1899), 14–15.
10. As I established in the introduction, Oppenheimer disputes the sonnet's supposed musical status, illustrating how the sonnet moves not toward but away from an already existing song form. While Barrett believed poetry differed from grief in its "singing" nature, she persistently called this assumption into question through her use of the sonnet form.
11. Marjorie Stone argues that "Barrett Browning clearly subscribed to many Romantic ideologies" (*Elizabeth Barrett Browning* 11). These include "the continuing attraction of Romantic Prometheanism, the Romantic cult of transcendent artistic genius, Romantic tropes of the sublime and the revisionary struggle with Milton and Dante" (10–11). However, Stone suggests that Barrett was also led to question many Romantic principles "given the critical distance fostered by her gender" (11). I agree with this line of argument and will use this chapter to further investigate Barrett's simultaneous attraction to and revision of Wordsworth's poetics.
12. Barrett's 1838 sonnet to Mitford deprecates, "I will not proudly say / As better poets use, 'These *flowers* I lay,'" and her final Portuguese sonnet concludes, "take [these verses], as I used to do / Thy flowers" (*The Complete Works,* vol. 2, 98; vol. 3, 248). In "Anthologies and the Making of the Poetic Canon," Natalie M. Houston points out that the "root meaning of the word *anthology* is a garland of flowers, or bouquet." See *A Companion to Victorian Poetry,* edited by Richard Cronin, Alison Chapman, and Antony H. Harrison (Boston: Blackwell, 2002), 367.
13. At the beginning of her article "Elizabeth Barrett Browning: Cross-Dwelling and the Reworking of Female Poetic Authority," Linda M. Shires reminds us of another famous writer's negative reaction to aspects of Barrett's poetry. As editor of the Cornhill magazine, William Makepeace Thackeray rejected one of Barrett's poems because he believed it to be "highly inappropriate for his audience"; Barrett's exchange with Thackeray in 1861 "forcefully exposes," as Shires makes evident, "not just literary values in crisis, but also authorship in crisis. In particular, the exchange exposes an enforced split between roles of the analytical poet and the domestic lady, a separation of roles which Barrett Browning's career both publicly exposed and dramatically reworked, but could not entirely evade." *Victorian Literature and Culture* 30:2 (2002): 327–28.
14. John Woolford makes the same observation about the double meaning of the word "ebb" in "Elizabeth Barrett and the Wordsworthian Sublime," *Essays in*

Criticism: A Quarterly Journal of Literary Criticism 45:1 (1995): 36–56.

15. The attention that Barrett draws to her own identity here serves to distinguish her writing from Charlotte Smith's; as we have seen, Smith speaks from the point of view of many ventriloquized voices.
16. In her sonnet to Haydon, Barrett echoes Wordsworth's own sonnets to the same painter—in particular, one published in 1816 that identifies the painter's skill with the poet's own, beginning "High is our calling, Friend!" and another on Haydon's picture of Napolean: "the one Man that laboured to enslave the World" much like the "unguilty Power" of the sun.
17. I take issue here with Jerome Mazzaro's opposing claim; where Mazzaro stresses Barrett's interest in sublimity, I see her interest as a framework for revision and critique. "Mapping Sublimity: Elizabeth Barrett Browning's *Sonnets from the Portuguese*," *Essays in Literature* 2 (1991): 166–79.
18. J. Hillis Miller, *The Linguistic Moment: From Wordsworth to Stevens* (Princeton, NJ: Princeton University Press, 1985), 74.
19. *The Prose Works of William Wordsworth*, vol. 2, edited by A. B. Grosart (London, 1876), 64; Karen Mills-Courts, *Poetry as Epitaph: Representation and Poetic Language* (Baton Rouge: Louisiana State University Press, 1990).
20. Jacques Derrida, *Writing and Difference*, translated by Alan Bass (Chicago: University of Chicago Press, 1978), 5.
21. In order to help him appreciate Wordsworth's poetry, Barrett writes in 1842 to her former Greek tutor, Hugh Stuart Boyd, "Read first, to put you into good humour, the sonnet written on Westminster bridge" (*BC* 6:126).
22. Wordsworth's sonnet abounds in death references: the "deep" calmness, the disinterest of nature ("at his own sweet will"), the "very houses" that "seem asleep," the stillness of "all that mighty heart," the exclamation to God, as if in despair.
23. Clearly, Wordsworth's City is "bare" in its link to death, but the extricability of silence from bareness here is also indicative of the oscillating motion his poetry enacts.
24. In "Sonnet and Sonnet Sequence," Alison Chapman uses two of Barrett's 1844 sonnets, "The Soul's Expression" and "Insufficiency," to argue that Barrett critiques Wordsworth's sonnet on the sonnet by communicating "the dangers of the transcendental sublime." *A Companion to Victorian Poetry*, edited by Richard Cronin, Alison Chapman and Antony H. Harrison (Boston: Blackwell, 2002), 101–2.
25. Barrett's 1838 sonnets find their counterparts in her 1844 collection. Like her "Bereavement" / "Consolation" pendant of 1838, "Grief" (1844) addresses the potentially incapacitating effect of mourning; in both "To Mary Russell Mitford in her garden" (1838) and "On a portrait of Wordsworth by B. R. Haydon" (1844), the speaker feigns inferiority with respect to a rival artist

who stands in closer proximity to nature than she does. The latter group of poems, however, shifts emphasis from the overcoming of limitations (those of grief, silence, conventional femininity, etc.) to the paralysis of "hopeless grief." If nature and its poetic embodiment are feminized and dismissed in Barrett's 1838 Mitford sonnet, this rejection develops in Barrett's 1844 Haydon sonnet into a critique of the Wordsworthian sublime.

26. Phelan also takes issue with recent critics who, in his words, "have described the *Sonnets from the Portuguese* as a narrative of self-emancipation" (56). Phelan argues that, instead, the *Sonnets* stage "the myth of rescue developed and sustained by Elizabeth Barrett and Robert Browning" (58). For reasons that will become clear in the rest of this chapter, I disagree with Phelan's line of argument as well as with easy narratives of transcendence and recuperation in the *Sonnets.*
27. Alison Chapman, "Mesmerism and Agency in the Courtship of Elizabeth Barrett and Robert Browning," *Victorian Literature and Culture* (1998): 313.
28. Sharon Smulders, "'Medicated Music': Elizabeth Barrett Browning's *Sonnets from the Portuguese,*" *Victorian Literature and Culture* 23 (1995): 200.
29. See "Love's Measurement in Elizabeth Barrett Browning's *Sonnets from the Portuguese,*" *Studies in Browning and His Circle* 21 (1997): 58
30. While the focus of Felman's book *The Scandal of the Speaking Body* is on speech rather than writing, many of her claims are relevant to Barrett's sonnets, which also address problems of speech as a *bodily* act. In her afterword to the new edition of Felman's book (Stanford, CA: Stanford University Press, 2003), Judith Butler writes, "The 'I' is thus embarrassed by its proclamation because it seeks to represent itself, but finds that it is more than can be represented. To the extent that this 'more' is signified by the body, it follows that the body interferes with every promise. The body is at once the organic condition of promise making and the sure guarantor of its failure" (119).
31. In *Giving an Account of Oneself* (New York: Fordham University Press, 2005), Butler relates her earlier theories of how both sex and gender are socially constructed to the difficulty with which she can give an account of herself: "There is a bodily referent here, a condition of me that I can point to, but that I cannot narrate precisely, even though there are no doubt stories about where my body went and what it did and did not do. The stories do not capture the body to which they refer. Even the history of this body is not fully narratable. To be a body is, in some sense, to be deprived of having a full recollection of one's life. There is a history to my body of which I can have no recollection" (38).
32. "This Living Hand, now Warm and Capable" in *John Keats: A Critical Edition of the Major Works,* edited by Frank Kermode (London: Oxford University Press, 1990), 331. Interesting work could be done on Barrett's revisions of the

sublime as mediated by Keats's own rewriting of Wordsworthian tropes.

33. Barbara Neri, "A Lineage of Love: The Literary Bloodlines of Elizabeth Barrett Browning's *Sonnets from the Portuguese,*" *Studies in Browning and His Circle: A Journal of Criticism, History, and Bibliography* 23 (2000): 61.
34. Dorothy Mermin, *Elizabeth Barrett Browning: The Origins of a New Poetry* (Chicago: University of Chicago Press, 1989), 130.
35. Ibid., 131. This tension between attraction and attractiveness has implications for speech and silence. In her article "The Female Poet and the Embarrassed Reader: Elizabeth Barrett Browning's *Sonnets from the Portuguese,*" Mermin pinpoints this strain: "Traditionally in English love poetry the man loves and speaks, the woman is beloved and silent. In *Sonnets from the Portuguese,* however, the speaker casts herself not only as the poet who loves, speaks, and is traditionally male, but also as the silent, traditionally female beloved." *ELH* 48:2 (1981): 352.
36. Paul de Man, *Blindness and Insight: Essays in the Rhetoric of Contemporary Criticism* (Minneapolis: University of Minnesota Press, 1971, reprinted 1983), 209.
37. Even though the "she" in "A slumber did my spirit seal" reads as distinct from the speaker of the poem, de Man points out that "Wordsworth is one of the few poets who can write proleptically about their own death and speak, as it were, from beyond their own graves" (225). This is the same dynamic that we saw earlier in this chapter—Wordsworth's treatment of self-consciousness in his sonnets. De Man explains that for this reason the "she" in the poem "is in fact large enough to encompass Wordsworth as well" (225).
38. Chapman, "Sonnet and Sonnet Sequence," 106.
39. In his chapter on melancholy in Barrett's poetry, David G. Riede comments that "Leighton, Mermin, and Cooper have all argued that the utterance, *I love thee,* from a woman speaker transforms the courtly love tradition by switching the amatory gender roles of lover and beloved, and for the first time makes a woman the subject rather than merely the object of loving" (128). And Riede adds to this discussion "that the lovers' exchanges all follow from the exchange of divine contemplation for earthly love. This is a choice to leave melancholy behind, and it is reiterated many times in the sonnets" (128). While Barrett appears to "leave melancholy behind" in her sonnets, I am arguing that she cleverly complicates this ostensibly celebratory progression with both the double use and the double meaning of the word "thee"—a maneuver that other critics have not observed.
40. See Angela Leighton, "Stirring 'a Dust of Figures': Elizabeth Barrett Browning and Love," in *Critical Essays on Elizabeth Barrett Browning,* edited by Sandra Donaldson (New York: G. K. Hall & Co., 1999), 218–32.
41. As we saw in Barrett's use of the word "ebb" in her sonnet on Wordsworth,

we might hear in the word "bare" another hint of self-referentiality. This anticipates what we will see in the following chapter, where I expose Christina Rossetti's equation of speechlessness with selfhood.

42. Mary B. Moore, *Desiring Voices: Women Sonneteers and Petrarchism* (Carbondale: Southern Illinois University Press, 2000), 191.

NOTES TO CHAPTER 3

1. Rossetti frames "*Monna Innominata*" with the explanation that had Barrett "only been unhappy instead of happy," she might have written such a sequence in place of her *Sonnets from the Portuguese* (2:3, 86); see *The Complete Poems of Christina Rossetti: A Variorum Edition,* 3 vols., edited by R. W. Crump (Baton Rouge: Louisiana State University Press, c. 1979–). From now on I will cite all of Rossetti's poetry from these volumes, and I will abbreviate citations accordingly. Marjorie Stone chooses not to discuss Barrett and Rossetti as mother/daughter figures but as sisters: "First, Rossetti's serious aspirations as a writer began in her adolescence during the 1840s, at a time when Barrett Browning's 1844 *Poems* had recently established their author as England's leading woman poet. Since Barrett Browning did not die until 1861, her career overlaps substantially with the first intense decade of Rossetti's writing career." See Stone's essay "Sisters in Art: Christina Rossetti and Elizabeth Barrett Browning," *Victorian Poetry* 32:3–4 (Autumn–Winter 1994): 341. In *Victorian Women Poets: Writing Against the Heart* (Charlottesville: University Press of Virginia, 1992), Angela Leighton points out that while Rossetti greatly admired Barrett's work, she "never met her great luminary, and William recalls that Barrett Browning herself never expressed any knowledge of Rossetti's work" (129).
2. Constance W. Hassett introduces her book, *Christina Rossetti: The Patience of Style* (Charlottesville: University of Virginia Press, 2005), with the following observation: "One might almost say that silence itself is Rossetti's medium" (1). In her book, Hassett uses the term "patience" to mean "something like the quality that readers have also called 'reticence' or 'reserve'" (1).
3. See Stuart Curran, "The Lyric Voice of Christina Rossetti," *Victorian Poetry* 9 (1971): 297–99.
4. I am using Butler's definition of "feminist"/"feminism": "Feminism is about the social transformation of gender relations. Probably we could all agree on that, even if 'gender' is not the preferred word for some" (*Undoing Gender* 204).
5. By drawing on Butler to talk about Rossetti, I do not mean to conflate twenty-first-century and Victorian views. However, I find Butler's terminology

useful here. In Victorian times as well as in the present tense, feminism has depended upon both an openness to the complexity of gender roles and a willingness to reconsider habitual presumptions about "what is possible in gendered life" (*Gender Trouble* viii).

6. William Whitla, "Questioning the Convention: Christina Rossetti's Sonnet Sequence 'Monna Innominata,'" in *The Achievement of Christina Rossetti*, edited by David A. Kent (Ithaca, NY: Cornell University Press, 1987), 131.
7. I am grateful to Anne Jamison who helped me to articulate the terms "stated" and "semantic" in my discussion of Rossetti's work.
8. Cynthia Scheinberg indicates a blindness in critics when it comes to assessing the religious forces that drive Victorian women's writing. She argues that while it may be tempting to read these forces as resulting in women's writing that is "didactic," "submissive," and "unenlightened," we need to be careful not to underestimate the technicalities of Tractarian poetics. See *Women's Poetry and Religion in Victorian England: Jewish Identity and Christian Culture* (Cambridge: Cambridge University Press, 2002), 9. Joseph Phelan follows Scheinberg's lead, viewing the sonnet as "a privileged point of intersection between feminine and Tractarian poetics" (93). In Rossetti's case, Phelan argues, "the well-established tradition of seeing the sonnet as a privileged vehicle for autobiographical utterance meets the Tractarian doctrine of reserve to produce poetry which is both deeply personal and carefully depersonalized" (94). Consequently, in Phelan's words, "Rossetti's is a quiet poetry which forces us to listen very carefully for minute changes in tone and texture" (98). Through my study of the interplay between "stated" and "semantic" silences in Rossetti's sonnets, I aim to make these "minute changes" audible in Rossetti's highly nuanced writing.
9. It is perhaps significant that Elizabeth Barrett's own turn to the sonnet occurred just four years earlier—in her 1844 collection—poetry from which the Rossettis surely drew inspiration.
10. Linda Marshall notes, "I count 227 sonnets in Crump, *Poems*, 1–3, in which the editor indicates that the total number of Rossetti's poems is 'more than eleven hundred' (I.XI)." See "'Abstruse the problems!': Unity and Divisions in Christina Rossetti's *Later Life: A Double Sonnet of Sonnets*." *Victorian Poetry* 32:3–4 (Autumn–Winter 1994): 312.
11. Gilbert and Gubar, *The Madwoman in the Attic*, 575.
12. Isobel Armstrong, *Victorian Poetry: Poetry, Poetics and Politics* (New York: Routledge, 1993), 339. In her book, *Recovering Christina Rossetti: Female Community and Incarnational Poetics* (New York: Palgrave, 2004), Mary Arseneau aims to supplement Armstrong's discussion by showing how "Rossetti's empowered and liberated statements, both poetic and political" emerge not in resistance to her religious faith but rather "in terms made available to her

by her religious faith" (3). Arseneau grounds Rossetti's withholding style in Tractarian poetic principles of reserve; according to these principles, "Intense emotion must be expressed indirectly; and this indirection, a veiling and guarding of meaning, is reserve" (Arseneau 69). In certain ways, Arseneau's approach intersects with Lynda Palazzo's; both Arseneau and Palazzo argue that Rossetti's theology functions as "female-centred, domestic, and infused with a reverence for the spirituality of daily life." (Arseneau 2). Also see Lynda Palazzo, *Christina Rossetti's Feminist Theology* (New York: Palgrave, 2002).

13. See *The British and Foreign Review* XIII (1842): 1–49. Mill's *Monthly Repository* article is quoted on p. 13.
14. Dora Greenwell, *Essays* (London and New York, 1866), 3–4.
15. All quotes from "Winter: My Secret" appear on the same page of Rossetti's *Complete Poems:* 1:1, 47.
16. Hassett also observes the echo to *Goblin Market* in this passage. See Hassett 61. She does not, however, relate the possibility of sexual aggressiveness to Rossetti's addressee in "Winter: My Secret."
17. As Foucault demonstrates in *The History of Sexuality, Volume I: An Introduction,* the repressive hypothesis that we associate with the silence and secrecy imposed on sexual practices during the Victorian regime resulted not in silence but in "a veritable discursive explosion" (17). It is in a similar way that I see Rossetti's repression of selfhood in her poems—as creating rather than eliminating an explosion of self references.
18. *The Complete Poems of Christina Rossetti: A Variorum Edition* 2:3, 122. Unless noted otherwise, all quotations from each sonnet appear on the single page the initial note provides.
19. Rossetti's use of "And I am," which she will repeat in the last line of her third sonnet ("I am, I am") recalls the ending of both Barrett's sonnet "Consolation" and Rilke's Sonnet II, 29 in *Sonnets to Orpheus.* These poets' reiteration of "I am" might intentionally recall not only the Bible but also Samuel Taylor Coleridge's definition of the primary imagination in his *Biographia Literaria:* the "repetition in the finite mind of the eternal act of creation in the infinite I AM" (167).
20. This line must be read in conjunction with Dante Gabriel Rossetti's definition of the sonnet as "a moment's monument." His words might be read, "*m*-o-*me*-nt's *mon* ("my" in French)-u-*me*-nt." To break this phrase down further, "u" sounds the same as "you," and "ment" is a homophone for "meant." The last word, then, becomes "my you meant" or the speaker's assumed possession of another's meaning. With their vagueness and ambiguity, Christina Rossetti's words read like an obvious revision of monumentality, and the references to selfhood that she embeds in her line overtake her brother's

self-references in his own.

21. Christina Rossetti, *The Face of the Deep: A Devotional Commentary on the Apocalypse* (London, 1892), 352.
22. Diane D'Amico, *Christina Rossetti: Faith, Gender and Time* (Baton Rouge: Louisiana State University Press, 1999), 149.
23. Margaret Homans, "'Syllables of Velvet': Dickinson, Rossetti, and the Rhetorics of Sexuality," *Feminist Studies* 11:3 (1985): 574.
24. Mary E. Finn, *Writing the Incommensurable: Kierkegaard, Rossetti, and Hopkins* (University Park: Pennsylvania State University Press, 1992), 147.
25. Antony Harrison, *Christina Rossetti in Context* (Chapel Hill: University of North Carolina Press, 1988), 153–54.
26. I will use the term "Rossetti" to name a possible speaker for the sonnets I discuss. I do not mean Rossetti's literal person here but simply her poetic counterpart—in particular, a woman poet who lived at the same time that she did.
27. *The Poetical Works of Christina Georgina Rossetti,* edited by William Michael Rossetti (London: Macmillan, 1904), 462.
28. Marjorie Stone argues that "[t]he richness of the biblical, classical, and literary allusions in '*Monna Innominata*' and the *Sonnets from the Portuguese* makes it all the more surprising that they were approached so uniformly as merely personal utterances, hidden behind the 'blinds' of their titles and, in Rossetti's case, of her preface. The predominance of such approaches manifests the inveterate nature of the gendered paradigms that both poets sought to deconstruct." See Stone's essay, "'*Monna Innominata*' and *Sonnets from the Portuguese:* Sonnet Traditions and Spiritual Trajectories" in *The Culture of Christina Rossetti: Female Poetics and Victorian Contexts,* edited by Mary Arseneau et al. (Athens: Ohio University Press, 1999), 67.
29. Finn explains that the "woman to whom *Monna Innominata* gives poetic voice (and for whom it imagines 'poetic attitude') precedes Beatrice and Laura, and therefore logically precedes Dante and Petrarch. The sonnet of sonnets reveals itself as a construct composed of parts that could not come together except in the fictional use of language" (147).
30. Other critics have suggested the double status of the speaker/addressee in "*Monna Innominata.*" Chapman maintains that "within a hyperconsciousness of restrictive poetic space, and the repeated emphatic staging of closure at the end of each sonnet, the sequence voices the position of loss, absence and longing both specifically as a sequence addressed to Rossetti's close friend Charles Cayley and generically as the unnamed lady of sonnet tradition" ("Sonnet and Sonnet Sequence" 108). And Sharon Bickle argues that there are two speakers of the sequence—the "translator" and the "poet": "The role of the translator is superimposed on the silenced woman, and the

translator's enterprise is the restoration of language to the silenced." See "A Woman of Women for 'A Sonnet of Sonnets': Exploring Female Subjectivity in Christina Rossetti's '*Monna Innominata*,'" in *Tradition and the Poetics of Self in Nineteenth-Century Women's Poetry,* edited by Barbara Garlick (New York: Editions Rodopi B.V., 2002), 128–29. The argument I am making in this chapter is more complex than a recognition of two possible speakers or two possible addressees. I am proposing that both the speaker and the addressee participate in an endless flux of shifting roles.

31. Like much of Rossetti's work, these sonnets have a strong homoerotic subtext. It is therefore important to take into account that the female addressee might not be a forgotten woman from history at all, but a same-tense female beloved.
32. I am using William Michael Rossetti's translations of Dante and Petrarch here, given in *The Poetical Works of Christina Georgina Rossetti* (462–63).
33. See Stone, *The Culture of Christina Rossetti,* 68. Stone ultimately argues that "despite their dramatically different conclusions, and despite the dramatically different lives of their authors, one might say that the 'roots' of '*Monna Innominata*' and of the *Sonnets from the Portuguese* are often intertwined" (68).
34. See Flowers's essay, "'Had Such a Lady Spoken for Herself': Christina Rossetti's '*Monna Innominata*'" in *Rossetti to Sexton: Six Women Poets at Texas,* edited by Dave Oliphant and Robin Bradford (Austin, TX: Harry Ransom Humanities Research Center, 1992), 29.

NOTES TO CHAPTER 4

1. Very little is known about Isabella Southern, which is unfortunate; I was able to examine her work at the British Library. She dedicates her book *Sonnets and Other Poems* (London: Walter Scott, 1891) "To My Father Thomas Pallister Barkas." More is known about her father who lived from 1819 to 1891, which means that he died the year Southern's book was published. He was also known as the pioneer of Phonography in the North of England—many reporters took from him their first lessons in shorthand. Furthermore, he was committed to the Investigation of Spiritualism, which used mediums to carry out test séances.
2. Maria Norris, "On Mrs. Browning," *The Ladies' Companion* No. 19 (August 1, 1851): 135. I examined this text at the British Library.
3. Angela Leighton and Margaret Reynolds, eds., *Victorian Women Poets: An Anthology* (Cambridge, MA: Blackwell, 1996), 286–87.
4. Samantha Matthews, "Entombing the Woman Poet: Tributes to Elizabeth Barrett Browning," *Studies in Browning and His Circle: A Journal of Criticism,*

History, and Bibliography 24 (2001): 31.

5. *A Variorum Edition of Elizabeth Barrett Browning's* Sonnets from the Portuguese, edited by Miroslava Wein Dow (Troy, NY: The Whitston Publishing Co., 1980), 75.
6. Leighton and Reynolds, eds., *Victorian Women Poets,* 291.
7. Eventually becoming lesbian lovers and lifetime partners, Katherine Bradley was born in 1846 and Edith Cooper was born in 1862; they died almost at the same time of cancer—Bradley in 1914 and Cooper in 1913. Bradley and Cooper wrote eight books of poetry under the name of Michael Field. Two more books of their poems were published under the same name after their death.
8. Leighton and Reynolds, eds., *Victorian Women Poets,* 506.
9. In *Recovering Christina Rossetti,* Mary Arseneau points out that Rossetti fails in Michael Field's sonnet to live up to an identification between Rossetti and Beatrice that has been proposed by other critics (212).
10. See Susan Conley, "'Poet's Right': Christina Rossetti as Anti-Muse and the Legacy of the 'Poetess,'" *Victorian Poetry* 32:3–4 (Autumn–Winter 1994): 365.
11. Marion Thain, *Michael Field and Poetic Identity: With a Biography* (London: The Eighteen Nineties Society, 2000), 7.
12. Felicity Nussbaum, *The Autobiographical Subject: Gender and Ideology in Eighteenth-Century England* (Baltimore: Johns Hopkins University Press, 1989), 1.
13. Joanne Shattock, ed., *Women and Literature in Britain, 1800–1900* (Cambridge: Cambridge University Press, 2001), 3.
14. E. A. Poe, review of *The Drama of Exile and other Poems* by Elizabeth Barrett Barrett, *The Broadway Journal* I (1845): 4–5. Quoted by Joanne Shattock, "The Construction of the Woman Writer," 8.
15. Linda Peterson, "Women Writers and Self-Writing," in *Women and Literature in Britain.*
16. Dow often takes issue with Barrett's easy reliance on religious themes and imagery in her poems. However, "Past and Future" is one poem that Dow feels works in a religious sense: "One of the few successful, genuinely religious poems is 'Past and Future'; the religious feeling is profound and essential. One does not wish to suggest that E.B.B.'s religious feelings were not strong and genuine, only that her use of them is sometimes mechanical and extrinsic to the poem" (*Variorum Edition* ix).
17. In "'Medicated Music': Elizabeth Barrett Browning's *Sonnets from the Portuguese,*" Sharon Smulders reads the ending of "Future and Past" differently than I do: "But while she charges the beloved to 'write me new my future's epigraph,' Barrett Browning in fact undertakes the task of revision herself. Writing anew the 1844 sonnets, she refigures the motif of imprisoning exclusion as one of saving inclusion" (208). According to my reading, the one

sense in which Barrett interferes with the revision process that she asks her beloved to undertake for her involves an underlying grief that will not disappear as a result of her love.

18. Barrett's choice to address her beloved as an "angel" involves some gender ambiguity. As Helen Cooper clarifies in *Elizabeth Barrett Browning, Woman and Artist,* "The 'angel,' culturally associated in the nineteenth century with woman, is here used in an ambiguous way—as the earlier Seraphim had been. Barrett draws on a Biblical and Miltonic tradition that considered the angel as male, and yet the asexual quality of the angel associates the 'new angel mine' as her muse with the young boy at the end of 'A Vision of Poets' and the little boy whose singing would be the inspiration for *Casa Guidi Windows*" (108).
19. In "'Some World's-Wonder in Chapel or Crypt': Elizabeth Barrett Browning and Disability," Christine Kenyon Jones draws attention to how Barrett makes no secret in her 1844 poems of the way that these poems were written by (and often use as their subject) "an author afflicted by sickness." *Nineteenth-Century Studies* 16 (2002): 24. Jones hypothesizes that as a woman poet Barrett may have stressed her own sickness so as to make herself less intimidating in the eyes of her critics: "The critical response to a woman poet who had dared to align herself with Milton, Dante, and other great poets and use their subject matter might easily in this period have been so censorious as to place her beyond the pale as far as publishers, critics, and readers were concerned. As it was, however, Barrett's openly acknowledged physical and emotional frailty made her seem much less threatening" (25).
20. In his essay, "Barrett Browning's Poetic Vocation: Crying, Singing, Breathing," Steve Dillon does a nice job of showing how attentive Barrett was in her poetry to moments when the human voice breaks into a cry. The cry in Dillon's essay does not necessarily result in tears; rather Dillon associates it with the "ecstatic shriek, painful shout, or despairing moan to God." *Victorian Poetry* 39:4 (2001): 510. Dillon shows how throughout Barrett's career, she "continues to explore the problematic articulation of poetic voice—at the boundary of noise and language, of volition and helplessness, of human and divine—through the manifold use of the cry" (528). However, Dillon's failure to account for any of the many instances in Barrett's sonnets (particularly in her grieving sonnets of 1844 and in her *Sonnets from the Portuguese*) where she equates "hopeless grief" with the absence both of tears and of speech renders his overall conclusions less convincing.
21. Southern's use of "less" as an ending to this word recalls both Wordsworth and Barrett. Wordsworth begins his description of the empty city in "Composed Upon Westminster Bridge" with a series of negations that include the word "smokeless"; like Wordsworth, Barrett fills her own octave in "Grief"

with negatives: "hopeless," "passionless," "desertness," "silent-bare." Southern changes this negation into a vacancy in her thirsty traveler's dreams.

22. Together with other late nineteenth-century female sonneteers, Isabella Southern foreshadows present-day feminist political theories of silence. As Wendy Brown explains in *Edgework: Critical Essays on Knowledge and Politics* (Princeton, NJ: Princeton University Press, 2005), while refusing to speak can serve as "a method of refusing colonization, of refusing complicity in injurious interpellation or in subjection through regulation," it would nevertheless "be a mistake to value this resistance too highly, for it is, like most rights claims, a defense in the context of domination, a strategy for negotiating domination, rather than a sign of emancipation from it" (97).
23. Siddal was Rossetti's model in many of his famous paintings (she also modeled for other members of Rossetti's Pre-Raphaelite Brotherhood). In 1862, Rossetti buried her with the only complete manuscript of his poems. He decided to recover the manuscript seven years later. The "Willowwood" sonnets appear in *The House of Life,* numbered 49–52; Rossetti introduces them into the collection toward the end of the "Youth and Change" section, which is the first part of the sequence. After Rossetti recovered the manuscript that he had buried with his wife, he published fifty of these sonnets in *Poems* (1870). His final version appeared in *Ballads and Sonnets* (1881). Rossetti's collected works then appeared in 1886 in two volumes (four years after his death at the age of fifty-three in 1882).
24. While Southern does not appear in Bristow's volume, I agree with his overarching conclusion about the poetry of the 1890s: "this much-misrecognized literary decade was not entirely a doom-laden affair that hurtled the Victorian age toward its terminal point. Instead, it was a time whose apparent freakishness and faddishness, naughtiness and neurosis, pretensions and perversions are better understood as signs of its authors' well-considered interest in devising fresh poetic models that could engage with the modern before further shifts in poetics became identifiably modernist." See *The Fin-de-Siècle Poem: English Literary Culture and the 1890s,* edited by Joseph Bristow (Athens: Ohio University Press, 2005), 39.

NOTES TO CONCLUSION

1. See Janis P. Stout, "Fretting Not: Multiple Traditions of the Sonnet in the Twentieth Century," *Concerning Poetry* 18:1–2 (1985): 21–35. Stout argues that "the sonnet has in fact flourished in the twentieth century. A great array of modern poets, major as well as minor, have worked substantially and well in the form" (21).

2. See Annie Finch, ed., *A Formal Feeling Comes: Poems in Form by Contemporary Women* (Ashland, OR: Story Line Press, 1994), 4.
3. See the opening quote to this book, which I take from Virginia Woolf's *To the Lighthouse* (London: Harcourt Brace and Co., 1927, reprint, 1955), 121.

WORKS CITED

Abrams, M. H. "Structure and Style in the Greater Romantic Lyric." In *From Sensibility to Romanticism,* edited by F. W. Hilles and Harold Bloom, 527–60. New York: Oxford University Press, 1965.

Armstrong, Isobel. *Victorian Poetry: Poetry, Poetics and Politics.* New York: Routledge, 1993.

Arseneau, Mary. *Recovering Christina Rossetti: Female Community and Incarnational Poetics.* New York: Palgrave, 2004.

Backsheider, Paula R. *Eighteenth-Century Women Poets and Their Poetry: Inventing Agency, Inventing Genre.* Baltimore: The Johns Hopkins University Press, 2005.

Barrett (Browning), Elizabeth. *The Brownings' Correspondence.* Edited by Philip Kelley, Ronald Hudson, and Scott Lewis. Winfield, KS: Wedgestone Press, 1984–.

———. *The Complete Works of Elizabeth Barrett Browning.* Edited by Charlotte Porter and Helen A. Clarke. 6 vols. New York: Thomas Y. Crowell & Co., 1900. Reprinted 1973. New York: AMS Press.

———. *The Letters of Elizabeth Barrett Browning.* Edited by Frederic Kenyon. 2 vols. London: Macmillan, 1897.

———. *The Letters of Elizabeth Barrett Browning to Her Sister Arabella.* Edited by Scott Lewis. 2 vols. Waco, TX: Wedgestone Press, 2002.

———. *A Variorum Edition of Elizabeth Barrett Browning's* Sonnets from the Portuguese. Edited by Miroslava Wein Dow. Troy, NY: The Whitston Publishing Co., 1980.

Behrendt, Stephen C. "Telling Secrets: The Sonnets of Anna Maria Smallpiece and Mary F. Johnson." *European Romantic Review* (Special Issue: The Romantic-Period Sonnet) 13 (2002): 393–410.

———. "In Search of Anna Maria Smallpiece." *Women's Writing* 7:1 (2000): 55–73.

Bickle, Sharon. "A Woman of Women for 'A Sonnet of Sonnets': Exploring Female Subjectivity in Christina Rossetti's '*Monna Innominata.*'" In *Tradition and the Poetics of Self in Nineteenth-Century Women's Poetry,* edited by Barbara Garlick, 117–35. New York: Editions Rodopi B.V., 2002.

Bowles, William Lisle. *Fourteen Sonnets, Elegiac and Descriptive.* 1789. Oxford: Woodstock, 1991.

Bristow, Joseph, ed. *The Fin-de-Siècle Poem: English Literary Culture and the 1890s.* Athens: Ohio University Press, 2005.

Brown, Wendy. *Edgework: Critical Essays on Knowledge and Politics.* Princeton, NJ: Princeton University Press, 2005.

Budick, Sanford, and Wolfgang Iser, eds. *Languages of the Unsayable: The Play of Negativity in Literature and Literary Theory.* New York: Columbia University Press, 1989.

Burke, Edmund. *A Philosophical Enquiry into the Origin of Our Ideas of the Sublime and Beautiful.* 1757. Edited by Adam Phillips. New York: Oxford University Press, 1990.

Butler, Judith. Afterword to *The Scandal of the Speaking Body,* by Shoshana Felman, 113–23. Stanford, CA: Stanford University Press, 2003.

———. *Gender Trouble: Feminism and the Subversion of Identity.* London: Routledge, 1990.

———. *Giving an Account of Oneself.* New York: Fordham University Press, 2005.

———. *Precarious Life: The Powers of Mourning and Violence.* New York: Verso, 2004.

———. *Undoing Gender.* London: Routledge, 2004.

Chapman, Alison. *The Afterlife of Christina Rossetti.* New York: St. Martin's Press, 2000.

———. "Mesmerism and Agency in the Courtship of Elizabeth Barrett and Robert Browning." *Victorian Literature and Culture* (1998): 303–19.

———. "Sonnet and Sonnet Sequence." In *A Companion to Victorian Poetry,* edited by Richard Cronin, Alison Chapman, and Antony H. Harrison, 99–114. Boston: Blackwell, 2002.

Cheng, Anne Anlin. *The Melancholy of Race.* Oxford: Oxford University Press, 2000.

Colebrook, Claire. *Gender.* New York: Palgrave, 2004.

Coleridge, Samuel Taylor. 1817. *Biographia Literaria.* Clarendon, VT: Charles E. Tuttle Co., 1975.

Collins, William. "The Passions: An Ode to Music." 1747. In *The Poems of Gray, Collins and Goldsmith,* edited by Roger Lonsdale, 477–85. London: Longmans, 1969.

Conley, Susan. "'Poet's Right': Christina Rossetti as Anti-Muse and the Legacy of the 'Poetess.'" *Victorian Poetry* 32:3–4 (Autumn–Winter 1994): 365–86.

Cooper, Helen. *Elizabeth Barrett Browning, Woman and Artist.* Chapel Hill: University of North Carolina Press, 1988.

Culler, Jonathan. "On the Negativity of Modern Poetry: Friedrich, Baudelaire, and the Critical Tradition." In *Languages of the Unsayable: The Play of Negativity in Literature and Literary Theory,* edited by Sanford Budick and Wolfgang Iser, 190–208. New York: Columbia University Press, 1989.

Curran, Stuart. "Charlotte Smith and British Romanticism." *South Central Review* 11.2 (1994): 64–78.

———. "The Lyric Voice of Christina Rossetti." *Victorian Poetry* 9 (1971): 287–99.

———. *The Poems of Charlotte Smith.* New York: Oxford University Press, 1993.

———. *Poetic Form and British Romanticism.* New York: Oxford University Press, 1986.

D'Amico, Diane. *Christina Rossetti: Faith, Gender and Time.* Baton Rouge: Louisiana State University Press, 1999.

de Man, Paul. *Blindness and Insight: Essays in the Rhetoric of Contemporary Criticism.* 1971. Minneapolis: University of Minnesota Press, 1983.

Derrida, Jacques. *Writing and Difference.* Translated by Alan Bass. Chicago: University of Chicago Press, 1978.

Dillon, Steve. "Barrett Browning's Poetic Vocation: Crying, Singing, Breathing." *Victorian Poetry* 39:4 (2001): 509–32.

Feldman, Paula R., and Daniel Robinson, eds. *A Century of Sonnets: The Romantic-Era Revival.* New York: Oxford University Press, 1999.

Felman, Shoshana. *The Scandal of the Speaking Body.* Stanford, CA: Stanford University Press, 2003.

Felski, Rita. *Literature after Feminism.* Chicago: University of Chicago Press, 2003.

Finch, Annie, ed. *A Formal Feeling Comes: Poems in Form by Contemporary Women.* Ashland, OR: Story Line Press, 1994.

Finn, Mary E. *Writing the Incommensurable: Kierkegaard, Rossetti, and Hopkins.* University Park: Pennsylvania State University Press, 1992.

Flowers, Betty. "'Had Such a Lady Spoken for Herself': Christina Rossetti's '*Monna Innominata.*'" In *Rossetti to Sexton: Six Women Poets at Texas,* edited by Dave Oliphant and Robin Bradford, 13–29. Austin, TX: Harry Ransom Humanities Research Center, 1992.

Foucault, Michel. *The History of Sexuality, Volume I: An Introduction.* Translated by Robert Hurley. New York: Vintage, 1980.

Fuller, John. "The Sonnet." No. 26 of the series *The Critical Idiom.* Edited by John D. Jump. London: Methuen & Co., 1972.

Gilbert, Sandra, and Susan Gubar. *The Madwoman in the Attic: The Woman Writer and the Nineteenth-Century Literary Imagination.* New Haven, CT: Yale University Press, 1979.

Glenn, Cheryl. *Unspoken: A Rhetoric of Silence.* Carbondale: Southern Illinois University Press, 2004.

Gray, Thomas. "Sonnet [On the Death of Mr. Richard West]." 1775. In *The Poems of Gray, Collins and Goldsmith,* edited by Roger Lonsdale, 67–68. London: Longmans, 1969.

Greenwell, Dora. *Essays.* London and New York, 1866.

Harrison, Antony. *Christina Rossetti in Context.* Chapel Hill: University of North Carolina Press, 1988.

Hassett, Constance W. *Christina Rossetti: The Patience of Style.* Charlottesville: University of Virginia Press, 2005.

Hayley, William, Esq. *Poems and Plays.* Vol. 1. London: T. Cadell, 1785.

Hedges, Elaine, and Shelley Fisher Fishkin, eds. *Listening to Silences: New Essays in Feminist Criticism.* New York: Oxford University Press, 1994.

Homans, Margaret. "'Syllables of Velvet': Dickinson, Rossetti, and the Rhetorics of Sexuality." *Feminist Studies* 11:3 (1985): 569–93.

Houston, Natalie M. "Affecting Authenticity: *Sonnets from the Portuguese* and

Modern Love." Studies in the Literary Imagination 35:2 (2002): 99–121.

———. "Anthologies and the Making of the Poetic Canon." In *A Companion to Victorian Poetry*, edited by Richard Cronin, Alison Chapman, and Antony H. Harrison, 361–77. Boston: Blackwell, 2002.

———. "Towards a New History: Fin-de-Siècle Women Poets and the Sonnet." In *Essays and Studies 2003: Victorian Women Poets*, edited by Alison Chapman, 145–64. Cambridge: D. S. Brewer, 2003.

Jones, Christine Kenyon. "'Some World's-Wonder in Chapel or Crypt': Elizabeth Barrett Browning and Disability." *Nineteenth-Century Studies* 16 (2002): 21–35.

Kant, Immanuel. *Critique of Judgment.* Translated by Werner S. Pluhar. Indianapolis: Hackett, 1987.

Keats, John. *John Keats: A Critical Edition of the Major Works.* Edited by Frank Kermode. Oxford: Oxford University Press, 1990.

Kennedy, Deborah. "Thorns and Roses: The Sonnets of Charlotte Smith." *Women's Writing* 2:1 (1995): 45–53.

Kintner, Elvan, ed. *The Letters of Robert Browning and Elizabeth Barrett Browning: 1845–46.* 2 vols. Cambridge, MA: Harvard University Press.

Knapp, Steven. *Personification and the Sublime: Milton to Coleridge.* Cambridge, MA: Harvard University Press, 1985.

Labbe, Jacqueline M. *Charlotte Smith: Romanticism, Poetry, and the Culture of Gender.* New York: Palgrave, 2003.

———. Selling One's Sorrows: Charlotte Smith, Mary Robinson and the Marketing of Poetry." *The Wordsworth Circle* 25:2 (Spring 1994): 68–71.

Laurence, Patricia Ondek. *The Reading of Silence: Virginia Woolf in the English Tradition.* Stanford, CA: Stanford University Press, 1991.

Leighton, Angela. *Elizabeth Barrett Browning.* Bloomington: Indiana University Press, 1986.

———. "Stirring 'a Dust of Figures': Elizabeth Barrett Browning and Love." In *Critical Essays on Elizabeth Barrett Browning*, edited by Sandra Donaldson, 218–32. New York: G. K. Hall & Co., 1999.

———. *Victorian Women Poets: Writing Against the Heart.* Charlottesville: University of Virginia Press, 1992.

Leighton, Angela, and Margaret Reynolds, eds. *Victorian Women Poets: An Anthology.* Cambridge, MA: Blackwell, 1996.

Lootens, Tricia. *Lost Saints: Silence, Gender, and Victorian Literary Canonization.* Charlottesville: University Press of Virginia, 1996.

Manning, Peter J. "Wordsworth and Gray's Sonnet on the Death of West." *SEL: Studies in English Literature* 22:3 (Summer 1982): 505–18.

Marshall, Linda. "'Abstruse the problems!': Unity and Divisions in Christina Rossetti's *Later Life: A Double Sonnet of Sonnets." Victorian Poetry* 32:3–4 (Autumn–Winter 1994): 299–314.

Matthews, Samantha. "Entombing the Woman Poet: Tributes to Elizabeth Barrett Browning." *Studies in Browning and His Circle: A Journal of Criticism, History, and Bibliography* 24 (2001): 31–53.

Mazzaro, Jerome. "Mapping Sublimity: Elizabeth Barrett Browning's *Sonnets from the Portuguese." Essays in Literature* 2 (1991): 166–79.

McGann, Jerome. *The Poetics of Sensibility: A Revolution in Literary Style.* Oxford:

Clarendon Press, 1996.

———. "The Religious Poetry of Christina Rossetti." In *Victorian Women Poets: Emily Bronte, Elizabeth Barrett Browning, Christina Rossetti,* edited by Joseph Bristow, 167–88. New York: St. Martin's Press, 1995.

Mellor, Anne K. *Romanticism & Gender.* New York: Routledge, 1993.

Mergenthal, Silvia. "Charlotte Smith and the Romantic Sonnet Revival." In *Feminist Contributions to the Literary Canon: Setting Standards of Taste,* edited by Susanne Fendler, 65–79. New York: The Edwin Mellen Press, 1997.

Mermin, Dorothy. *Elizabeth Barrett Browning: The Origins of a New Poetry.* Chicago: University of Chicago Press, 1989.

———. "The Female Poet and the Embarrassed Reader: Elizabeth Barrett Browning's Sonnets from the Portuguese." *ELH* 48:2 (1981): 351–67.

Miller, J. Hillis. *The Linguistic Moment: From Wordsworth to Stevens.* Princeton, NJ: Princeton University Press, 1985.

Mills-Courts, Karen. *Poetry as Epitaph: Representation and Poetic Language.* Baton Rouge: Louisiana State University Press, 1990.

Milton, John. *The Complete Poetry and Selected Prose of John Milton.* New York: The Modern Library, 1950.

Mitford, Mary Russell. *Recollections of a Literary Life.* New York: Harper and Brothers, 1852.

Moore, Mary B. *Desiring Voices: Women Sonneteers and Petrarchism.* Carbondale: Southern Illinois University Press, 2000.

Neri, Barbara. "A Lineage of Love: The Literary Bloodlines of Elizabeth Barrett Browning's *Sonnets from the Portuguese.*" *Studies in Browning and His Circle: A Journal of Criticism, History, and Bibliography* 23 (2000): 50–69.

Norris, Maria. "On Mrs. Browning." *The Ladies' Companion* No. 19 (August 1, 1851): 135.

Nussbaum, Felicity. *The Autobiographical Subject: Gender and Ideology in Eighteenth-Century England.* Baltimore: Johns Hopkins University Press, 1989.

Olsen, Tillie. *Silences.* New York: Delacorte Press, 1978.

Oppenheimer, Paul. *The Birth of the Modern Mind: Self, Consciousness, and the Invention of the Sonnet.* New York: Oxford University Press, 1989.

Palazzo, Lynda. *Christina Rossetti's Feminist Theology.* New York: Palgrave, 2002.

Peterson, Linda. "Women Writers and Self Writing." In *Women and Literature in Britain, 1800–1900,* edited by Joanne Shattock, 209–30. Cambridge: Cambridge University Press, 2001.

Phelan, Joseph. *The Nineteenth-Century Sonnet.* New York: Palgrave, 2005.

Pinch, Adela. *Strange Fits of Passion: Epistemologies of Emotion, Hume to Austen.* Stanford, CA: Stanford University Press, 1996.

Ramazani, Jahan. *Poetry of Mourning: The Modern Elegy from Hardy to Heaney.* Chicago: The University of Chicago Press, 1994.

Raycroft, Brent. "From Charlotte Smith to Nehemiah Higginbottom: Revising the Genealogy of the Early Romantic Sonnet." *European Romantic Review* 9:3 (Summer 1998): 363–92.

Reynolds, Margaret. "Love's Measurement in Elizabeth Barrett Browning's *Sonnets from the Portuguese.*" *Studies in Browning and His Circle* 21 (1997): 53–67.

Riede, David G. *Allegories of One's Own Mind: Melancholy in Victorian Poetry.* Columbus: The Ohio State University Press, 2005.

Robinson, Daniel. "*Elegiac Sonnets:* Charlotte Smith's Formal Paradoxy." *Papers on Language and Literature: A Journal for Scholars and Critics of Language and Literature* 39:2 (Spring 2003): 185–220.

———. *A Century of Sonnets: The Romantic-Era Revival.* Edited by Paula R. Feldman and Daniel Robinson. New York: Oxford University Press, 1999.

———. "Reviving the Sonnet: Women Romantic Poets and the Sonnet Claim." *European Romantic Review* 6:1 (Summer 1995): 98–127.

Rossetti, Christina. *The Complete Poems of Christina Rossetti: A Variorum Edition.* 3 vols. Edited by R. W. Crump. Baton Rouge: Louisiana State University Press, c. 1979– .

———. *The Face of the Deep: A Devotional Commentary on the Apocalypse.* London, 1892.

———. *The Poetical Works of Christina Georgina Rossetti.* Edited by William Michael Rossetti. London: Macmillan, 1904.

Rossetti, Dante Gabriel. *The House of Life.* Cambridge, MA: Harvard University Press, 1928.

Scheinberg, Cynthia. *Women's Poetry and Religion in Victorian England: Jewish Identity and Christian Culture.* Cambridge: Cambridge University Press, 2002.

Schiesari, Juliana. *The Gendering of Melancholia: Feminism, Psychoanalysis, and the Symbolics of Loss in Renaissance Literature.* Ithaca, NY: Cornell University Press, 1992.

Schor, Esther. *Bearing the Dead: The British Culture of Mourning from the Enlightenment to Victoria.* Princeton, NJ: Princeton University Press, 1994.

Scott, Joan W. "Experience." In *Feminists Theorize the Political,* edited by Judith Butler and Joan W. Scott, 22–40. New York: Routledge, 1992.

Shattock, Joanne, ed. *Women and Literature in Britain 1800–1900.* Cambridge: Cambridge University Press, 2001.

Shires, Linda M. "Elizabeth Barrett Browning: Cross-Dwelling and the Reworking of Female Poetic Authority." *Victorian Literature and Culture* 30:2 (2002): 327–43.

Sibelman, Simon P. *Silence in the Novels of Elie Wiesel.* New York: St. Martin's Press, 1995.

Smallpiece, Anna Maria. *Original Sonnets, and Other Small Poems.* London: J. Johnson, 1805.

Smith, Charlotte. *The Collected Letters of Charlotte Smith.* Ed. Judith Phillips Stanton. Bloomington: Indiana University Press, 2003.

———. *Elegiac Sonnets: 1789.* New York: Woodstock Books, 1992.

———. *The Old Manor House.* 1793. New York: Garland Publishing, 1974.

———. *The Poems of Charlotte Smith.* Edited by Stuart Curran. Oxford: Oxford University Press, 1993.

———. *The Young Philosopher.* 1798. Lexington: The University Press of Kentucky, 1999.

Smulders, Sharon. "'Medicated Music': Elizabeth Barrett Browning's *Sonnets from the Portuguese.*" *Victorian Literature and Culture* 23 (1995): 193–213.

Southern, Isabella J. *Sonnets and Other Poems.* London: Walter Scott, 1891.

Stone, Marjorie. *Elizabeth Barrett Browning.* London: Macmillan, 1995.

———. "'*Monna Innominata*' and *Sonnets from the Portuguese:* Sonnet Traditions and Spiritual Trajectories." In *The Culture of Christina Rossetti: Female Poetics and Victorian Contexts,* edited by Mary Arseneau et al., 46–74. Athens: Ohio University Press, 1999.

———. "Sisters in Art: Christina Rossetti and Elizabeth Barrett Browning." *Victorian Poetry* 32:3–4 (Autumn–Winter 1994): 339–64.

Stout, Janis P. "Fretting Not: Multiple Traditions of the Sonnet in the Twentieth Century." *Concerning Poetry* 18:1–2 (1985): 21–35.

———. *Strategies of Reticence: Silence and Meaning in the Works of Jane Austen, Willa Cather, Katherine Anne Porter, and Joan Didion.* Charlottesville: University of Virginia Press, 1990.

Thain, Marion. *Michael Field and Poetic Identity: With a Biography.* London: The Eighteen Nineties Society, 2000.

Thomson, James. *The Seasons.* 1727. London: Nonesuch Press, 1927.

Todd, Janet. *Sensibility: An Introduction.* London: Methuen, 1986.

Toker, Leona. *Eloquent Reticence: Withholding Information in Fictional Narrative.* Lexington: University Press of Kentucky, 1993.

Wagner, Jennifer. *A Moment's Monument: Revisionary Poetics and the Nineteenth-Century English Sonnet.* London: Associated University Presses, 1996.

White, Daniel. "Autobiography and Elegy: The Early Romantic Poetics of Thomas Gray and Charlotte Smith." In *Early Romantics: Perspectives in British Poetry from Pope to Wordsworth,* edited by Thomas Woodman, 57–69. New York: St. Martin's Press, 1998.

Whitla, William. "Questioning the Convention: Christina Rossetti's Sonnet Sequence 'Monna Innominata.'" In *The Achievement of Christina Rossetti,* edited by David A. Kent, 82–132. Ithaca, NY: Cornell University Press, 1987.

Williams, Helen Maria. *Julia; a novel.* New York: Garland Publishing, 1974.

———. *Poems, Moral, Elegant and Pathetic: And Original Sonnets.* London, 1796.

Wimsatt, W. K. "The Structure of Romantic Nature Imagery." In *The Verbal Icon,* 103–16. Louisville: University Press of Kentucky, 1954.

Woolf, Virginia. *To the Lighthouse.* 1927. London: Harcourt Brace and Co., 1981.

Woolford, John. "Elizabeth Barrett and the Wordsworthian Sublime." *Essays in Criticism: A Quarterly Journal of Literary Criticism* 45:1 (1995): 36–56.

Wordsworth, William. *The Poetical Works of Wordsworth.* 1904. Edited by Thomas Hutchinson. New York: Oxford University Press, 1960.

———. *The Prose Works of William Wordsworth.* c. 1876. Edited by A. B. Grosart. London: E. Moxon, Son and Co., 1967.

———. *William Wordsworth: The Major Works.* Edited by Stephen Gill. Oxford: Oxford University Press, 2000.

Zimmerman, Sarah. "Charlotte Smith's Letters and the Practice of Self-Presentation." *Princeton University Library Chronicle* 53 (1991): 50–77.

———. *Romanticism, Lyricism, and History.* New York: State University of New York Press, 1999.

INDEX